Conversations with Hunter S. Thompson

Literary Conversations Series
Peggy Whitman Prenshaw
General Editor

Hunter S. Thompson, courtesy Gary Isaacs

Conversations with Hunter S. Thompson

Edited by
Beef Torrey and Kevin Simonson

University Press of Mississippi
Jackson

www.upress.state.ms.us

The University Press of Mississippi is a member of the Association of American University Presses.

∞
Library of Congress Cataloging-in-Publication Data

Thompson, Hunter S.
  Conversations with Hunter S. Thompson / edited by Beef Torrey and Kevin Simonson.
      p. cm. — (Literary conversations series)
  Compilation of selected personal interviews.
  Includes index.
  ISBN 978-1-934110-76-8 (cloth : alk. paper) — ISBN 978-1-934110-77-5 (pbk. : alk. paper) 1. Thompson, Hunter S. — Interviews.   2. Authors, American — 20th century — Interviews.   3. Journalists—United States—Interviews.   I. Torrey, Beef.   II. Simonson, Kevin.   III. Title.
  PS3570.H62Z46 2008
  070.92—dc22
  [B]
                                                                              2007049191

British Library Cataloging-in-Publication Data available

Books by Hunter S. Thompson

Hells Angels: A Strange and Terrible Saga, New York: Random House (1966). Reprinted, New York: Modern Library (1999).

Fear and Loathing in Las Vegas: A Savage Journey to the Heart of the American Dream, illustrated by Ralph Steadman, New York: Random House (1971). Reprinted with an introduction by P. J. O'Rourke as *Fear and Loathing in Las Vegas and Other American Stories,* New York: Modern Library (1996).

Fear and Loathing: On the Campaign Trail '72, San Francisco: Straight Arrow Books (1973).

The Great Shark Hunt: Strange Tales from a Strange Time, The Gonzo Papers, Volume 1, New York: Summit Books (1979).

The Curse of Lono, illustrated by Ralph Steadman. New York: Bantam Books (1983). Reprinted in London, United Kingdom: Taschen (2005).

Generation of Swine: Tales of Shame and Degradation in the '80s, The Gonzo Papers, Volume 2, New York: Summit Books (1988).

Songs of the Doomed: More Notes on the Death of the American Dream, The Gonzo Papers, Volume 3, New York: Summit Books (1990).

Screwjack and Other Stories, Santa Barbara, CA: Neville Press (1991). Issued in a trade edition, New York: Simon & Schuster (2000).

Better Than Sex: Confessions of a Political Junkie, The Gonzo Papers, Volume 4, New York: Random House (1994).

The Proud Highway: The Saga of a Desperate Southern Gentleman 1955–1967, The Fear and Loathing Letters, Vol. 1, edited by Douglas Brinkley, foreword by William J. Kennedy, New York: Random House, (1997).

The Rum Diary, New York: Simon & Schuster (1999).

Fear and Loathing in America: The Brutal Odyssey of an Outlaw Journalist 1968–1976, Vol. 2, New York: Simon & Schuster (2001).

Kingdom of Fear: Loathsome Secrets of a Star-Crossed Child in the Final Days of the American Century, New York: Simon & Schuster (2003).

Hey Rube: Blood Sport, the Bush Doctrine, and the Downward Spiral of Dumbness Modern History from the Sports Desk, New York: Simon & Schuster (2004).

Fire in the Nuts, illustrated by Ralph Steadman, Woody Creek/Loose Valley/Blue Grass/High Desert Gonzo International/Steam Press/Petro III Graphics/Sylph Publications (2004).

The Mutineer: Rants, Ravings, and Missives from the Mountaintop 1977–2005, New York: Simon & Schuster (2009).

Contents

Introduction

In 1971, the outlandish originator of gonzo journalism, Hunter S. Thompson (1937–2005) burst into the international literary limelight with his best-selling comic masterpiece, *Fear and Loathing in Las Vegas.*

Thompson needs no introduction. Accounts of his anomalous behavior, sinister shenanigans, and menacing persona are wildly strewn throughout the mass media. He displayed an uncanny flair for inserting himself into the epicenter of major sociopolitical events of his generation, and his provocative commentary has reached millions of readers.

In his work, Thompson provided readers with a brutally entertaining chronicle of American culture and its political landscape, giving voice to a cast of unforgettable characters (real and imagined). His fertile and anything-but-banal musings make his writing style instantly recognizable. Although Thompson blurred the lines between fact and fiction, there was never a doubt as to his seriousness as a writer and cultural critic of our generation. The notorious and unabashed Thompson became a potent and powerful force, who never blinked or flinched in the face of America's worst excesses.

Conversations with Hunter S. Thompson is the first compilation of selected interviews that spans the full trajectory of his writing career. These engaging exchanges reveal Thompson's self-determination, self-indulgence, energy, wit, and passions as he discusses his life and career. They reveal the intriguing development of the infamous outlaw journalist's raging, wild mind, and his unique contribution to American literature.

Thompson was born in Louisville, Kentucky, in 1937. Thompson's mother, a librarian, ensured that the writer's childhood home was filled with books. Despite a difficult and delinquent youth, the charismatic adolescent devoured them and acquired a ravenous appetite for the works of Hemingway, Fitzgerald, Faulkner, and Kerouac—writers who had an irrevocable impact on the aspiring author. *The Great Gatsby,* in particular, was a huge influence. "*Gatsby* is

possibly the Great American Novel, if you look at it as a technical achievement,"
Thompson states. "It's about 55,000 words, which was astounding to me. In
[*Fear and Loathing in Las*] *Vegas,* I tried to compete with that. . . . It was one
of the basic guiding principles for my writing. I've always competed with
that. Not a wasted word. This has been a main point to my literary thinking
all my life."[1]

Not only was Thompson well read, but he was an unashamed self-
promoter—resolute, from the get-go, to stake his claim in literary history. In
a 3 June 1959 letter—one of over three hundred (out of a total of over twenty
thousand carbons he stowed away and safeguarded) reprinted in *The Proud
Highway*—he writes: "As things stand now, I am going to be a writer. I'm not
sure that I'm going to be a good one or even a self-supporting one, but until
the dark thumb of fate presses me to the dust and says 'you are nothing,' I
will be a writer."[2] Thompson's destiny was ordained. He set out to learn the
trade and make his mark, and he devised atypical training techniques to
achieve the desired effect: ". . . one of the things I stumbled on early . . . was
typing other writers . . . a page of Hemingway or a page of Faulkner. Three
pages. I learned a tremendous amount about rhythm in that way. I see
writing really as music. And I see my work as essentially music."[3] And the
music never stopped. Thompson's only son, Juan reflects: "I . . . deeply miss
reading out loud in the kitchen—just his works in recent years—as he moved
his hand rhythmically back and forth like an orchestra conductor, keeping
the beat and always reminding me to slow down, slow down, to speak louder,
speak louder. For him, cadence was a crucial part of writing well, and if a
piece did not read well out loud, it was not written well."[4]

From inauspicious beginnings as a drifting young adult, the unflappable
Thompson cleverly crafted a daring and innovative style that soon made him
one of the most talked-about writers of his generation, and a commercial
force of modern nonfiction. He was skeptical of the straight press and
traditional journalistic tenets—who, what, why, when, where, and how—and
created his own brand of first-person journalism. Thompson acknowledges:
"I'm not a reporter, I'm a writer. Nobody gives Norman Mailer shit. I've
never tried to pose as a goddamn reporter. I don't defend what I do in the
context of straight journalism, and . . . some people regard me as a reporter
who's gone bad rather than a writer who's just doing his job."[5]

Thompson's preferred writing subjects were ominous and ventured into
perilous terrain. His first book, *Hell's Angels: The Strange and Terrible Saga of*

the Outlaw Motorcycle Gangs (1966), chronicled the exploits of the Hells Angels and provided readers with a taste of things to come. Thompson next focused his sights on two other corrupt and blighted institutions: Las Vegas and American politics. Thompson's persona as an earnest, briefcase-carrying journalist was transmogrified into that of a raving, madcap bard on the pages of his next book: *Fear and Loathing in Las Vegas.* This image, for good or for ill, stayed with Thompson for the rest of his career.

Thompson achieved cult status and never felt quite comfortable in the role. Rarely was Thompson seen in public without his trademark aviator shades, hat, and cigarette holder with a dangling Dunhill. His drinking bouts and manic behavior became as noticeable as his prose. "In the rough use of the word, I became a public figure," Thompson said in a 1980 profile. "Somehow the author has become larger than the writing. And it sucks."[6]

Historian Douglas Brinkley, who edited three volumes of Thompson's correspondence, adds: "In public, Hunter was never his true self. He was playing [Marlon] Brando-gone-mad, a true, dyed-in-the-wool, 100 percent showman. His core genius was that he created one of the greatest living protagonists in American folklore/literature: 'The Hunter Figure.' "[7]

Thompson's persona did, however, have some connection with his actual life. He worked ungodly hours, kept lots of firearms, and consumed copious amounts of drugs and alcohol. He contends: "Whether it's negative or not, the reality of it is, you start playing with drugs, the numbers aren't on your side for coming up smelling like roses and being President of the United States."[8] He further elaborates that "Wild Turkey and tobacco are the only drugs I use regularly when I write. . . . The only drug I really count on is adrenaline. I'm basically an adrenaline junkie."[9] Nevertheless, his widow Anita Thompson indicated concern about his habits: "I worried about him, but I never told him to stop. That was an agreement we made."[10]

Thompson's reputation balanced precariously between his provocative, virtuosic writing and his hell-raising ways. Fellow writers and interviewers often expressed disbelief and amazement at Thompson's chosen lifestyle. The late Kurt Vonnegut sums it up best: "As for those who wish to know more about Thompson and his ideals, his frazzled nervous system, his self-destructiveness, and all that—he is unabridgeable. He is that rare sort of American author who must be read. . . . They must be experienced. They can't be paraphrased."[11]

Or as Tim Cahill, gonzo journalism's heir apparent, concludes: "Hunter represents freedom. He has confidence, plus size, plus a certain undeniable fearlessness. We all have a kind of Peter Pan ideal in our lives when we're about twelve. We're going to do this, we're going to do that, and it gets beaten out of us. It gets beaten out of us sometime between puberty and our first job. People often regret the things they didn't do. Hunter is the alter ego who got to do *everything*."[12]

Thompson's famous visage can be partly attributed to Ralph Steadman's distinct, ink-splattered drawings of him which illustrate numerous Thompson books. It was an assignment for the short-lived *Scanlan's* that brought Steadman (a then-unknown Welsh artist) and Thompson together for the first time to cover the Kentucky Derby and America's Cup. According to Steadman these trips solidified Thompson's style: "It remains a defining moment in the evolution of gonzo and without a doubt, a dress rehearsal for *Fear and Loathing in Las Vegas.* For Hunter it provided living proof that going crazy as a journalistic style was possible."[13] Steadman's work illustrated Thompson's articles and books for most of the writer's career, and the art helped contribute to Thompson's persona as a chain-smoking madman.

Steadman adds: "[Hunter] was a real live American of the noble kind: a pioneer, a frontiersman, the last of the cowboys . . . with a huge and raging mind. . . . I had the good fortune to work with one of the great originals of American literature. Maybe he is the Mark Twain of the late twentieth century. Maybe not. Time will sort the bastard out, and I leave it to others more qualified than I to assess and appraise his legacy."[14]

"Gonzo"—Thompson's contribution to the English language and the pop lexicon—is not only a word, but a lifestyle, and now an industry. Thompson explains: "I never intended gonzo journalism to be any more than just a differentiation of new journalism. I kind of knew it wasn't that. Bill Cardoso—then working for the *Boston Globe*—wrote me a note about the Kentucky Derby thing saying, 'Hot damn. Kick ass. It was pure gonzo.' . . . It's a Portuguese word, and it translates almost exactly to what the Hells Angels would have said was 'off the wall.' "[15]

The creation of gonzo—a highly subjective and personal form of journalism that allowed room for satirical devices and fictional asides— allowed Thompson the freedom to discourse wildly on the topic at hand while still achieving insight. Some critics accused him of making the stories up as he went along—an assertion that he vehemently denies: "Truth is easier. And weirder. And funnier. . . . You can't fall back on a story you made up, because then you start to wonder if it is good or funny or right. . . . The only way I can get away with the gonzo thing is by telling the truth."[16]

Writer William McKeen offers his assessment: "Thompson's work stands as a vital chronicle of a turbulent time in American history. In the end, his may be the truest telling of the story of the 1960s and 1970s."[17]

Our first meeting with Thompson was in 1990, when we booked him to speak at the University of Nebraska in Lincoln. Our paths crossed multiple times during the ensuing years: visits to Owl Farm and Thompson's always-bustling command central/kitchen; meals and drinks at the Woody Creek Tavern; early morning drives in "the Great Red Shark," Thompson's red Chevy convertible. Our last sojourn to Owl Farm was on August 20, 2005, to attend Thompson's memorial service—six months to the day after he took his own life.

Thompson never made interviewing an easy task. Indeed, he granted very few interviews, and those who were granted admission into his inner circle had to tolerate Thompson's world of sixty-hour work weeks fueled by Chivas and the ear-piercing squawks of his peacocks. "I have a theory that the truth is never told across a desk. Or during the nine-to-five hours," Thompson explains about his nocturnal timetable. "Even on the telephone, I call people at night."[18]

The interviews presented here come from a range of sources. Along with lengthy interviews from *Playboy, High Times,* and the *Paris Review,* there are pieces from online journals and features from now-defunct publications. These selections illuminate the panoply of Thompson's preoccupations, interests, indulgences, antics, energy, ire, and his incessant mumbling monologues and tirades. Taken as a whole, these interviews clearly indicate the degree of attention Thompson has generated during the last three decades of his life.

It will become readily apparent that the term "interview" is used loosely within this collection. Some of the selections follow the traditional question-and-answer format, others include quasi-interviews, author profiles, and edited conversations—all of which employ quotations from Thompson (abridged or verbatim). Furthermore the interviews took place in various locales, several over extended periods of time. As customary with all books in University Press of Mississippi's Literary Conversations series, the interviews herein have not been edited. Consequently the reader will at times encounter repetitions of both questions and answers, but it is the belief that the significance of the same questions being asked and the consistency (or inconsistency) of responses will prove of value to readers. With the exceptions of emendations made to correct errors of fact, spelling, and punctuation, the pieces herein are reprinted as they originally appeared.

Thompson's words have taken on special meaning to his widow. A former assistant at Thompson's Owl Farm compound in Colorado, Anita wed Hunter in April 2003: "If you read his work now, it has a new sparkle. Perhaps because now we only have a finite amount of words. Imagine if, in some twisted world, he'd taken his words with him; if we picked up his books, and there were only empty pages; if every box in the basement held only blank manuscripts. So obviously, he's still with us."[19]

Thompson ended his life as violently as he lived it, with a self-inflicted gunshot wound in 2005. At age sixteen, he wrote what amounts to a justification of his cartwheeling life and provocative work: "So we shall let the reader answer the question for himself. Who is the happier man, he who has braved the storm of life and lived, or he who has stayed securely on shore and merely existed?"[20]

Thompson braved the storm. The American literary landscape is richer, and wilder, for it.

This book would not have been possible without the assistance, encouragement and support of numerous individuals, in fact, far too many to name individually. In short, we have amassed tremendous personal indebtedness in the completion of this project.

Special tributes go out to:

Our dear friend, Ralph Steadman.

The interviewers and publishers who granted their permission to reprint the interviews selected for this volume, specifically, Ron Rosenbaum, Peter O. Whitmer, Curtis Wilkie, William McKeen, Matthew Hahn, Jeff Kass, Seth Mnookin, J. Rentilly, and John Glassie, who each went above and beyond the call of duty in assisting us.

Our families: Ken, Marian, and Kurt Torrey; Doug, Donna, Mark, and Kristine Simonson, who have always been there for me from our days in Wahoo on . . . (And to Niamh Murphy, Anna, Biggs, and our lovely gang of nieces and nephews).

Our very special friends for their support: Adam Raby, Jan Seng, Gregg Orr, KC Engdahl, Linda Melton, Dinah Henderson, Liz Whitlow (wherever you are?), Randy Gerdts, Jay Quinn, Lanie Jacob, Jeff Norenberg, Gary Sadlemyer, Tom Becka, Brandon Howell, Ted Grau, Ray Trujillo, Beth Govaerts, Chris Pafford, Heather Pond, Dan Beckmann, Leslie Prisbell, the gang at Sullivan's and The Boston Boys (including the memory of our dear friend, Ron McArdle).

Julie, Kat, Dana and Deborah (former assistants of Hunter's) for ensuring that we survived all our encounters with Hunter.

Former colleagues and professors at Doane College in Crete, Nebraska, for their assistance and expertise: Dr. Liam Purdon, Dr. Betty Levitov and Tammy Roach at Perkins Library.

Numerous college classmates for their friendship and input, including J.R. Hansen, David Stamm, Chris Conrad (and his daughters, Carrie Beth and Abbie), Ed Flanagan, Trout, and Gern.

The late Kurt Vonnegut, Tim Cahill, and Cande Carroll for their contributions.

Dennis Baumert, CPA, legal advice of James H. Lee, Bob Dattila, Kevin Rogers, Joe Duggan, and Jack Pokorny, a special thanks for the various roles they played in making this a reality.

Former students during my Tishomingolian exile: Dr. Mark Walling, Kent Stewart, Mark Finley and Ace Collier.

Professional peers Dr. Hal Thaut, Dr. Shawn Bryant, and Cathy Ray for their encouragement and praise.

All the staff of University Press of Mississippi: director Seetha Srinivasan, our editor Walter Biggins, and Anne Stascavage and Shane Gong, for insuring the manuscript progressed from start to finish.

Anita Thompson and Juan Thompson, a special heartfelt recognition.

Gary Isaacs, with deep appreciation for the use of the cover photograph.

The American tobacco and coffee industries and the Woody Creek Tavern.

Lastly, this book is dedicated to our dear friend, the late Hunter S. Thompson, who despite his early exit, fought the good fight. May he rest in peace (which isn't likely).

BT and KS

Notes

1. P. J. O'Rourke, "Dr. Hunter S. Thompson," *Rolling Stone* November 28, 1996, p. 70.
2. Hunter S. Thompson, *The Proud Highway: The Saga of a Desperate Southern Gentleman 1955–1967*, The Fear and Loathing Letters, Vol. 1. New York, Random House: 1997, p. 165.

3. O'Rourke, p. 96.

4. Juan Thompson, "My Father," *Rolling Stone,* March 24, 2005, p. 72.

5. Craig Vetter, "*Playboy* Interview: Hunter Thompson," *Playboy,* November 1974, p. 246.

6. Dave Felton, "Hunter Thompson Has Cashed His Check," *Rolling Stone College Papers,* #2 (1980), p. 49.

7. Douglas Brinkley, "Contentment Was Not Enough," *Rolling Stone,* March 24, 2005, p. 38.

8. O'Rourke, p. 66.

9. Vetter, p. 246.

10. Rachel Cooke, "A Lonely Legacy," *London Observer,* October 23, 2005.

11. Kurt Vonnegut, *Wampeters, Foma & Granfalloons (Opinions),* New York: Delacorte Press/Seymour Lawrence, 1974, pp. 234–35.

12. E. Jean Carroll, *Hunter: The Strange and Savage Life of Hunter S. Thompson,* New York: Dutton, 1993, p. 278.

13. Ralph Steadman, *The Joke's Over: Bruised Memories: Gonzo, Hunter Thompson and Me,* New York: Harcourt Books, 2006, p. 63.

14. Ralph Steadman with Hunter S. Thompson, "Smashing Windows: An Epistolary Lesson in Raising Sons and Making Art," *Playboy,* September 2006, p. 64.

15. O'Rourke, p. 72.

16. P. J. O'Rourke, "Hunter S. Thompson," *Rolling Stone,* (20th Anniversary Issue, November 5–December 10, 1987), p. 237.

17. William McKeen. *Hunter S. Thompson,* Boston: Twayne Publishers, 1991, p. 16.

18. O'Rourke (1987), p. 232.

19. Cooke.

20. Carroll, p. 279.

Chronology

1937	Hunter Stockton Thompson is born on July 18 in Louisville, Kentucky, the first of three sons born to Virginia Ray and Jack R. Thompson.
1948	Listed as "reporter" on the masthead of *Southern Star,* a mimeographed newspaper.
1952	Thompson's father dies unexpectedly of a heart attack during Hunter's sophomore year in high school.
1954	Inducted into the Louisville Athenaeum Literary Association and writes for its literary magazine *The Spectator.*
1955	Sentenced on June 16 to sixty days in the Jefferson County Jail by the juvenile court judge. He is released after serving thirty days, on the condition that he enlist in the armed forces. Thompson misses his high school graduation.
1956	Enlists in the U.S. Air Force, completing boot camp at Kelly Air Force Base in San Antonio, Texas. Serves as Airman Second Class, sports editor and columnist for the Eglin Air Force Base paper, *The Command Courier,* in Florida. Writes sports column under the pen name "Thorne Stockton" for *Playground News* in Fort Walton Beach.
1957	Honorably discharged. Works a few weeks at *Jersey Shore Times* in Pennsylvania.
1959	Enrolls in night classes at Columbia University taking courses on short story writing. Hired by *Time* as a copyboy. Serves as Caribbean correspondent for the *New York Herald Tribune* and *Middletown Daily Record.* Meets his future wife, Sandra Dawn Conklin, in New York City.
1960	Moves to San Juan, Puerto Rico, writing for the sporting magazine *El Sportive.* Completes the novel *Prince Jellyfish* (never published, but later excerpted in *Songs of the Doomed*).
1961	Completes the novel *The Rum Diary.* First magazine feature is published in *Rogue.*

1962   Serves as South American correspondent for the *National Observer.*
1963   Returns to the United States. Marries Conklin on May 19.
1964   Moves with his wife to the Haight-Ashbury district of San Francisco. Birth of his son, Juan Fitzgerald. Named West Coast correspondent for the *Nation* (through 1966).
1965   Begins hanging out with the Hells Angels to research an article. Takes the Angels to Ken Kesey's ranch in La Honda. Publishes article "Motorcyle Gangs: Losers and Outsiders" in the *Nation* and is besieged with book contracts.
1966   Publication of *Hell's Angels: A Strange and Terrible Saga.*
1967–68 Moves family to Owl Farm in Woody Creek, Colorado; he resides in this "heavily fortified compound" for the rest of his life. Attorney Oscar Acosta accompanies Thompson on a trip to Las Vegas to cover the Mint 400 motorcycle race for *Sports Illustrated.*
1970   Thompson draws national attention on his nearly successful run for sheriff of Pitkin County, Colorado, on the Freak Power ticket. First collaboration of Thompson and illustrator Ralph Steadman entitled "The Kentucky Derby Is Decadent and Depraved" appears in *Scanlan's Monthly.*
1971   "Fear and Loathing in Las Vegas" first appears in *Rolling Stone* as a two-part series written by Raoul Duke (Thompson's pseudonym and alter ego). Later that year released by Random House, entitled *Fear and Loathing in Las Vegas: A Savage Journey to the Heart of the American Dream.*
1972   Covers the Nixon-McGovern presidential campaign for *Rolling Stone.*
1973   Publication of *Fear and Loathing: On the Campaign Trail '72.* Publication of Tom Wolfe's *The New Journalism,* a collection of essays and articles by Thompson, Truman Capote, Norman Mailer, and other practitioners of New Journalism.
1974   "A Conversation on Ralph Steadman and His Book, 'America,' with Dr. Hunter S. Thompson" in Ralph Steadman's *America.* Thompson covers the Watergate affair and the Ali-Foreman fight in Zaire, Africa.
1975   Covers the fall of Saigon for *Rolling Stone.*
1976   Thompson characterized as "Uncle Duke" in political cartoonist Garry Trudeau's *Doonesbury* comic strip. Appointed to the Pitkin County sheriff's advisory committee (through 1981).

1977   Thompson becomes extremely popular on the college lecture
circuit. Thompson and Steadman star in the BBC documentary *Fear
and Loathing on the Road to Hollywood.* Release of *The Life of Fiction*
by literary critic, Jerome Klinkowitz, the first critical discussion
of Thompson's work as postmodernist. Includes chapters on
Thompson, Kurt Vonnegut, Jr., Russell Banks, among others.

1979   Publication of *The Great Shark Hunt: Strange Tales from a Strange
Time* (Gonzo Papers, Volume 1).

1980   Divorces Conklin. Release of the film *Where the Buffalo Roam,*
depicting Thompson's adventures while writing stories about
both the Super Bowl and the 1972 presidential election; it stars
Bill Murray as Raoul Duke and Peter Boyle as Oscar Acosta;
original screenplay by John Kaye, produced and directed by Art
Linson. Thompson covers the Honolulu Marathon, with Ralph
Steadman, for *Running* magazine.

1981   Release of John Hellman's *Fables of Fact: The New Journalism as
New Fiction.*

1982   First stage production of *Fear and Loathing in Las Vegas,* adapted
by Lou Stein, opens in London. Friend John Belushi dies.

1983   Publication of *The Curse of Lono.* Covers the Roxanne Pulitzer
divorce trial in Florida for *Rolling Stone.*

1984   Contributor to *Russell Chatham.*

1985   Named media critic/columnist for the *San Francisco Examiner.*
Release of the movie *The Crazy Never Die* starring Thompson.

1987   Annie Leibovitz photographs Thompson for the twentieth-
anniversary edition of *Rolling Stone.* Release of *Aquarius Revisited:
Seven Who Created the Sixties Counterculture That Changed
America* by Peter O. Whitmer, discussing the ideas and writings of
seven key figures: Thompson, William Burroughs, Allen Ginsberg,
Ken Kesey, Timothy Leary, Norman Mailer, and Tom Robbins.

1988   Publication of *Generation of Swine: Tales of Shame and
Degradation in the '80s* (Gonzo Papers, Volume 2). Named
editor-at-large, for the short-lived magazine *Smart,* edited by
Terry McDonell. Thompson serves as a freelance political analyst
for various European magazines.

1989   Thompson becomes popular on the talk show circuit over the
next several years with multiple appearances on *Late Show with*

David Letterman, Late Night with Conan O'Brien, and The Charlie
Rose Show. Publication of Interview with Dr. Hunter S. Thompson
by Ralph Steadman.

1990   Publication of Songs of the Doomed: More Notes on the Death of
          the American Dream (Gonzo Papers, Volume 3). Arrested for
          assault of former porn queen Gail Palmer-Slater at Owl Farm;
          charges of sexual assault and possession of controlled substances
          and incendiary devices are later dismissed. Thompson later forms
          the Fourth Amendment Foundation. Audio version of Songs from
          the Doomed, recorded by Thompson, is released. Writes the
          foreword to On the Bus: The Complete Guide to the Legendary Trip
          of Ken Kesey and the Merry Pranksters and the Birth of the
          Counterculture by Paul Perry, which marked the twenty-fifth
          anniversary of Tom Wolfe's Electric Kool-Aid Acid Test.

1991   Publication of Screwjack and Other Stories. Release of William
          McKeen's Hunter S. Thompson, part of the ongoing Twayne's
          United States Author Series. Thompson has his first solo exhibit at
          the Aspen Art Gallery. Stage production of Fear and Loathing in Las
          Vegas, opens at The Gallery in Chicago, by New Crime Productions.
          Produced by John Cusack, with Jeremy Piven as Dr. Gonzo.

1992   Release of Paul Perry's Fear and Loathing: The Strange and Terrible
          Saga of Hunter S. Thompson. Inducted into the Louisville Male
          High School Hall of Fame.

1993   Release of Peter O. Whitmer's When the Going Gets Weird: The
          Twisted Life and Times of Hunter S. Thompson and E. Jean Carroll's
          Hunter: The Strange and Savage Life of Hunter S. Thompson.
          Appears on ABC's In Concert and interviews Keith Richards.

1994   Death of Thompson's brother, James. Publication of Better Than
          Sex: Confessions of a Political Junkie (Gonzo Papers, Volume 4).
          Named correspondent-at-large for Big Sky Journal.

1995   Thompson and Steadman collaboratively design label for "Road
          Dog Ale," brewed by Flying Dog Brewery LCC in Denver,
          Colorado, sporting a fanged and perhaps rabid dog scowling
          through dark blue sunglasses with the caption: "Good Beer, No
          Shit." The beer and label were pulled from the market by the
          Liquor Enforcement Division of the Colorado Department of
          Revenue, because of "consumer-unfriendly language." The new
          label read: "Good Beer, No Censorship."

1996   Thompson named a Kentucky Colonel by the governor of
            Kentucky and receives the keys to the city of Louisville.
            Publication of The Modern Library Edition of *Fear and Loathing
            in Las Vegas and Other American Stories*, with an introduction by
            P. J. O'Rourke. Audio version of *Fear and Loathing in Las Vegas*
            released, featuring music by Todd Snider and voices of Harry
            Dean Stanton, Jimmy Buffett, Jim Jarmusch, and Buck Henry.

1997   Publication of *The Proud Highway: The Saga of a Desperate
            Southern Gentleman* (1955–1967). Thompson appears in the
            documentary *Anthem: An American Road Story*, produced by
            Shainee Gabel and Kristin Hahn. Transcript of the same title
            published by Avon Books. Contributes story lines for "Nash
            Bridges" (television series starring his neighbor Don Johnson).

1998   Release of the film adaptation of *Fear and Loathing in Las Vegas*.
            Directed by Monty Python veteran Terry Gilliam, starring Johnny
            Depp as Raoul Duke and Benicio Del Toro as Dr. Gonzo.
            Thompson appears in a cameo scene. Writes the foreword for
            Ralph Steadman's *Gonzo: The Art*.

1999   Death of Thompson's mother, Virginia. Publication of
            Thompson's first novel, *The Rum Diary*. Anita Beymuk begins
            working as Thompson's assistant.

2000   Thompson is the first living author ever featured on the cover of
            Paris Review (illustrated by his longstanding cohort, Ralph
            Steadman). Thompson appears in yet another commissioned
            caricature by Steadman on the cover of the *New York Times Book
            Review*. Begins writing "Hey Rube" column for ESPN.

2001   Publication of *Fear and Loathing in America: The Brutal Odyssey
            of an Outlaw Journalist, 1968–1976*. Death of longtime friend Ken
            Kesey.

2002   Thompson's short essay "Walking with the King" appears in
            Spit in the Ocean #7, a tribute to the late Ken Kesey, edited by
            Ed McClanahan. Co-wrote the song "You're a Whole Different
            Person When You're Scared," on the Warren Zevon album
            My Ride's Here.

2003   Marries Anita Beymuk, April 24. Publication of *Kingdom of Fear:
            Loathsome Secrets of a Star-Crossed Child in the Final Days of the
            American Century*. Release of the documentary *Breakfast with
            Hunter*, directed by Wayne Ewing.

2004   Publication of *Hey Rube: Blood Sport, the Bush Doctrine, and the Downward Spiral of Dumbness—Modern History from the Sports Desk*. Publication of *Fire in the Nuts*.

2005   Thompson dies of a self-inflicted gunshot wound on February 20, at his home in Woody Creek, Colorado. *Rolling Stone* and *Doonesbury* publish tributes to Thompson. August 20: Thompson's ashes are blasted from a 155-foot Gonzo fist during the invitation-only ceremony at the Owl Farm, financed by Johnny Depp. Release of the documentary *When I Die* by Wayne Ewing. Flying Dog Brewery releases "Gonzo Imperial Porter" a microbrewed beer with the label designed by Ralph Steadman, featuring a caricature of Thompson. Thompson's will calls for the Gonzo Trust, a group of three trustees (attorneys Hal Haddon and George Tobia and historian Douglas Brinkley) to manage his archives and literary estate. Publication of *The Gang That Wouldn't Shoot Straight: Wolfe, Thompson, Didion and the New Journalism* by Marc Weingarten.

2006   Thompson is named Editor Emeritus of *The Woody Creeker* which is edited by his widow Anita. Release of the documentary *Buy the Ticket, Take the Ride*, produced by Starz Entertainment Group and directed by Tom Thurman. October release of Steadman's memoir *The Joke's Over: Bruised Memories: Gonzo, Hunter S. Thompson and Me*. December release of *GONZO*, a collection of Thompson photographs and memorabilia. Release of the documentary *Free Lisl: Fear & Loathing in Denver*, directed by Wayne Ewing.

2007   Publication of *Gonzo: The Oral History of Hunter S. Thompson* by Jann Wenner and Corey Seymour; and *The Gonzo Way: A Celebration of Dr. Hunter S. Thompson* by Anita Thompson.

2008   Scheduled release of *The Kitchen Readings: Untold Stories of Hunter S. Thompson* by Michael Cleverly and Bob Braudis; *Outlaw Journalist: The Life and Times of Hunter S. Thompson* by William McKeen and *Who Killed Hunter Thompson?*, a collection of essays by Thompson's friends and co-conspirators, edited by Warren Hinckle.

2009   Scheduled release of Thompson's third volume of personal letters: *The Mutineer: Rants, Ravings, and Missives from the Mountaintop 1977–2005*.

Conversations with Hunter S. Thompson

Playboy Interview: Hunter Thompson
Craig Vetter / 1974

Hunter Stockton Thompson was born and grew up in Louisville, Kentucky, and for the past fifteen years he has worked as a free-lance writer. He began it all in the Air Force by lying his way into a job as sports editor of the base newspaper. He was fired and threatened with duty in Iceland when his superiors discovered that he was also writing about sports for a civilian paper under another name. After he was discharged, he took writing jobs and was fired from them in Pennsylvania (for destroying his editor's car), in Middletown, New York (where he insulted an advertiser and kicked a candy machine to death), at *Time* magazine (for his attitude) and in Puerto Rico, where the bowling magazine he was working for failed and he decided to give up journalism. He moved to Big Sur, where his wife, Sandy, made motel beds while he wrote a novel that was never published.

His first real success as a writer came when he moved to South America and began sending stories on tin miners, jungle bandits and smugglers back to *The National Observer,* which was printing them on the front page and paying him well for them. He continued to write for it when he returned to the States but quit finally in a bitter dispute with his editors over coverage of the Berkeley Free Speech Movement. After another try at a novel, this time in San Francisco, he wrote a story for *The Nation* on a gang of motorcycle outlaws that he turned into his first book, *Hell's Angels: A Strange and Terrible Saga.* He continued to write for magazines, developing his wide-open, often-criticized style. Then, in 1971, he turned two abortive magazine assignments into a stunning romp called *Fear and Loathing in Las Vegas: A Savage Journey to the Heart of the American Dream;* which earned him an almost immediate reputation as one of the toughest and funniest writers in America.

3

Since then, he has written about football and power politics for *Rolling Stone* and his dispatches written during the 1972 Presidential campaign became his third book, *Fear and Loathing: On the Campaign Trail '72.*

Early in the year, PLAYBOY sent Craig Vetter to interview Thompson. Vetter's report:

"This interview was hammered and stitched together over seven months, on the road, mostly, in Mexico and Washington, San Clemente and Colorado, and as I write this, we are in Chicago, where tornado warnings are out, and we are up against a hell-fire deadline that has me seeing ghosts and has Dr. Thompson locked in a penthouse full of mirrors on the twentieth floor of an Astor Street high-rise. He has the heavy steel window louvers cranked shut, there is a lamp behind him that has had its neck snapped off and he is bent over a coffee table cursing. We are trying to salvage this interview, making changes, corrections, additions—all of them unnecessary until nine days ago, when Richard Nixon quit. Thompson is mumbling that the motor control in his pen hand is failing and he is not kidding. You can't read his Rs anymore and all five vowels may become illegible soon. We might have finished this thing like gentlemen, except for Richard Nixon, who might as well have sent the plumbers' unit to torch the entire second half, the political half, of the manuscript we have worked on so long. All of it has had to be redone in the past few sleepless days and it has broken the spirit of nearly everyone even vaguely involved.

"Thompson is no stranger to this sort of madness. In fact, he has more than once turned scenes like this into art: Gonzo Journalism, his own wild and dangerous invention, was born in the fires of a nearly hopeless deadline crisis and although no one can storm his demons and win every time out, the mad and speedy Doctor does it more often and with more humor than any other journalist working today. He's still talking to himself over there, chewing on his cigarette holder, and a few minutes ago he said, 'When this is over, I'm going back to Colorado and sleep like an animal,' and he wasn't kidding about that, either. Because for the past two weeks, Nixon's last few weeks, Thompson has suffered and gone sleepless in Washington with another deadline on an impeachment story that was finally burned to a cinder by the same fire storm that gutted the White House. Finally it has been too much even for the man they call 'the quintessential outlaw journalist.' We have been forced over the course of this epic to use certain drugs in such quantity that he has terminated his personal drug research for good and in the same desperate fit, he has severed all connection with national politics and is returning, for new forms of energy, to his roots.

"We're well into the thirtieth hour now and there won't be many more, no matter what. Thompson is working over his last few answers, still talking to himself, and I think I just heard him say, 'The rest will have to be done by God,' which may mean that he is finished.

"And though this long and killing project is ending here in desperate, guilty, short-tempered ugliness, it began all those months ago, far from this garden of agony, on a sunshine island in the Caribbean where Thompson and Sandy and I had gone to begin taping.

"The first time I turned on the tape recorder, we were sitting on a sea wall, in damp, salty bathing suits, under palm trees. It was warm, Nixon was still our President and Thompson was sucking up bloody marys, vegetables and all, and he had just paid a young newsboy bandit almost one dollar American for a paper that would have cost a straighter, more sober person twenty-four cents."

Playboy: You just paid as much for your morning paper as you might for a good hit of mescaline. Are you a news junkie, too?
Thompson: Yeah, I *must* have the news. One of these mornings, I'm gonna buy a paper with a big black headline that says, "RICHARD NIXON COMMITTED SUICIDE LAST NIGHT." Jesus . . . can you imagine *that* rush?

Playboy: Do you get off on politics the same way you get off on drugs?
Thompson: Sometimes. It depends on the politics, depends on the drugs . . . there are different kinds of highs. I had this same discussion in Mexico City one night with a guy who wanted me to do Zihuatanejo with him and get stoned for about ten days on the finest flower tops to be had in all of Mexico. But I told him I couldn't do that; I had to be back in Washington.

Playboy: That doesn't exactly fit your image as the drug-crazed outlaw journalist. Are you saying you'd rather have been in the capital, covering the Senate Watergate hearings or the House Judiciary Committee debate on Nixon's impeachment, than stoned on the beach in Mexico with a bunch of freaks?
Thompson: Well—it depends on the timing. On Wednesday, I might want to go to Washington; on Thursday, I might want to go to Zihuatanejo.

Playboy: Today must be Thursday, because already this morning you've had two bloody marys, three beers and about four spoons of some white substance and you've been up for only an hour. You don't deny that you're heavily into drugs, do you?

Thompson: No, why should I deny it? I like drugs. Somebody gave me this white powder last night. I suspect it's cocaine, but there's only one way to find out—look at this shit! It's already crystallized in this goddamn humidity. I can't even cut it up with the scissors in my Swiss-army knife. Actually, coke is a worthless drug, anyway. It has no edge. Dollar for dollar, it's probably the most inefficient drug on the market. It's not worth the effort or the risk or the money—at least not to me. It's a social drug; it's more important to offer it than it is to use it. But the world is full of cocamaniacs these days and they have a tendency to pass the stuff around, and this morning I'm a little tired and I have this stuff, so. . . .

Playboy: What do you like best?

Thompson: Probably mescaline and mushrooms: That's a genuine high. It's not just an up—you know, like speed, which is really just a motor high. When you get into psychedelics like mescaline and mushrooms, it's a very clear kind of high, an *interior* high. But really, when you're dealing with psychedelics, there's only one king drug, when you get down to it, and that's acid. About twice a year you should blow your fucking tubes out with a tremendous hit of really good acid. Take seventy-two hours and just go completely amuck, break it all down.

Playboy: When did you take your first acid trip?

Thompson: It was while I was working on the Hell's Angels book. Ken Kesey wanted to meet some of the Angels, so I introduced him and he invited them all down to his place in La Honda. It was a horrible, momentous meeting and I thought I'd better be there to see what happened when all this incredible chemistry came together. And, sure as shit, the Angels rolled in—about forty or fifty bikes—and Kesey and the other people were offering them acid. And I thought, "Great creeping Jesus, what's going to happen now?"

Playboy: Had the Angels ever been into acid before that?

Thompson: No. That was the most frightening thing about it. Here were all these vicious bikers full of wine and bennies, and Kesey's people immediately started giving them LSD. They didn't know what kind of violent crowd they were dealing with. I was sure it was going to be a terrible blood, rape and pillage scene, that the Angels would tear the place apart. And I stood there, thinking, "Jesus, I'm responsible for this, I'm the one who did it." I watched those lunatics gobbling the acid and I thought, "Shit, if it's gonna get this heavy I want to be as fucked up as possible." So I went to one of Kesey's friends and I said, "Let me have some of that shit; we're heading into a very serious night. Perhaps even ugly." So I took what he said was about 800 micrograms, which almost blew my head off at the time . . . but in a very fine way. It was nice. Surprised me, really. I'd heard all these stories when I lived in Big Sur a couple of years before from this psychiatrist who'd taken the stuff and wound up running naked through the streets of Palo Alto, screaming that he wanted to be punished for his crimes. He didn't know what his crimes were and nobody else did, either, so they took him away and he spent a long time in a loony bin somewhere, and I thought, "That's not what *I* need." Because if a guy who seems levelheaded like that is going to flip out and tear off his clothes and beg the citizens to punish him, what the hell might *I* do?

Playboy: You didn't beg to be scourged and whipped?
Thompson: No . . . and I didn't scourge anybody else, either, and when I was finished, I thought, "Jesus, you're not so crazy, after all; you're not a basically violent or vicious person like they said." Before that, I had this dark fear that if I lost control, all these horrible psychic worms and rats would come out. But I went to the bottom of the well and found out there's nothing down there I have to worry about, no secret ugly things waiting for a chance to erupt.

Playboy: You drink a little, too, don't you?
Thompson: Yeah . . . obviously, but I drink this stuff like I smoke cigarettes; I don't even notice it. You know—a bird flies, a fish swims, I drink. But you notice I very rarely sit down and say, "Now I'm going to get wasted." I never eat a tremendous amount of any one thing. I rarely get drunk and I use drugs pretty much the same way.

Playboy: Do you like marijuana?
Thompson: Not much. It doesn't mix well with alcohol. I don't like to get stoned and stupid.

Playboy: What would you estimate you spend on drugs in a year?
Thompson: Oh, Jesus. . . .

Playboy: What the average American family spends on an automobile, say?
Thompson: Yeah, at least that much. I don't know what the total is; I don't even *want* to know. It's frightening, but I'll tell you that on a story I just did, one of the sections took me seventeen days of research and $1400 worth of cocaine. And that's just what *I* spent. On *one section* of *one* story.

Playboy: What do you think the drugs are doing to your body?
Thompson: Well, I just had a physical, the first one in my life. People got worried about my health, so I went to a very serious doctor and told him I wanted every fucking test known to man: EEG, heart, everything. And he asked me questions for three hours to start with, and I thought, "What the hell, tell the truth, that's why you're here." So I told him exactly what I'd been doing for the past ten years. He couldn't believe it. He said, "Jesus, Hunter, you're a goddamn mess"—that's an exact quote. Then he ran all the tests and found I was in perfect health. He called it a "genetic miracle."

Playboy: What about your mind?
Thompson: I think it's pretty healthy. I think I'm looser than I was before I started to take drugs. I'm more comfortable with myself. Does it *look* like it's fucked me up? I'm sitting here on a beautiful beach in Mexico; I've written three books; I've got a fine hundred-acre fortress in Colorado. On that evidence, I'd have to *advise* the use of drugs. . . . But of course I wouldn't, never in hell—or at least not *all* drugs for *all* people. There are some people who should never be allowed to take acid, for instance. You can spot them after about ten minutes: people with all kinds of bad psychic baggage, stuff they haven't cleaned out yet, weird hostilities, repressed shit—the same kind of people who turn into mean drunks.

Playboy: Do you believe religious things about drugs?
Thompson: No, I never have. That's my main argument with the drug culture. I've never believed in that guru trip; you know, God, nirvana, that kind of oppressive, hipper-than-thou bullshit. I like to just gobble the stuff right out in the street and see what happens, take my chances, just stomp on my own accelerator. It's like getting on a racing bike and all of a sudden

you're doing 120 miles per hour into a curve that has sand all over it and you think, "Holy Jesus, here we go," and you lay it over till the pegs hit the street and metal starts to spark. If you're good enough, you can pull it out, but sometimes you end up in the emergency room with some bastard in a white suit sewing your scalp back on.

Playboy: Is that what you call "edge work"?
Thompson: Well, that's one aspect of it, I guess—in that you have to be *good* when you take nasty risks, or you'll lose it, and then you're in serious trouble.

Playboy: Why are you smiling?
Thompson: Am I smiling? Yeah, I guess I am . . . well, it's fun to lose it sometimes.

Playboy: What kind of flack do you get for being so honest about the drugs you use?
Thompson: I'm not too careful about what I say. But I'm careful in other ways. I never sell any drugs, for instance; I never get involved in the traffic or the marketing end of the drug business. I make a point of not even knowing about it. I'm very sensitive about maintaining my deniability, you know—like Nixon. I never deal. Simple use is one thing—like booze in the Twenties—but selling is something else: They come after you for that. I wouldn't sell drugs to my mother, for any reason . . . no, the only person I'd sell drugs to would be Richard Nixon. I'd sell him whatever the fucker wanted . . . but he'd pay heavy for it and damn well remember the day he tried it.

Playboy: Are you the only journalist in America who's ridden with both Richard Nixon and the Hell's Angels?
Thompson: I *must* be. Who else would claim a thing like that? Hell, who else would admit it?

Playboy: Which was more frightening?
Thompson: The Angels. Nobody can throw a gut-level, king-hell scare into you like a Hell's Angel with a pair of pliers hanging from his belt that he uses to pull out people's teeth in midnight diners. Some of them wear the teeth on their belts, too.

Playboy: Why did you decide to do a book on the Hell's Angels?
Thompson: Money. I'd just quit and been fired almost at the same time by *The National Observer.* They wouldn't let me cover the Free Speech thing at Berkeley and I sensed it was one of the biggest stories I'd ever stumbled onto. So I decided, "Fuck journalism," and I went back to writing novels. I tried driving a cab in San Francisco, I tried every kind of thing. I used to go down at five o'clock every morning and line up with the winos on Mission Street, looking for work handing out grocery-store circulars and shit like that. I was the youngest and healthiest person down there, but nobody would ever select me. I tried to get weird and rotten-looking; you know—an old Army field jacket, scraggly beard, tried to look like a bad wino. But even then, I never got picked out of the line-up.

Playboy: You couldn't even get wino's work?
Thompson: No, and at that point I was *stone*-broke, writing fiction, living in a really fine little apartment in San Francisco—looking down on Golden Gate Park, just above Haight Street. The rent was only $100 a month—this was 1965, about a year before the Haight-Ashbury madness started—and I got a letter from Carey McWilliams, the editor of *The Nation,* and it said, "Can you do an article on the Hell's Angels for us for $100?" That was the rent, and I was about ready to get back into journalism, so I said, "Of course. I'll do *anything* for $100."

Playboy: How long did the article take?
Thompson: I worked about a month on it, put about $3000 worth of effort into it, got no expenses—and about six weeks after the fucker came out, my mailbox piled up with book offers. My phone had been cut off by then. I couldn't believe it: editors, publishers, people I'd never heard of. One of them offered me $1500 just to sign a thing saying that if I decided to write the book, I'd do it for them. Shit, at that point I would have written the definitive text on hammer-head sharks for the money—and spent a year in the water with them.

Playboy: How did you first meet the Angels?
Thompson: I just went out there and said, "Look, you guys don't know me, I don't know you, I heard some bad things about you, are they true?" I was wearing a fucking madras coat and wing tips, that kind of thing, but

I think they sensed I was a little strange—if only because I was the first writer who'd ever come out to see them and talk to them on their own turf. Until then, all the Hell's Angels stories had come from the cops. They seemed a little stunned at the idea that some straight-looking writer for a New York literary magazine would actually track them down to some obscure transmission shop in the industrial slums of south San Francisco. They were a bit off balance at first, but after about fifty or sixty beers, we found a common ground, as it were. . . . Crazies always recognize each other. I think Melville said it, in a slightly different context: "Genius all over the world stands hand in hand, and one shock of recognition runs the whole circle round." Of course, we're not talking about genius here, we're talking about crazies—but it's essentially the same thing. They *knew* me, they saw right through all my clothes and there was that instant karmic flash. They seemed to *sense* what they had on their hands.

Playboy: Had you been into motorcycles before that?
Thompson: A little bit, not much. But when I got the advance on the book, I went out and bought the fastest bike ever tested by *Hot Rod* magazine: a BSA 650 Lightning. I thought, "If I'm gonna ride with these fuckers, I want the fastest bike known to man."

Playboy: They all rode Harley-Davidsons, right?
Thompson: Yeah, and they didn't like it that I was riding a BSA. They kept offering to get me hot bikes. You know—a brand-new Harley Sportster for $400, stuff like that. No papers, of course, no engine numbers—so I said no. I had enough trouble as it was. I was always getting pulled over. Jesus, they canceled my car insurance because of that goddamn bike. They almost took my driver's license away. I never had any trouble with my car. I drove it full bore all over San Francisco all the time, just wide open. It was a good car, too, a little English Ford. When it finally developed a crack in one of the four cylinders, I took it down to a cliff in Big Sur and soaked the whole interior with ten gallons of gasoline, then executed the fucker with six shots from a .44 magnum in the engine block at point-blank range. After that, we rolled it off the cliff—the radio going, lights on, everything going—and at the last minute, we threw a burning towel in. The explosion was ungodly; it almost blew us into the ocean. I had no idea what ten gallons of gas in an English Ford could do. The car was a mass of twisted, flaming metal. It bounced

about six times on the way down—pure movie-stunt shit, you know. A sight like that was worth the car; it was beautiful.

Playboy: It seems pretty clear you had *something* in common with the Angels. How long did you ride with them?
Thompson: About a year.

Playboy: Did they ever ask you to join?
Thompson: Some of them did, but there was a very fine line I had to maintain there. Like when I went on runs with them, I didn't go dressed as an Angel. I'd wear Levis and boots but always a little different from theirs; a tan leather jacket instead of a black one, little things like that. I told them right away I was a *writer*, I was doing a book and that was it. If I'd joined, I wouldn't have been able to write about them honestly, because they have this "brothers" thing. . . .

Playboy: Were there moments in that year when you wondered how you ever came to be riding with the meanest motorcycle outlaws in the world?
Thompson: Well, I figured it was a hard dollar—maybe the hardest—but actually, when I got into it, I started to like it. My wife, Sandy, was horrified at first. There were five or six from the Oakland and Frisco chapters that I got to know pretty well, and it got to the point that they'd just come over to my apartment any time of the day or night—bring their friends, three cases of stolen beer, a bunch of downers, some bennies. But I got to like it; it was my life, it wasn't just working.

Playboy: Was that a problem when you actually started to write?
Thompson: Not really. When you write for a living and you can't do anything else, you know that sooner or later that the deadline is going to come screaming down on you like a goddamn banshee. There's no avoiding it—not even when you have a fine full-bore story like the Angels that's still running . . . so one day you just don't appear at the El Adobe bar anymore; you shut the door, paint the windows black, rent an electric typewriter and become the monster you always were—the writer. I'd warned them about that. I'd said, "It's going to come, I'm not here for the fun of it, it's gonna happen." And when the time came, I just did it. Every now and then, somebody like Frenchy or Terry would drop by at night with some girls or

some of the others, but even when I'd let them read a few pages of what I'd written, they didn't really believe I was actually writing a book.

Playboy: How long did it take?
Thompson: About six months. Actually it took six months to write the first half of the book and then four days to write the second half. I got terrified about the deadline; I actually thought they were going to cancel the contract if I didn't finish the book exactly on time. I was in despair over the thing, so I took the electric typewriter and about four quarts of Wild Turkey and just drove north on 101 until I found a motel that looked peaceful, checked in and stayed there for four days. Didn't sleep, ate a lot of speed, went out every morning and got a hamburger at McDonald's and just wrote straight through for four days—and that turned out to be the best part of the book.

Playboy: In one of the last chapters, you described the scene where the Angels finally stomped you, but you described it rather quickly. How did it happen?
Thompson: Pretty quickly. . . . I'd been away from their action for about six months, I'd finished most of the writing and the publisher sent me a copy of the proposed book cover and I said, "This sucks. It's the worst fucking cover I've seen on *any* book"—so I told them I'd shoot another cover if they'd just pay the expenses. So I called Sonny Barger, who was the head Angel, and said, "I want to go on the Labor Day run with you guys; I've finished the book, but now I want to shoot a book cover." I got some bad vibes over the phone from him. I knew something was not right, but by this time I was getting careless.

Playboy: Was the Labor Day run a big one?
Thompson: Shit, yes. This was one of these horrible things that scare the piss out of everybody—two hundred bikes. A mass Hell's Angels run is one of the most terrifying things you'll ever hope to see. When those bastards come by you on the road, *that's* heavy. And being a part of it, you get this tremendous feeling of humor and madness. You see the terror and shock and fear all around you and you're laughing all the time. It's like being in some kind of horror movie where you know that sooner or later the actors are going to leap out of the screen and burn the theater down.

Playboy: Did the Angels have a sense of humor about it?

Thompson: Some of them did. They were running a trip on everybody. I mean, you don't carry pliers and pull people's teeth out and then wear them on your belt without knowing you're running a trip on somebody. But on that Labor Day, we went up to some beach near Mendocino and I violated all my rules: First, never get stoned with them. Second, never get really drunk with them. Third, never argue with them when you're stoned and drunk. And fourth, when they start beating on each other, *leave*. I'd followed those rules for a year. But they started to pound on each other and I was just standing there talking to somebody and I said my bike was faster than his, which it was—another bad mistake—and all of a sudden, I got it right in the face, a terrific whack; I didn't even see where it came from, had no idea. When I grabbed the guy, he was small enough so that I could turn him around, pin his arms and just hold him. And I turned to the guy I'd been talking to and said something like, "Jesus Christ, look at this nut, he just hit me in the fucking face, get him away from here," and the guy I was holding began to scream in this high wild voice because I had him helpless, and instead of telling him to calm down, the *other* guy cracked *me* in the side of the head—and then I knew I was in trouble. That's the Angels' motto: One on all, all on one.

Playboy: Were there police around or other help?

Thompson: No, I was the only nonbiker there. The cops had said, "All right, at midnight we seal this place off and anybody who's not a part of this crowd get the hell out or God's mercy on him." So here I was, suddenly rolling around on the rocks of that Godforsaken beach in a swarm of stoned, crazy-drunk bikers. I had this guy who'd hit me in a death grip by now, and there were people kicking me in the chest and one of the bastards was trying to bash my head in with a tremendous rock . . . but I had this screaming Angel's head right next to mine, and so he had to be a little careful. I don't know how long it went on, but just about the time I *knew* I was going to die, Tiny suddenly showed up and said, "That's it, stop it," and they stopped as fast as they started, for no reason.

Playboy: Who was Tiny?

Thompson: He was the sergeant at arms and he was also one of the guys who I knew pretty well. I didn't know the bastards I was fighting with. All the Angels I might have counted on for help—the ones I'd come to think of as friends by that time—had long since retired to the bushes with their old ladies.

Playboy: How badly were you hurt?

Thompson: They did a pretty good job on my face. I went to the police station and they said, "Get the fuck out of here—you're bleeding in the bathroom." I was wasted, pouring blood, and I had to drive sixty miles like that to Santa Rosa, where I knew a doctor. I called him, but he was in Arizona and his partner answered the phone and said something like, "Spit on it and run a lap"; you know, that old football-coach thing. I'll never forgive him for that. So then I went to the emergency room at the Santa Rosa hospital and it was one of the worst fucking scenes I'd ever seen in my life. A bike gang called the Gypsy Jokers had been going north on Labor Day and had intersected with this horrible train of Angels somewhere around Santa Rosa and these fuckers were all over the emergency room. People screaming and moaning, picking up pieces of jawbones, trying to fit them back in, blood everywhere, girls yelling, "He's dying, please help us! Doctor, doctor! I can't stop the bleeding!" It was like a bomb had just hit.

Playboy: Did you get treatment?

Thompson: No, I felt guilty even being there. I had only been *stomped*. These other bastards had been cranked out with pipes, run over, pinned against walls with bikes—mangled, just mangled. So I left, tried to drive in that condition, but finally I just pulled over to the side of the road and thought, "I'd better set this fucking nose, because tomorrow it's going to be hard." It felt like a beanbag. I could hear the bone chips grinding. So I sat there and drank a beer and did my own surgery, using the dome light and the rearview mirror, trying to remember what my nose had looked like. I couldn't breathe for about a year, and people thought I was a coke freak before I actually was, but I think I did a pretty good job.

Playboy: Who are the Hell's Angels, what kind of people?

Thompson: They're rejects, losers—but losers who turned mean and vengeful instead of just giving up, and there are more Hell's Angels than anybody can count. But most of them don't wear any colors. They're people who got moved out—you know, musical chairs—and they lost. Some people just lie down when they lose; these fuckers come back and tear up the whole game. I was a Hell's Angel in my head for a long time. I was a failed writer for ten years and I was always in fights. I'd do things like go into a bar with a fifty-pound sack of lime, turn the whole place white and then just take on anyone who came at me. I always got stomped, never won a fight. But I'm not into that anymore. I lost a lot of my physical aggressiveness when I started to sell what I wrote. I didn't need that trip anymore.

Playboy: Some people would say you didn't lose all your aggressiveness, that you come on like journalism's own Hell's Angel.
Thompson: Well, I don't see myself as particularly aggressive or dangerous. I tend to act weird now and then, which makes people nervous if they don't know me—but I think that's sort of a stylistic hangover from the old days . . . and I suppose I get a private smile or two out of making people's eyes bulge once in a while. You might call that a Hell's Angels trait—but otherwise, the comparison is ugly and ominous. I reject it—although I definitely feel myself somewhat *apart*. Not an outlaw, but more like a natural freak . . . which doesn't bother me at all. When I ran for sheriff of Aspen on the Freak Power ticket, that was the point. In the rotten fascist context of what was happening to America in 1969, being a freak was an honorable way to go.

Playboy: Why did you run for sheriff?
Thompson: I'd just come back from the Democratic Convention in Chicago and been beaten by vicious cops for no reason at all. I'd had a billy club rammed into my stomach and I'd seen innocent people beaten senseless and it really jerked me around. There was a mayoral race a few months later in Aspen and there was a lawyer in town who'd done some good things in local civil rights cases. His name is Joe Edwards and I called him up one midnight and said, "You don't know me and I don't know you, but you've got to run for mayor. The whole goddamn system is getting out of control. If it keeps going this way, they'll have us all in pens. We *have* to get into politics—if only in self-defense." Now, this guy was a bike rider, a head and a freak in the same sense I am. He said, "We'll meet tomorrow and talk about it." The next day, we went to see *The Battle of Algiers* and when we came out, he said, "I'll do it; we're going to bust these bastards."

Playboy: How close did you come?
Thompson: Edwards lost by six votes. And remember, we're talking about an apolitical town and the hardest thing was to get our people to register. So one of the gigs I used to get people into it was to say, "Look, if you register and vote for Edwards, I'll run for sheriff next year, if he wins." Well, he didn't win,

but when the next county elections came up, I found myself running for sheriff anyway. I didn't take it seriously at first, but when it began to look like I might win, *everybody* took it seriously.

Playboy: As a matter of fact, you announced you were going to eat drugs in the sheriff's office if you won, didn't you?

Thompson: Yeah and that scared a lot of people. But I'd seen the ignorant hate vote that the Edwards campaign brought out the year before. You know, when the freaks get organized, the other side gets scared and they bring out people on stretchers who are half dead, haven't voted for twenty-five years. And I thought, "Well, if they want somebody to hate, I'll give them one they can *really* hate." And meanwhile, on the same ticket, I figured we could run a serious candidate for a county commissioner, which is the office we really wanted. Hell, I didn't want to be sheriff, I wanted to scare the piss out of the yahoos and the greed-heads and make our county-commissioner candidate look like a conservative by contrast. That's what we did, but then this horrible press coverage from all over the goddamn world poured in and we finally couldn't separate the two races.

Playboy: There was a whole Freak Power slate, wasn't there?

Thompson: Yeah, a friend of mine, who lived next door at the time, ran for coroner, because we found out the coroner was the only official who could fire the sheriff. And we decided we needed a county clerk, so we had somebody running for that. But finally, my lightning rod, hate-candidate strategy backlashed on them, too. It got a little heavy. I announced that the new sheriff's posse would start tearing up the streets the day after the election—every street in Aspen, rip 'em up with jackhammers and replace the asphalt with sod. I said we were going to use the sheriff's office mainly to harass real-estate developers.

Playboy: Sounds like that could heat up a political contest.

Thompson: Indeed. The greedheads were terrified. We had a series of public debates that got pretty brutal. The first one was in a movie theater, because that was the only place in town that could hold the crowd. Even then, I arrived a half hour early and I couldn't get in. The aisles were jammed, I had to walk over people to get to the stage. I was wearing shorts, with my head shaved completely bald. The yahoos couldn't handle it. They were convinced the Anti-christ had finally appeared—right there in Aspen. There's something ominous about a totally shaved head. We took questions from the crowd and sort of laid out our platforms. I was not entirely comfortable, sitting up there with the incumbent sheriff and saying, "When I drive this corrupt thug out of office, I'm going to go in there and maybe eat a bit of mescaline on slow nights. . . ." I figured from then on I *had* to win, because if I lost, it was going to be the hammer for me. You just don't admit that kind of thing on camera, in front of a huge crowd. There was a reporter from *The New York Times* in the front row, NBC, an eight-man team from the BBC filming the whole thing, the *Los Angeles Times, The Washington Post*—incredible.

Playboy: You changed the pitch toward the end, toned it down, didn't you?
Thompson: Yeah, I became a creature of my own campaign. I was really surprised at the energy we could whip up for that kind of thing, latent political energy just sitting around.

Playboy: What did your platform finally evolve into?
Thompson: I said I was going to function as an Ombudsman, create a new office—unsalaried—then turn my sheriff's salary over to a good experienced lawman and let him do the job. I figured once you got control of the sheriff's office, you could let somebody else carry the badge and gun—under your control, of course. It almost worked.

Playboy: What was the final vote?
Thompson: Well, there were six precincts that mattered and I won the three in town, broke even in number four and then got stomped brutally in the two precincts where most of the real-estate developers and subdividers live.

Playboy: Are you sorry you lost?
Thompson: Well, I felt sorry for the people who worked so hard on the campaign. But I don't miss the job. For a while, I thought I was going to win, and it scared me.

Playboy: There's been talk of your running for the Senate from Colorado. Is that a joke?
Thompson: No. I considered it for a while, but this past year has killed my appetite for politics. I might reconsider after I get away from it for a while. *Somebody* has to change politics in this country.

Playboy: Would you run for the Senate the same way you ran for sheriff?
Thompson: Well, I might have to drop the mescaline issue, I don't think there'd be any need for that—promising to eat mescaline on the Senate floor. I found out last time you can push people too far. The backlash is brutal.

Playboy: What if the unthinkable happened and Hunter Thompson went to Washington as a Senator from Colorado? Do you think you could do any good?
Thompson: Not much, but you always do some good by setting an example—you know, just by proving it can be done.

Playboy: Don't you think there would be a strong reaction in Washington to some of the things you've written about the politicians there?
Thompson: Of course. They'd come after me like wolverines. I'd have no choice but to haul out my secret files—all that raw swill Ed Hoover gave me just before he died. We were good friends. I used to go to the track with him a lot.

Playboy: You're laughing again, but that raises a legitimate question: Are you trying to say you know things about Washington people that you haven't written?
Thompson: Yeah, to some extent. When I went to Washington to write *Fear and Loathing: On the Campaign Trail '72,* I went with the same attitude I take anywhere as a journalist: hammer and tongs—and God's mercy on anybody who gets in the way. Nothing is off the record, that kind of thing. But I finally realized that some things *have* to be off the record. I don't know where the line is, even now. But if you're an indiscreet blabber-mouth and a fool, nobody is going to talk to you—not even your friends.

Playboy: What was it like when you first rode into Washington in 1971?
Thompson: Well, nobody had ever heard of *Rolling Stone,* for one thing. "Rolling what? . . . Stones? I heard them once; noisy bastards, aren't they?" It was a nightmare at first, nobody would return my calls. Washington is a horrible town, a cross between Rome, Georgia, and Toledo, Ohio—that kind of mentality. It's basically a town full of vicious, powerful rubes.

Playboy: Did they start returning your calls when you began writing things like "Hubert Humphrey should be castrated" so his genes won't be passed on?
Thompson: Well, that was a bit heavy, I think—for reasons I don't want to get into now. Anyway, it didn't take me long to learn that the only time to call

politicians is very late at night. *Very* late. In Washington, the truth is never told in daylight hours or across a desk. If you catch people when they're very tired or drunk or weak, you can usually get some answers. So I'd sleep days, wait till these people got their lies and treachery out of the way, let them relax, then come on full speed on the phone at two or three in the morning. You have to wear the bastards down before they'll tell you anything.

Playboy: Your journalistic style has been attacked by some critics—most notably, the *Columbia Journalism Review*—as partly commentary, partly fantasy and partly the ravings of someone too long into drugs.
Thompson: Well, fuck the *Columbia Journalism Review*. They don't pay my rent. That kind of senile gibberish reminds me of all those people back in the early Sixties who were saying, "This guy Dylan is giving Tin-Pan Alley a bad name—hell, he's no musician. He can't even carry a tune." Actually, it's kind of a compliment when people like that devote so much energy to attacking you.

Playboy: Well, you certainly say some outrageous things in your book on the 1972 Presidential campaign; for instance, that Edmund Muskie was taking Ibogaine, an exotic form of South American speed or psychedelic, or both. That wasn't true, was it?
Thompson: Not that I know of, but if you read what I wrote carefully, I didn't *say* he was taking it. I said there was a rumor around his headquarters in Milwaukee that a famous Brazilian doctor had flown in with an emergency packet of Ibogaine for him. Who would believe that shit?

Playboy: A lot of people did believe it.
Thompson: Obviously, but I didn't realize that until about halfway through the campaign—and it horrified me. Even some of the reporters who'd been covering Muskie for three or four months took it seriously. That's because they don't know anything about drugs. Jesus, nobody running for President would *dare* touch a thing like Ibogaine. Maybe.' I would, but no normal politician. It would turn his brains to jelly. He'd have to be locked up.

Playboy: You also said that John Chancellor took heavy hits of black acid.
Thompson: Hell, that was such an obvious heavy-handed joke that I *still* can't understand how anybody in his right mind could have taken it seriously. I'd infiltrated a Nixon youth rally at the Republican Convention

and I thought I'd have a little fun with them by telling all the grisly details of the time that John Chancellor tried to kill me by putting acid in my drink. I also wrote that if I'd had more time, I would have told these poor yo-yos the story about Walter Cronkite and his white-slavery racket with Vietnamese orphan girls—importing them through a ranch in Quebec and then selling them into brothels up and down the East Coast . . . which is true, of course; *Collier's* magazine has a big story on it this month, with plenty of photos to prove it. . . . What? You don't *believe* that? Why not? All those other waterheads did. Christ, writing about politics would paralyze my brain if I couldn't have a slash of weird humor now and then. And, actually, I'm pretty careful about that sort of thing. If I weren't, I would have been sued long ago. It's one of the hazards of Gonzo Journalism.

Playboy: What *is* Gonzo Journalism?
Thompson: It's something that grew out of a story on the Kentucky Derby for *Scanlan's* magazine. It was one of those horrible deadline scrambles and I ran out of time. I was desperate. Ralph Steadman had done the illustrations, the cover was printed and there was this horrible hole in the magazine. I was convinced I was finished, I'd blown my mind, couldn't work. So finally I just started jerking pages out of my notebook and numbering them and sending them to the printer. I was sure it was the last article I was ever going to do for anybody. Then when it came out, there were massive numbers of letters, phone calls, congratulations, people calling it a "great breakthrough in journalism." And I thought, "Holy shit, if I can write like this and get away with it, why should I keep trying to write like *The New York Times?*" It was like falling down an elevator shaft and landing in a pool full of mermaids.

Playboy: Is there a difference between Gonzo and the new journalism?
Thompson: Yeah, I think so. Unlike Tom Wolfe or Gay Talese, for instance, I almost never try to *reconstruct* a story. They're both much better *reporters* than I am, but then I don't really think of myself as a reporter. Gonzo is just a word I picked up because I liked the sound of it—which is not to say there isn't a basic difference between the kind of writing I do and the Wolfe / Talese style. They tend to go back and re-create stories that have already happened, while I like to get right in the middle of whatever I'm writing about—as

personally involved as possible. There's a lot more to it than that, but if we have to make a distinction, I suppose that's a pretty safe way to start.

Playboy: Are the fantasies and wild tangents a necessary part of your writing?
Thompson: Absolutely. Just let your mind wander, let it go where it wants to. Like with that Muskie thing; I'd just been reading a drug report from some lab in California on the symptoms of Ibogaine poisoning and I thought, "I've seen that style before, and not in West Africa or the Amazon; I've seen those symptoms very recently." And then I thought, "Of course: rages, stupors, being able to sit for days without moving—that's Ed Muskie."

Playboy: Doesn't that stuff get in the way of your serious political reporting?
Thompson: Probably—but it also keeps me sane. I guess the main problem is that people will believe almost *any* twisted kind of story about politicians or Washington. But I can't help that. Some of the truth that *doesn't* get written is a lot more twisted than any of my fantasies.

Playboy: You were the first journalist on the campaign to see that McGovern was going to win the nomination. What tipped you off?
Thompson: It was the energy; I could feel it. Muskie, Humphrey, Jackson, Lindsay—all the others were dying on the vine, falling apart. But if you were close enough to the machinery in McGovern's campaign, you could almost see the energy level rising from one week to the next. It was like watching pro-football teams toward the end of a season. Some of them are coming apart and others are picking up steam; their timing is getting sharper, their third-down plays are working. They're just starting to peak.

Playboy: The football analogy was pretty popular in Washington, wasn't it?
Thompson: Yes, because Nixon was into football very seriously. He used the language constantly; he talked about politics and diplomacy in terms of power slants, end sweeps, mousetrap blocks. Thinking in football terms may be the best way to understand what finally happened with the whole Watergate thing: Coach Nixon's team is fourth and 32 on their own ten, and he finds out that his punter is a junkie. A sick junkie. He looks down the bench: "OK, big fella—we need you *now!*" And this guy is stark white and vomiting, can't even stand up, much less kick. When the game ends in

disaster for the home team, then the fans rush onto the field and beat the players to death with rocks, beer bottles, pieces of wooden seats. The coach makes a desperate dash for the safety of the locker room, but three hit men hired by heavy gamblers nail him before he gets there.

Playboy: You talked football with Nixon once, didn't you, in the back seat of his limousine?

Thompson: Yeah, that was in 1968 in New Hampshire; he was just starting his comeback then and I didn't take him seriously. He seemed like a Republican echo of Hubert Humphrey: just another sad old geek limping back into politics for another beating. It never occurred to me that he would ever be President. Johnson hadn't quit at that point, but I sort of sensed he was going to and I figured Bobby Kennedy would run—so that even if Nixon got the Republican nomination, he'd just take another stomping by another Kennedy. So I thought it would be nice to go to New Hampshire, spend a couple of weeks following Nixon around and then write his political obituary.

Playboy: You couldn't have been too popular with the Nixon party.

Thompson: I didn't care what they thought of me. I put weird things in the pressroom at night, strange cryptic threatening notes that they would find in the morning. I had wastebaskets full of cold beer in my room in the Manchester Holiday Inn. Oddly enough, I got along pretty well with some of the Nixon people—Ray Price, Pat Buchanan, Nick Ruwe—but I felt a lot more comfortable at Gene McCarthy's headquarters in the Wayfarer, on the other side of town. So I spent most of my spare time over there.

Playboy: Then why did Nixon let you ride alone with him?

Thompson: Well, it was the night before the vote and Romney had dropped out. Rockefeller wasn't coming in, so all of a sudden the pressure was off and Nixon was going to win easily. We were at this American Legion hall somewhere pretty close to Boston. Nixon had just finished a speech there and we were about an hour and a half from Manchester, where he had his Learjet waiting, and Price suddenly came up to me and said, "You've been wanting to talk to the boss? OK, come on." And I said, "What? What?" By this time I'd given up; I knew he was leaving for Key Biscayne that night and I was wild-eyed drunk. On the way to the car, Price said, "The boss wants to relax and talk football; you're the only person here who claims to be an expert on that subject, so you're it. But if you mention *anything* else—*out*. You'll be hitchhiking back to Manchester. No talk about Vietnam, campus riots— nothing political; the boss wants to talk football, period."

Playboy: Were there awkward moments?
Thompson: No, he seemed very relaxed. I've never seen him like that before or since. We had a good, loose talk. That was the only time in twenty years of listening to the treacherous bastard that I knew he wasn't lying.

Playboy: Did you feel any sympathy as you watched Nixon go down, finally?
Thompson: Sympathy? No. You have to remember that for my entire adult life, Richard Nixon has been the national boogeyman. I can't remember a time when he wasn't around—always evil, always ugly, fifteen or twenty years of fucking people around. The whole Watergate chancre was a monument to everything he stood for: This was a cheap thug, a congenital liar. . . . What the Angels used to call a gunsel, a punk who can't even pull off a liquor-store robbery without shooting somebody or getting shot, or busted.

Playboy: Do you think a smarter politician could have found a man to cover it up after the original break-in? Could Lyndon Johnson have handled it, say?
Thompson: Lyndon Johnson would have burned the tapes. He would have burned everything. There would have been this huge wreck out on his ranch somewhere—killing, oddly enough, all his tape technicians, the only two Secret Servicemen who knew about it, his executive flunky and the Presidential tapemeisters. He would have had a van go over a cliff at high speed, burst into flames and they'd find all these bodies, this weird collection of people who'd never had any real reason to be together, lying in a heap of melted celluloid at the bottom of the cliff. Then Johnson would have wept— all of his trusted assistants—"Goddamn it, how could they have been in the same van at the same time? I warned them about that."

Playboy: Do you think it's finally, once and for all, true that we won't have Richard Nixon to kick around anymore?

Thompson: Well, it looks like it, but he said an incredible thing when he arrived in California after that last ride on Air Force One. He got off the plane and said to his crowd that was obviously rounded up for the cameras— you know: winos, children, Marine sergeants . . . they must have had a hell of a time lashing that crowd together. No doubt Ziegler promised to pay well, and then welshed, but they had a crowd of two thousand or three thousand and Nixon said: "It is perhaps appropriate for me to say very simply this, having completed one task does not mean that we will just sit and enjoy this marvelous California climate and do nothing." Jesus Christ! Here's a man who just got run out of the White House, fleeing Washington in the wake of the most complete and hideous disgrace in the history of American politics, who goes out to California and refers to "having completed one task." It makes me think there must have been another main factor in the story of his downfall, in addition to greed and stupidity; I think in the past few months he was teetering on the brink of insanity. There were hints of this in some of the "inside reports" about the last days; Nixon didn't want to resign and he didn't understand why he had to; the family *never* understood. He probably still thinks he did nothing wrong, that he was somehow victimized, ambushed in the night by his old and relentless enemies. I'm sure he sees it as just another lost campaign, another cruel setback on the road to greatness; so now it's back to the bunker for a while—lick the wounds and then come out fighting again. He may need one more whack. I think we should chisel his tombstone *now* and send it to him with an epitaph, in big letters, that says, HERE LIES RICHARD NIXON: HE WAS A QUITTER.

Playboy: Do you think that his resignation proves that the system works?
Thompson: Well, that depends on what you mean by "works." We can take some comfort, I guess, in knowing the system was so finely conceived originally—almost two hundred years ago—that it can still work when it's absolutely *forced* to. In Nixon's case, it wasn't the system that tripped him up and finally destroyed his Presidency; it was Nixon himself, along with a handful of people who actually took it upon themselves to act on their own— a bit outside the system, in fact; maybe even a bit above and beyond it. There were a lot of "highly respected" lawyers, for instance—some of them alleged experts in their fields—who argued almost all the way to the end that Judge Sirica exceeded his judicial authority when he acted on his own instinct and put the most extreme kind of pressure on the original Watergate burglars to

keep the case from going into the books as the cheap-Jack "third-rate burglary" that Nixon, Haldeman and Ehrlichman told Ziegler to call it when the news first broke. If Sirica had gone along with the system, like the original Justice Department prosecutors did, McCord would never have cracked and written that letter that opened the gates to the White House. Sirica was the flywheel in that thing, from start to finish, when he put the final nail in the coffin by forcing James St. Clair, Nixon's lawyer of last resort, to listen to those doomsday tapes that he had done everything possible to keep from hearing. But when he heard the voices, that pulled the rip cord on Nixon, once St. Clair went on record as having listened to the tapes—which proved his client guilty beyond any doubt—he had only two choices: to abandon Nixon at the eleventh hour or stay on and possibly get dragged down in the quicksand himself. Sirica wasn't the only key figure in Nixon's demise who could have played it safe by letting the system take its traditional course. *The Washington Post* editors who kept Woodward and Bernstein on the story could have stayed comfortably within the system without putting their backs to the wall in a show-down with the whole White House power structure and a vengeful bastard of a President like Nixon. Leon Jaworski, the special prosecutor, couldn't even find a precedent in the system for challenging the President's claim of "Executive privilege" in the U. S. Supreme Court.

Hell, the list goes on and on . . . but in the end, the Nixon Watergate saga was written by mavericks who worked the loneliest outside edges of the system, not by the kind of people who played it safe and followed the letter of the law. If the system worked in this case, it was almost in spite of itself. Jesus, what else *could* the Congress have done—faced with the spectacle of a President going on national TV to admit a felony? Nixon dug his own grave, then made a public confession. If his resignation somehow proves the system works, you have to wonder how well that same system might have worked if we'd had a really blue-chip, sophisticated criminal in the White House— instead of a half-mad used-car salesman. In the space of ten months, the two top executives of this country resigned rather than risk impeachment and trial; and they wouldn't even have had to do that if their crimes hadn't been too gross to ignore and if public opinion hadn't turned so massively against them. Finally, even the chickenshit politicians in Congress will act if the people are outraged enough. But you can bet that if the public-opinion polls hadn't gone over 50 percent in favor of his impeachment, he'd still be in the White House.

Playboy: Is politics going to get any better?

Thompson: Well, it can't get much worse. Nixon was so bad, so obviously guilty and corrupt, that we're already beginning to write him off as a political mutant, some kind of bad and unexplainable accident. The danger in that is that it's like saying, "Thank God! We've cut the cancer out . . . you see it? . . . It's lying there . . . just sew up the wound . . . cauterize it. . . . No, no, don't bother to look for anything else . . . just throw the tumor away, burn it," and then a few months later the poor bastard dies, his whole body rotten with cancer. I don't think purging Nixon is going to do much to the system except make people more careful. Even if we accept the idea that Nixon himself was a malignant mutant, his Presidency was no accident. Hell, Ford is our accident. He's never been elected to anything but Congress. . . . But Richard Nixon has been elected to every national office a shrewd mutant could aspire to: Congressman, Senator, Vice-President, President. He should have been impeached, convicted and jailed, if only as a voter-education project.

Playboy: Do you think that over the course of the Watergate investigation, Congress spent as much energy covering up its own sins as it did in exposing Richard Nixon's?

Thompson: Well, that's a pretty harsh statement; but I'm sure there've been a lot of tapes and papers burned and a lot of midnight phone calls, saying things like, "Hello, John, remember that letter I wrote you on August fifth? I just ran into a copy in my files here and, well, I'm burning mine, why don't you burn yours, too, and we'll just forget all about that matter? Meanwhile, I'm sending you a case of Chivas Regal and I have a job for your son here in my office this summer—just as soon as he brings me the ashes of that fucking letter."

Playboy: Does Gerald Ford epitomize the successful politician?

Thompson: That's pretty obvious, isn't it? Somehow he got to be President of the U. S. without ever running for the office. Not only that but he appointed his own Vice-President. This is a bizarre syndrome we're into: For six years we were ruled by lunatics and criminals, and for the next two years we're going to have to live with their appointees. Nixon was run out of town, but not before he named his own successor.

Playboy: It's beginning to look as if Ford might be our most popular President since Eisenhower. Do you think he'll be tough to beat in 1976?

Thompson: That will probably depend on his staff. If it's good, he should be able to maintain this Mr. Clean, Mr. Good Guy, Mr. Reason image for two years; and if he can do that, he'll be very hard to beat.

Playboy: Will you cover the 1976 campaign?
Thompson: Well, I'm not looking forward to it, but I suspect I will. Right now, though, I need a long rest from politics—at least until the '76 campaign starts. Christ, now *there's* a junkie talking—"I guess I'll try one more hit . . . this will be the last, mind you. I'll just finish off what's here and that's it." No, I don't want to turn into a campaign junkie. I did that once, but the minute I kicked it, I turned into a Watergate junkie. That's going to be a hard one to come down from. You know, I was actually *in* the Watergate the night the bastards broke in. Of course, I missed the whole thing, but I was there. It still haunts me.

Playboy: What part of the Watergate were you in?
Thompson: I was in the bar.

Playboy: What kind of a reporter are you, anyway, in the bar?
Thompson: I'm not a reporter, I'm a writer. Nobody gives Norman Mailer this kind of shit. I've never tried to pose as a goddamn reporter. I don't defend what I do in the context of straight journalism, and if some people regard me as a reporter who's gone bad rather than a writer who's just doing his job—well, they're probably the same dingbats who think John Chancellor's an acid freak and Cronkite is a white slaver.

Playboy: You traveled to San Clemente with the White House press corps on the last trip Nixon made as President, and rumor had it that you showed up for one of the press conferences in pretty rocky shape.
Thompson: Rocky? Well, I suppose that's the best interpretation you could put on it. I'd been up all night and I was wearing a wet Mexican shirt, swimming trunks, these basketball shoes, dark glasses. I had a bottle of beer in my hand, my head was painfully constricted by something somebody had put in my wine the night before up in L.A. and when Rabbi Korff began his demented rap about Nixon's being the most persecuted and maligned President in American history, I heard myself shouting, "Why *is* that, Rabbi? . . . Why? . . . Tell *us* why. . . ." And he said something like, "I'm only a smalltime

rabbi," and I said, "That's all right, nobody's bigoted here. You can talk." It got pretty ugly—but then, ugliness was a sort of common denominator in the last days of the Nixon regime. It was like a sinking ship with no ratlines.

Playboy: How did the press corps take your behavior?
Thompson: Not too well. But it doesn't matter now. I won't be making any trips with the President for a while.

Playboy: What *will* you do? Do you have any projects on the fire other than the political stuff?
Thompson: Well, I think I may devote more time to my ministry, for one thing. All the hellish running around after politicians has taken great amounts of time from my responsibilities as a clergyman.

Playboy: You're not a real minister, are you?
Thompson: What? Of course I am. I'm an ordained doctor of divinity in the Church of the New Truth. I have a scroll with a big gold seal on it hanging on my wall at home. In recent months we've had more converts than we can handle. Even Ron Ziegler was on the brink of conversion during that last week in San Clemente, but the law of kàrma caught up with him before he could take the vows.

Playboy: How much did it cost you to get ordained?
Thompson: I prefer not to talk about that. I studied for years and put a lot of money into it. I have the power to marry people and bury them. I've stopped doing marriages, though, because none of them worked out. Burials were always out of the question; I've never believed in burials except as an adjunct to the Black Mass, which I still perform occasionally.

Playboy: But you *bought* your scroll, didn't you?
Thompson: Of course I did. But so did everybody else who ever went to school. As long as you understand that. . . .

Playboy: What's coming up as far as your writing goes?
Thompson: My only project now is a novel called *Guts Ball,* which is almost finished on tape but not written yet. I was lying in bed one night, the room was completely black, I had a head full of some exotic weed and all of a

sudden it was almost as if a bright silver screen had been dropped in front of me and this strange movie began to run. I had this vision of Haldeman and Ehrlichman and a few other Watergate-related casualties returning to California in disgrace. They're on a DC-10, in the first-class cabin; there's also a Secret Serviceman on board whose boss has just been gunned down by junkies in Singapore for no good reason and he's got the body in the baggage bowels of the plane, taking it home to be buried. He's in a vicious frame of mind, weeping and cursing junkies, and these others have their political disaster grinding on them, they're all half crazy for vengeance—and so to unwind, they start to throw a football around the cabin. For a while, the other passengers go along with it, but then the game gets serious. These crewcut, flinty-eyed buggers begin to force the passengers to play, using seats as blockers; people are getting smacked around for dropping passes, jerked out of the line-up and forced to do push-ups if they fumble. The passengers are in a state of terror, weeping, their clothes are torn. . . . And these thugs still have all their official White House identification, and they put two men under arrest for refusing to play and lock them in the bathroom together. A man who can't speak English gets held down in a seat and shot full of animal tranquilizer with a huge hypodermic needle. The stewardesses are gobbling tranquilizers. . . . You have to imagine this movie unrolling: I was hysterical with laughter. I got a little tape recorder and laid it on my chest and kept describing the scene as I saw it. Just the opening scenes took about forty-five minutes. I don't know how it's going to end, but I like it that way. If I knew how it ended, I'd lose interest in the story.

Playboy: When you actually sit down to start writing, can you use drugs like mushrooms or other psychedelics?

Thompson: No. It's impossible to write with anything like that in my head. Wild Turkey and tobacco are the only drugs I use regularly when I write. But I tend to work at night, so when the wheels slow down, I occasionally indulge in a little speed—which I deplore and do not advocate—but you know, when the car runs out of gas, you have to use something. The only drug I really count on is adrenaline. I'm basically an adrenaline junkie. I'm addicted to the rush of the stuff in my own blood and of all the drugs I've ever used, I think it's the most powerful. [Coughing] Mother of God, here I go. [More coughing] Creeping Jesus, this is it . . . choked to death by a fucking . . . poisoned Marlboro. . . .

Playboy: Do you ever wonder how you have survived this long?

Thompson: Yes. Nobody expected me to get much past twenty. Least of all me. I just assume, "Well, I got through today, but tomorrow might be different." This is a very weird and twisted world; you can't afford to get careless; don't fuck around. You want to keep your affairs in order at all times.

Hunter Thompson: The Good Doctor Tells All . . . about Carter, Cocaine, Adrenaline, and the Birth of Gonzo Journalism

Ron Rosenbaum / 1977

From *High Times*, September 1977, pp. 30–39. Reprinted with permission of Ron Rosenbaum.

The first time I met Hunter Thompson was back in 1970, at the America's Cup yacht race where Hunter had chartered a huge power yacht and was preparing to sail it full steam right into the middle of the race course. (This was shortly after his spectacular but unsuccessful run for the office of the sheriff of Aspen, Colorado, on a mescaline-eating "Capitalist Freak Power" ticket.) When I arrived on board the huge yacht, I found Thompson ensconced on the command deck, munching on a handful of psilocybin pills and regarding the consternation of the snooty Newport sailing establishment with amusement.

We never did manage to cross the path of the cup contenders and *Scanlan's* magazine went bankrupt before Hunter wrote up the whole fiasco, but I did learn one thing: this is a guy who understands the importance of *perspective*. He rode with the Hell's Angels—and got himself a nasty beating in the process of getting a unique perspective on them. He loaded his car, his bloodstream and his brain cells full of dangerous drugs to cover a conference of drug-busting D.A.'s and turned that experience into *Fear and Loathing in Las Vegas*, a brilliant exploration of the dark side of the drug scene at the peak of Nixon's power.

When he covered the 1972 presidential campaign as national affairs editor for *Rolling Stone*. Thompson's special deadline-and-drug-crazed. "Gonzo" journalism—his own patented mix of paranoia, nightmare, recklessness and black humor—would fill nervous secret service agents with fear and loathing on the campaign trail. Ever since then, Thomson's become a kind of national character with millions of people following the exploits of "Uncle Duke" in the *Doonesbury* comic strip.

This year too, Thompson had another very special but very different perspective: he's widely reported to have become close to Jimmy Carter and to Carter's inner circle from the time back in 1974 when he heard Carter's now-famous Law Day speech. But curiously, there have been more articles speculating about Thompson—his relations with Jimmy Carter and Jann Wenner—this year than by him. He's never put his own role into perspective until now.

Rosenbaum: How have your attitudes toward politics changed since you wrote about the '72 presidential election in Fear and Loathing on the Campaign Trail?
Thompson: Well, I think the feeling that I've developed since '72 is that an ideological attachment to the presidency or the president is very dangerous. I think the president should be a businessman; probably he should be hired. It started with Kennedy, where you got sort of a personal attachment to the president, and it was very important that he agree with you and you agree with him and you knew he was on your side. I no longer give a fuck if the president's on my side, as long as he leaves me alone or doesn't send me off to any wars or have me busted. The president should take care of business, mind the fucking store and leave people alone.

Rosenbaum: So you developed a tired-of-fighting-the-White-House theory?
Thompson: I think I've lost my sense that it's a life or death matter whether someone is elected to this, that or whatever. Maybe it's losing faith in ideology or politicians—or maybe both. Carter, I think, is an egomaniac, which is good because he has a hideous example of what could happen if he fucks up. I wouldn't want to follow Nixon's act, and Carter doesn't either. He has a whole chain of ugly precedents to make him careful—Watergate, Vietnam, the Bay of Pigs—and I think he's very aware that even the smallest blunder on his part could mushroom into something that would queer his image forever in the next generation's history text . . . if there is a next generation.
    I don't think it matters much to Carter whether he's perceived as a "liberal" or a "conservative," but it does matter to him that he's perceived— by the voters today and by historians tomorrow—as a successful president. He didn't run this weird Horatio Alger trip from Plains, Georgia, to the White House, only to get there and find himself hamstrung by a bunch of

hacks and fixers in the Congress. Which is exactly what's beginning to happen now, and those people are making a very serious mistake if they assume they're dealing with just another political shyster, instead of the zealot he really is. Jimmy Carter is a *true believer*, and people like that are not the ones you want to cross by accident.

I'm not saying this in defense of the man, but only to emphasize that anybody in Congress or anywhere else who plans to cross Jimmy Carter should take pains to understand the real nature of the beast they intend to cross. He's on a very different wavelength than most people in Washington. That's one of the main reasons he's president, and also one of the first things I noticed when I met him down in Georgia in 1974—a total disdain for political definition or conventional ideologies.

His concept of populist politics is such a strange mix of total pragmatism and almost religious idealism that every once in a while—to me at least, and especially when I listen to some of the tapes of conversations I had with him in 1974 and '75—that he sounds like a borderline anarchist . . . which is probably why he interested me from the very beginning; and why he still does, for that matter. Jimmy Carter is a genuine original. Or at least he was before he got elected. God only knows what he is now, or what he might turn into when he feels he's being crossed—by Congress, the Kremlin, Standard Oil or anything else. He won't keep any enemies list on paper, but only because he doesn't have to; he has a memory like a computerized elephant.

Rosenbaum: Did you ever have any ideology in the sense of being a liberal, a conservative . . . or were you an anarchist all along?
Thompson: I've always considered myself basically an anarchist, at least in the abstract, but every once in a while you have to come out of the closet and deal with reality. I am interested in politics, but not as ideology, simply as an art of self-defense-that's what I learned in Chicago. I realized that you couldn't afford to turn your back on the bastards because that's what they would do—run amok and beat the shit out of you—and they had the power to do it. When I feel it's necessary to get back into politics, I'll do it, either writing about it or participating in it. But as long as it's not necessary, there are a lot of better ways to spend your time. Buy an opium den in Singapore, or a brothel somewhere in Maine; become a hired killer in Rhodesia or some kind of human Judas Goat in the Golden Triangle. Yeah, a soldier of fortune, a professional geek who'll do anything for money.

Rosenbaum: You've received a lot of flak for your enthusiasm about Jimmy Carter's Law Day speech in Athens, Georgia. Do you still like Carter?
Thompson: Compared to most other politicians, I do still like Carter. Whether I agree with him on everything, that's another thing entirely. He'd put me in jail in an instant if he saw me snorting coke in front of him. He would not, however, follow me into the bathroom and try to catch me snorting it. It's little things like that.

Rosenbaum: In that Law Day speech, Carter quoted Bob Dylan. Do you really think Carter cares about Bob Dylan's music the way we do?
Thompson: I listened to Bob Dylan records in his house, but that was mainly because his sons had them. I don't think he goes upstairs to the bedroom at night, reads the Bible in Spanish while listening to *Highway 61*.

Rosenbaum: Why haven't you written anything about Carter and the '76 campaign trail?
Thompson: I was going to write a book on the '76 campaign, but even at the time I was doing research, I started to get nervous about it. I knew if I did another book on the campaign. I'd somehow be trapped.

I was the most obvious journalist—coming off my book on the 1972 campaign—to inherit Teddy White's role as a big-selling chronicler of presidential campaigns. I would have been locked into national politics as a way of life not to mention as a primary source of income. . . . And there's no way you can play that kind of Washington Wizard role from a base in Woody Creek, Colorado. I'd have had to move to Washington, or at least to New York . . . and, Jesus, life is too short for that kind of volunteer agony. I've put a lot of work into living out here where I do and still making a living, and I don't want to give it up unless I absolutely have to. I moved to Washington for a year in 1972, and it was a nightmare.

Yeah, there was a definite temptation to write another campaign book— especially for a vast amount of money in advance—but even while I was looking at all that money, *I knew* it would be a terminal mistake. It wasn't until I actually began covering the campaign that I had to confront the reality of what I was getting into. I hadn't been in New Hampshire two days when I knew for certain that I just couldn't make it. I was seeing my foot-prints everywhere I went. All the things that were of interest last time—even the small things, the esoteric little details of a presidential campaign—seemed like jibberish the second time around. Plus, I lost what looks more and more like a tremendous advantage of anonymity. That was annoying, because in '72 I could stand against a wall somewhere—and I'd select some pretty weird walls to stand against—and nobody knew who I was. But in '76, Jesus, at press conferences, I had to sign more autographs than the candidates.

Through some strange process, I came from the '72 campaign an unknown reporter, a vagrant journalist, to a sort of media figure in the '76 campaign. It started getting so uncomfortable and made it so hard to work that even the alleged or apparent access that I had to this weird peanut farmer from Georgia became a disadvantage.

Rosenbaum: You became a public figure?
Thompson: Thanks to our friend Trudeau.

Rosenbaum: Did Garry Trudeau consult you before he started including you as the Uncle Duke character in *Doonesbury*?
Thompson: No, I never saw him; I never talked to him, It was a hot, nearly blazing day in Washington, and I was coming down the steps of the Supreme Court looking for somebody, Carl Wagner or somebody like that. I'd been inside in the press section, and then all of a sudden I saw a crowd of people and I heard them saying. "Uncle Duke." I heard the words *Duke, Uncle*; it didn't seem to make any sense. I looked around, and I recognized people who were total strangers pointing at me and laughing. I had no idea what the fuck they were talking about. I had gotten out of the habit of reading funnies when I started reading the *Times*. I had no idea what this outburst meant. It was a weird experience, and as it happened I was sort of by myself up there on the stairs, and I thought: What in the fuck madness is going on? Why am I being mocked by a gang of strangers and friends on the steps of the Supreme Court? Then I must have asked someone, and they told me that Uncle Duke had appeared in the *Post* that morning.

Rosenbaum: So all this public notoriety was a burden in trying to return to the campaign?
Thompson: It was impossible because there was no way for me to stay anonymous, to carry on with what I consider my normal behavior, which is usually—in terms of a campaign—either illegal or dangerous or both. . . . It was generally assumed that I was guilty—which I was.

Rosenbaum: So eventually you found that refuge in a kind of band of brothers?

Thompson: What? No, I have never had much faith in concepts like "a band of brothers"—especially in politics. What we're talking about here is a new generation of highly competent professional political operatives and also a new generation of hot-rod political journalists who are extremely serious and competitive during the day, but who happened to share a few dark and questionable tastes that could only be mutually indulged late at night, in absolute privacy. . . .

Because no presidential candidate even *wants to know*, much less have to explain at a press conference, why rumors abound that many of his speech writers, strategists and key advance men are seen almost nightly—and sometimes for nine or ten nights in a row—frequenting any of the two or three motel rooms in the vortex of every primary campaign that are known to be "dope dens," "orgy pads" and "places of deep intrigue."

They simply don't want to hear these things, regardless of how true they may be—and in 1976 they usually were, although not in the sense that we were running a movable dope orgy, right in the bowels of a presidential campaign—but it *was* true that for the first time, there was a sort of midnight drug underground that included a few ranking staff people, as well as local workers and volunteers, from almost every democratic candidate's staff, along with some of the most serious, blue-chip press people . . . and it was also true that some of the most intelligent and occasionally merciless conversations of the whole campaign took place in these so-called dope dens.

Hell, it was a fantastic luxury to be able to get together at night with a few bottles of Wild Turkey or Chivas Regal and a big tape deck with portable speakers playing Buffett or Jerry Jeff or The Amazing Rhythm Aces . . . yeah, and also a bag of ripe Colombian tops and a gram or two of the powder; and to feel relaxed enough with each other, after suffering through all that daytime public bullshit, to just hang out and talk honestly about what was *really* happening in the campaign. . . . You know, like which candidate was fatally desperate for money, which one had told the most ridiculous lie that day, who was honest and who wasn't.

In a lot of ways it was the best part of the campaign, the kind of thing I'd only be able to do with a very few people in 1972 and '68. But in '76 we were able—because there were enough of us—to establish a sort of midnight-to-dawn truce that transcended all the daytime headline jibberish, and I think it helped all of us to get a better grip on what we were really doing.

   I could illustrate this point a lot better by getting into names and specific situations, but I can't do that now for the same reason I couldn't write about it during the campaign. We all understand that, and the very few times I even hinted at this midnight underground, I did it in code phrases—like "tapping the glass."

Rosenbaum: Tapping the glass, I wonder if you could explain that?
Thompson: Well, that's one of those apparently meaningless code phrases that I use in almost everything I write. It's a kind of lame effort to bridge the gap between what I know and what I can write without hurting my friends— sort of working on two or three levels at the same time.

Rosenbaum: So if you go back and read your stories, a scene where you talk about "tapping the glass" with Carter campaign staffer "X" . . .
Thompson: Right. That means chopping up rocks of cocaine on a glass coffee table or some mirror we jerked off the wall for that purpose—but not necessarily with one of Carter's people. The whole point of this wretched confession is that there were so many people tapping the glass in the '76 campaign that you never knew *who* might turn up at one of those midnight sessions. They were dangerously nonpartisan. On any given night you would meet Udall and Shriver staffers, along with people from the Birch Bayh and Fred Harris campaigns. Even George Wallace was represented from time to time; and, of course, there was always the hard corps of press dopers.

Rosenbaum: That's amazing. You were covering this media-saturated presidential campaign during the day, then snorting coke at night with all those hotshot politicos?
Thompson: They weren't very hotshot then.

Rosenbaum: Ok. But since we're talking about drug use during the '76 campaign, it's obvious we're talking about people who are now in the White House, right?
Thompson: Well . . . some of them, yes. But let's get a grip on ourselves here. We don't want to cause a national panic by saying that a gang of closet coke

freaks are running the country—although that would probably be the case, no matter who had won the election.

Rosenbaum: Times are definitely changing, eh? But since Carter *won* the election, let's focus on him for a moment.
Thompson: Well, why not? Let's see how thin a wire we can walk here, without getting ourselves locked up. . . . Indeed, and meanwhile let's rent a big villa in the mountains of Argentina, just in case my old friend Jimmy is as mean as I always said he was. Anyway, yeah, we're talking about at least a few people in the White House inner circle; not Cy and Ziggy and that crowd, the professional heavies who would have gone to work for anybody—Carter. Humphrey, Brown. Shit, they'd even work for me, if I'd won the election.

Rosenbaum: The inner circle of Carter's people are serious drug users?
Thompson: Wait a minute, I didn't say that. For one thing, a term like serious users has a very weird and menacing connotation; and, for another, we were talking about a few people from almost everybody's staff. Across the board. . . . Not junkies or freaks, but people who were just as comfortable with drugs like weed, booze or coke as we are—and we're not weird, are we? Hell no, we're just overworked professionals who need to relax now and then, have a bit of the whoop and the giggle, right?

Rosenbaum: Weren't they nervous, or were you nervous, when you first started doing coke together?
Thompson: Well, I suppose I should have expected the same kind of difference between say, the '72 and '76 campaigns as I saw between '68 and '72. When I went to New Hampshire in '68 I was a genuine unknown. I was the only person except for Bill Cardoso who would smoke weed, ever. I mean in the press. In '72 it was a revolution in that sense, and people in the press openly smoked hash and did coke. So I should have expected it in '76, but I hadn't really thought of it. It stunned me a little bit in '76 that coke was as common as weed had been in '72 and almost right out in the open, used in a very cavalier fashion. As I say, in 1972 it was a fairly obvious consistent use of the weed by McGovern's people, in '68 it was McCarthy, but this time it was across the board.

Rosenbaum: In a way, what you're saying is that it was a kind of truth-telling substrata of drug users, and that's why you couldn't write stories about it.

Thompson: Yes, for the first time I was really faced with the problem of knowing way too much.

Rosenbaum: Was this a good or a bad thing?
Thompson: I think it was good. It allowed people who would never under the circumstances have been able to sit down, get stoned and talk honestly about whether they should even be working there.

Rosenbaum: People are always asking how did you get away with it. Why aren't you in jail with all the stuff you write about drugs on the campaign trail? Do you feel that the secret service was specifically tailing you after you started writing these articles about all the dope you had taken?
Thompson: No. I made my peace with the secret service early in '72 when I went to a party in the Biltmore Hotel here in New York after McGovern's primary victory, and there were about ten agents in a room. Three of them were obviously passing a joint around. The look on their faces when I walked in there . . . all of them turning to look when I walked in . . . it was a wonderful moment of confrontation. I didn't want to be there, *they* didn't want me in there. Immediately they just crushed the joint and tried to ignore it. But the room was obviously full of marijuana smoke.

Rosenbaum: And everybody knew that you knew.
Thompson: Oh yeah, of course. But I decided not to write about it—at least not right away.

Rosenbaum: Was there ever any kind of trouble with the secret service after that?
Thompson: No trouble at all, except when they tried to bar me from the White House during the impeachment thing. I called the guards Nazi cocksuckers or something, and in order to get in the White House I had to promise not to call anybody Nazi cocksuckers. I just waved my hand at the White House itself, you know, with Haldeman inside. I kind of got off that hook. And then I promised not to call anyone Nazi cocksuckers, and they let me in.

Rosenbaum: Some of your fans wonder if you ever make up some of the bizarre incidents you describe. You've said that all the outrageous drugs you

did and things you did in your Las Vegas book were true, except the
notorious incident where you supposedly paralyzed yourself with
adrenochrome extract from live human adrenal glands.
Thompson: If I admitted that it was true, it was tantamount to admitting
that I was a first-degree murderer of the foulest sort, that somebody would
kill a child in order to suck out the adrenaline.

Rosenbaum: But in the book you didn't say that you killed the kid. You just
said that you got it.
Thompson: That's right. I said that my attorney had gotten it from a client of
his. What I was doing was taking what you normally feel from shooting
adrenaline into the realm of the extremely weird.

Rosenbaum: Have you ever had that feeling? Shooting adrenaline?
Thompson: Oh, yes. Whenever it was necessary. Sometimes nothing else
works. When you really have to stay up for the fifth day and fifth night . . .
and nothing will work, not even black beauties. Then you shoot adrenaline.
But you have to be very careful with it. First don't ever shoot it into a vein.
That's doom. But even then, you've got to be very careful because you can
drive yourself completely berserk, and I'm sure it would be just the way I
described it in *Las Vegas*.

Rosenbaum: I always thought you were talking in metaphorical terms when
you said, "I like to work on the adrenaline."
Thompson: Yeah, but usually my own. I'm really an adrenaline junkie; I
never get anything done without the pressure of some impossible deadline.

Rosenbaum: How would you describe the adrenaline high?
Thompson: At its best it's one of the most functional of all the speed sort of
drugs in that it has almost no rush unless you overdo it, and almost no crash.
I never considered speed fun. I use speed as fuel, a necessary evil. Adrenaline
is much smoother and much more dangerous if you fuck up. I fucked up one
time in a motel in Austin, Texas, I was very careless, and I just whacked the
needle into my leg without thinking. I'd forgotten the vein thing, and after I
pulled the little spike out, I noticed something was wrong. In the bathroom
the tile was white, the curtain was white—but in the corner of my eye in the
mirror I looked down and saw a hell of a lot of red. Here was this little tiny

puncture, like a leak in a high-powered hose. . . . You could barely see the stream. It was going straight from my leg and hitting the shower curtain at about, thigh level, and the whole bottom of the curtain was turning red.

I thought, oh Jesus Christ, what now? And I just went in and lay down on the bed and told the people in the room to get out without telling them why; then I waited twenty minutes and all I could think of was these horrible Janis Joplin stories: you know, ODing in a motel . . . Jim Morrison . . . Jimi Hendrix . . . needles. And I thought, oh fuck, what a sloppy way to go—I was embarrassed by it. But after twenty minutes nothing happened. Then I really began to get nervous and I thought, oh God, it's going to come all at once. It's a delayed thing, like those acid flashbacks they've been promising all these years.

Rosenbaum: When are we going to have them?
Thompson: I've been waiting for a long time.

Rosenbaum: Once I asked a friend of yours why you are so attracted to Carter, and this guy says, well, Carter's basically in a lot of ways a conservative good old boy and so is Hunter. Do you think that's true in some ways, or that you're a good old boy that's gone weird?
Thompson: That sounds better. Good old boy gone weird. That's a good line anyway. I wouldn't deny that; I would just as soon admit it.

Rosenbaum: You had a fairly straight upbringing in Louisville, Kentucky, didn't you?
Thompson: Well, I was a juvenile delinquent, but a straight juvenile delinquent. The kind that wore white bucks, buttoned-down Oxford cloth shirts, suits. It was a good cover to use to rob crowded liquor stores.
I discovered then that it helps to have a cover. If you act as weird as you are, something terrible is bound to happen to you, if you're as weird as I am.
I mean if I looked like I thought, I wouldn't be on the streets for very long.

Rosenbaum: Were you ever busted?
Thompson: Yeah, repeatedly. I learned about jails a lot earlier than most people. On about ages fifteen through eighteen I was in and out of jails continually. Usually for buying booze under age or for throwing fifty-five-gallon oil drums through filling station windows—you know, those big plate

glass windows. And then I was expelled from school once—for rape, I think. I wasn't guilty, but what the hell. We were in the habit of stealing five or six cases of beer on weekends to drink. That night was the Friday night after my expulsion. We did our normal run and stole about five or six cases. We took one of them and put it on the superintendent of schools' lawn at one o'clock in the morning and very carefully put twenty whole bottles right through every pane in the front of his house. We heard them exploding inside, and they must have gone mad—you hear them in the bedrooms, in the living room, every window was broken I mean, what kind of thugs would do that? Twenty-four hand beer bottle grenades . . . to wake up and hear the whole house exploding! Which window is going to be hit next? We deliberately took about ten minutes to put them through there because we knew they'd never get the cops there in ten minutes.

Rosenbaum: Makes you feel someone's out to get you. Twenty-four bottles of beer, that's heavy. So you were into over-kill when making statements?
Thompson: That wasn't overkill. It was massive retaliation, the court of final resort. I was expelled for something I hadn't done or even thought about doing.

Rosenbaum: What is your favorite drug experience?
Thompson: Well, there are very few things that can really beat driving around the Bay Area on a good summer night—big motorcycle, head full of acid—wearing nothing but a T-shirt and a pair of shorts and getting on that Highway 1 going 120 miles an hour. That's a rush of every kind—head, hands—it's everything put in a bundle. Because first of all, it's a rush, and also it's maintaining control and see how far I can go, how weird I can get and still survive, even though I'm seeing rats in front of me instead of cops. Rats with guns on . . .

Rosenbaum: How do you handle something like that?
Thompson: I never know. It's interesting, always a different way. Mainly it's figuring out real fast whom you are dealing with, and what their rules are. One of the few times I ever got in trouble, I wasn't drunk or pumped up. I had a loaded.44 magnum in the glove compartment, a bottle of Wild Turkey open on the seat beside me, and I said, well, this is a good time to try that advice a hippie lawyer gave me once—to pull down the window just a crack

and stick out my driver's license. So I started to do that. I was just getting it out, when all of a sudden the door on the other side opened. I looked around, and here was a flashlight glaring right in my face, and right beside the flashlight was a big, dirty .57 magnum pointed at me. They didn't give a fuck about my license. They jerked me out of the car and pushed me up against the side. I said something about my constitutional rights, and they said, "Well, sue us" or something and kicked my legs. So I gave it up and eventually I paid a thirty-five-dollar fine, because it's easier than arguing. I had just bought the car. It was a Saab. The night before I had pushed my English Ford off a cliff in Big Sur, four hundred feet down to the ocean, to get even with the bastard for all the trouble it caused me. We filled it with gasoline and set it on fire just before it went over the edge.

Ever since then I have made it a point to be polite to the California Highway Patrol. I have a National Rifle Association sticker on the back window of my car, so that any cop on the driver's side has to pass that and see it. I used to carry a police badge in a wallet, and that helped a lot.

Rosenbaum: I reread *Fear and Loathing in Las Vegas* last summer. I loved it, but I felt it was really a sad book filled with regret for the passing of the San Francisco scene.
Thompson: No, not really. But I think almost any kind of humor I like always has a touch of melancholy or weirdness in it. I seem to be alone, for instance, in considering Joseph Conrad one of history's great humorists.

Rosenbaum: Were you also down on the drug experience in that book?
Thompson: No. I kind of assumed that this was sort of a last fling; that Nixon and Mitchell and all those people would make it very soon impossible for anybody to behave that way and get away with it. It wouldn't be a matter of a small fine. Your head would be cut off.

Rosenbaum: So it's a real exploration of terminal paranoia.
Thompson: Well . . . It was kind of a weird celebration for an era that I figured was ending.

Rosenbaum: Maybe you can tell us the true story of the birth of Gonzo journalism. It was the Kentucky Derby story you did for *Scanlan's* magazine in 1969, right?

Thompson: I guess it's important to take it all the way back to having dinner in Aspen with Jim Salter, a novelist who had sort of a continental style. It was one of those long European dinners with lots of wine, and Salter said something like, "Well, the Derby's coming up. Aren't you going to be there?" And I thought, well, I'll be damned. That's a good idea.

I was working at the time for Warren Hinckle at *Scanlan's* magazine. So I immediately called Hinckle and said, "I have a wonderful idea, we must do the derby. It's the greatest spectacle the country can produce." It was 3:30 in the morning or something like that, but Hinckle go right into it. By that time I'd learned to hate photographers; I still do. I can't stand to work with them. So I said we've got to get an illustrator for this, and I had Pat Oliphant in mind. Hinckle, said fine, you know, do it.

In an hour's time the whole thing was settled. Oliphant wasn't available, but Ralph Steadman was coming over on his first trip to the U.S. and it was all set up that I would go to Louisville and do the advance work, and Ralph would meet me there later.

I think I took off the next day. The whole thing took less than twenty-four hours. I got there and of course found that the place was jammed, there were no rooms and it was out of the question to get a press pass. The deadline had been three months earlier. It took me about two days to get two whole press kits. I'm not sure exactly how I did it. I traded off the outrage, which was so gross, that somebody from a thing called *Scanlan*, which we told them was an Irish magazine famous all over the world, was sending a famous European artist to illustrate the derby for the British Museum, weird stuff like that. They agreed to give me two of everything except passes to the clubhouse and the drunk tank—I mean the blue-blood drunk tank at the center of the clubhouse. That's where Goldwater and all the movie stars and those people sit. The best seats in the house. They wouldn't give us those. So I think we stole those.

In any case, we got total access to everything, including a heavy can of mace . . . Now this is bad, this is ugly. The press box is on the roof, directly over the governor's box. And I had this can of mace, I'm not sure why . . . maybe for arguments; mace is a very efficient way of ending arguments. So I'd been fondling the can in my pocket, but we couldn't find any use for it— nobody threatened me. I was kind of restless. Then just before the derby started we were standing in the front row of the press box, up on the roof, and just for the hell of it I blasted the thing about three times about a hundred feet straight down to the governor's box. Then I grabbed Ralph and said let's get out of here. Nobody maces the governor in the press box. It's not done. It's out of the question. I have no idea what the hell went on in the box when the stuff hit because we took off. That was sort of the end of the story.

About two days later, Ralph had all the drawings done, and I stayed on to write the story, but I couldn't get much done. That goddamned Kent State thing happened the Monday after the derby; that was all I could think of for a while. So I finally flew up to New York, and that's when the real fear started. Most of the magazine was either printed or on the press out in San Francisco—except for my story, which was the lead story, which was also the cover story, and I was having at the time what felt to me like a terminal writer's block, whatever the hell that means.

I would lie in the bathtub at this weird hotel. I had a suite with everything I wanted—except I couldn't leave. After three days of not writing more than two pages, this kind of anxiety/depression syndrome builds up, and it really locks you up. They were sending copy boys and copy girls and people down every hour to see what I had done, and the pressure began to silently build like a dog whistle kind of scream, you know. You couldn't hear it but it was everywhere.

After the third day of that horrible lockup, I'd lie in the tub for three hours in the morning drinking White Horse scotch out of the bottle—just lying in the tub, feeling like, "Well, I got away with it for a while, but this time I've pushed it too far." But there was no alternative; something had to go in.

Finally I just began to tear the pages out of my notebooks since I write constantly in the notebooks and draw things, and they were legible. But they were hard to fit in the telecopier. We began to send just torn pages. When I first sent one down with the copy boy, I thought the phone was going to ring any minute, with some torrent of abuse from whoever was editing the thing in the New York office. I just sort of sat back and watched TV.

I was waiting for the shit to hit the fan . . . . But almost immediately the copy boy was back and wanted more. And I thought. "Ah, ha, what's this?" Here's the light at the end of the tunnel. Maybe they're crazy, but why worry? I think I actually called Hinckle in San Francisco and asked him if he wanted any more pages and he said, "Oh, yeah. It's wonderful stuff . . . wonderful." So I just began to tear the fucking things out. And sometimes I would have to write handwritten inserts—I just gave up on the typewriter—sending page after page right out of the notebook, and of course Hinckle was happy as twelve dogs. But I was full of grief and shame; I thought this was the end, it was the worst hole I had ever gotten into. And I always had been almost pretty good about making deadlines—scaring people to death, but making them. This time I made it, but in what I considered the foulest and cheapest way, like Oakland's unclean touchdown against Miami—off balance. . . they did it all wrong . . . six seconds to go . . . but it worked.

They printed it word for word, even with the pauses, thoughts and jagged stuff like that. And I felt nice that I hadn't sunk the magazine by failing to get the story done right, and I slunk back to Colorado and said oh fuck, when it comes out I'm going to take a tremendous beating from a lot of people.

But exactly the opposite happened. Just as soon as the thing came out, I started getting calls and letters. People were calling it a tremendous breakthrough in journalism, a stroke of genius. And I thought, *What in the shit?*

One of the letters came from Bill Cardoso, who was the editor of the *Boston Globe* Sunday Magazine at the time. I'd heard him use the word *Gonzo* when I covered the New Hampshire primary in '68 with him. It meant sort of "crazy," "off-the-wall"—a phrase that I always associate with Oakland. But Cardozo said something like, "Forget all the shit you've been writing, this is it; this is pure Gonzo. If this is a start, keep rolling." Gonzo. Yeah, of course. That's what I was doing all the time. Of course, I might be crazy.

Rosenbaum: Is it sheer intelligence?
Thompson: Well, it's more than that . . . Let's not forget now I've had at least ten years of paying dues. I know I have some talent, whatever that means. Some people are good at money and some people are good at basketball. I can use words to my advantage, which is a great trick to have.

Rosenbaum: Are there some things in your notebooks you can't put in your stories?
Thompson: All the best stories are unwritten. More and more I find that I can't tell the whole truth about events. I have one book I'd like to write, and the rest will have to be done to pay the fucking rent. That'll be the one where there'll be no question if anybody's lying. Well, there will be some question, but the truth is usually a lot weirder than anything you can make up. I'll make sure that it dooms as many people as possible—an absolutely true account, including my own disaster and disappearances. To hell with the American Dream. Let's write it off as a suicide.

Hunter Thompson: Still Crazy after All These Years?

Peter O. Whitmer / 1984

From *Saturday Review*, January–February 1984, pp. 19–21, 60. Reprinted with permission of Peter O. Whitmer.

He's at it again. Look at him sweat and lie, try to cheat his way out of a monstrous cocaine rap. "It was on orders from George Shultz, Your Honor. After all, I was a special envoy to the Chinese government," he shouts, fabricating another lie out of terminal desperation. Beads of perspiration pop out as he writhes in a cold, kinetic sweat.

Suddenly, he sings (Yes, it's Raoul Duke singing to the jury, with Zonker and B.D., and Joanie Caucus):

> I'm guilty!
> I'm just a man who's been misunderstood—
> of caring and sharing too much
> for my own good!©
>
> G.B. TRUDEAU

Garry Trudeau might be on sabbatical this year, but his cartoon character, Raoul Duke, is working up a lather as the lights come down and the curtain goes up on the new Broadway musical, *Doonesbury*.

It's no great secret, even on Broadway, that Raoul Duke is *not* just a cartoon character. He is a caricature of a real-life journalist whose fame stems from his reportage of a filthy motorcycle gang, a city of ill-repute, and a resigned president. His name is Hunter S. Thompson, author of *Hell's Angels, Fear and Loathing in Las Vegas, Fear and Loathing on the Campaign Trail, The Great Shark Hunt,* and his current best seller, *The Curse of Lono.* He is the founding father and sole practitioner of Gonzo Journalism. Winner of Tom Wolfe's "All-Time Freelance Writers Brass Stud Award" for contributions beyond the call of duty to New Journalism, Thompson is America's quintessential outlaw journalist.

To arrange to meet with Thompson, I have to track him down, following his zigzag trail like an obsessed bloodhound. He is not on his Colorado ranch, where he practices musical target-shooting, using Chinese gongs as targets. Following his directions, I head southeast to the Florida Keys, where he says he is holed up, getting in the mood to write his new novel, *Rum Diary*. We agree to meet on a coral chip of an island closer to Havana than Miami.

Two days go by slowly with only the television and air conditioner to keep me company, as I wait for Thompson to show himself. The weather in the Keys hangs heavily ominous; I sit and sweat. Sunset on the second day brings free entertainment. With a noise I have never heard before—a great, wet, crunching sound—a tornado rips across Sugarloaf Key fifty yards from my room. A four-wheel drive vehicle sails overhead, along with the remnants of several new houses. All electricity stops, and the TV set glows as though covered with a blue rhinestone paste. The air conditioner oozes a frosty fog and does nothing. The door has blown open, and from out of the dusk walks Thompson. "What the f–k was that?" he spits out, summing up the chaos of the past few minutes. He is tall, lean, and tan. In his tennis shoes and Hawaiian shirt, he looks like an off-duty split end for the Miami Dolphins. He strides to the television, slopping a little beer from his Heineken bottle, and stands staring at the phosphorescent set as immobile as a cigar-store Indian.

"Tornado," I say.

"Yeah, the lights were out all the way down here. Let's get some dinner," he says, turning and heading out the door, with the arrogance of a guy who just caught the winning touchdown pass against his former teammates.

And so at midnight, Hunter S. Thompson and I sit eating dinner in a restaurant on a tornado-scarred key. He is just waking up after writing for three days straight. As we talk, he drinks and slowly comes to life. After the original six-pack of Heinekens come two more. As the evening progresses, he leaves me in his suds. He orders and consumes two Bloody Marys, each with a side of black coffee. Chemically, this does not make sense, but the waitress knows him, and much of the drink ordering is non-verbal. As night becomes dawn, he sucks down four tall glasses of Chivas before heading to my room with a bottle of Wild Turkey to complete the interview.

Thompson, crawling back to consciousness after sleeping off thirty-six hours of anger with typewriter and telephone, is fascinating to observe. He is a tough guy to penetrate. He is, inside his ever-present trademarks of Hawaiian shirt and cigarette holder, very tightly wrapped—pressurized and strangely mechanical. Without the other part of his trademark, his mirrored sunglasses, he seems uncomfortable. His eye contact is fleeting; he does most of his talking while staring at his uneaten side order of tomatoes and onions.

Thompson admits a key to his behavior could be his "hillbilly" roots. The barefoot Kentucky mountain man graduated from high school, got an early release from the Air Force in 1957 for behavior "not guided by policy or personal advice, for poor judgment, and for talented but controversial written material," and spent four years in the Caribbean and in South America as a journalist for the *New York Herald Tribune* and *National Observer*, a career that combined his passions for excitement, travel, and writing. For him, journalism always seemed a good way "to get someone else to pay to get me where the action really is," he says.

He liked snooping around and writing about it so much that while struggling with the constraints of the Air Force, he took on pen names to write for local small-town papers. Articles by "Sebastian Owl" and "Thorne Stockton" are long-lost testimony to his zeal to explore and report.

In 1956, as an impressionable teenager, Thompson read Nelson Algren's *A Walk on the Wild Side* and was never quite the same. He saw a lot of himself in the hero, Dove Linkhorn, a marijuana-smoking country boy out on the road for sheer adventure. Algren portrayed the seamy realism of life with a vividness that bordered on the grotesque. Thompson says, "I admired Algren and still do. I thought at the time that no living American had written any two books better than *The Man with the Golden Arm* and *A Walk on the Wild Side*."

Thompson never finished college. He explains, "I played around with college and then I figured out that . . . there is only so much to learn and that's *how* to learn. There are no certificates that writers need."

Armed only with his discharge from the Air Force and a Dow Jones line of credit as a reporter for the *National Observer*, Thompson headed through the Caribbean and around South America. It took a few years, a few beatings, several brushes with penniless vagrancy, and a near nervous breakdown over "what to do with my life" before he was drawn back to the United States.

He came home in 1963. "Rio was the end of the foreign correspondent's tour," he explains. "I found myself twenty-five years old, wearing a white suit, and rolling dice at the Domino Club—the foreign correspondent's club.

And here I thought, 'Jesus Christ, what am I gonna do now?' Then, I would roll dice more and write less and worry about it until I'd have a nervous breakdown. It kinda makes you change whatever you're doing. So, I just came back here, in a sort of frenzy of patriotism—Kennedy, Peace Corps."

When writing for the *National Observer* and *Scanlon's* in Latin America and back home in the United States, Thompson more often than not chose to champion the underdog. A close look at some of his "prefame" work shows a man with as much heart as curiosity and more insight and prescience than one would expect from a writer who later seemed to drop skill for hype. Looking back now, his foresight can be spine-chilling.

In the early 1960s, he documented the improbability that Latin America would ever grasp the concept of democracy, let alone implement it. In 1965, in his first book, *Hell's Angels*, he warned the U.S. auto industry about its chances of losing market shares to the Japanese. He called it "The Honda Nightmare." John DeLorean was his target in a 1970 article about the huckstered rush to sell Z-28 Camaros by pairing the winning spirits of O.J. Simpson and Jean-Claude Killy. Thompson saw DeLorean's blitzkrieg approach as dehumanizing, tasteless, racial, opportunistic, successful, and all-American.

A favorite target of Thompson's was Richard Nixon. Thompson spent an hour with Nixon in his limousine during the 1971 campaign tour and discovered Nixon's pathological obsession with football, which only later surfaced publicly. Thompson learned that the most powerful man in the world was not only monomaniacally concerned with winning, but had a childlike admiration for a bunch of twenty-five-year-olds encased in plastic breaking each other's tibias.

Thompson quit the *National Observer* when the editors disagreed with his prediction that the Free Speech Movement at the University of California was only the beginning of something big. It was an article he wrote for *The Nation* on the controversial motorcycle gang, the Hell's Angels, that changed his lifestyle, changed his literary style, and essentially saved him from the end of what he had predicted would be a short life.

"By the age of twenty-seven," Thompson explains, "I had gone through about six or seven lives. I have had a few since then. But it is puzzling when you live beyond a time when you figure it will all be over. It is like budgeting $1 million to spend by Christmas. When you find you're still around, the budget is all screwed up and you have to reschedule."

The Nation article led to a mailbox jammed with book offers. One publishing house offered him $1,500 simply to sign a statement of intent. "Christ! For $1,500, I'd have done the definitive text on hammerhead sharks and stayed with them in the water for three months," he exclaims.

In little more than a year, Thompson went from being an unemployed journalist to being the author of a fast-selling book. Along the way he was nearly killed by the Angels, who assumed that anyone who wrote a book became an instant millionaire; they turned on him for not sharing his riches. He also met Ken Kesey, already the author of two smashing successes, introduced Kesey to Tom Wolfe, who was then writing part time for the *New York Herald Tribune*, and introduced the Hell's Angels to Ken Kesey.

The caustic, self-centered, no-holds-barred lifestyle for which Thompson is infamous originated with his own contempt for his journalistic peers' misrepresentation of the Hell's Angels. Thompson actually dove into the deep end to find out what life looked like from the bottom up, a method that became a trademark of his work to come and a common denominator of the school of New Journalism. At one point he was no longer sure if he was "doing research on the Hell's Angels or being slowly absorbed by them."

Immersed in the Hell's Angels, he finally found some larger-than-Algren characters, the truth-is-stranger-than-fiction people he had been looking for since leaving Louisville. Their ability to maintain an excessive and irreverent lifestyle that startled the American public gave him a sense of direction.

There was Smackey Jack, the Western world's most unorthodox orthodontist, practicing ad-lib extractions of others' or even his own teeth with a rusty pair of pliers he kept stuck in his belt. Bartenders would stand transmogrified in a clammy sweat while Jack jerked out a bloody incisor and plopped it on the counter. Anyone not giving him a free drink just to get rid of him was crazier still.

Thompson met Preetam Bobo, the renaissance man from the wrong side of the tracks, a motorcycle outlaw who was also a karate expert and writer. Rounding out this group was Sonny Barger, the Hell's Angels' president, who looked like George Carlin with muscles and without a sense of humor. Barger nearly rewrote Shakespeare with his definition of love as "the feelin' you get when you like somethin' as much as your motorcycle." Despite this display of emotionality, he ended up in Folsom Prison for killing an Oakland cop. This was a part of Americana where few dared venture, yet many appreciated the entertainment that Thompson's descriptions provided.

If this was the point where Thompson's journalism turned to "gonzo," it was because he came to realize the media's power to create monsters. The Hell's Angels were a microscopic spot of decay until the press discovered them. Once on the cover of *The Saturday Evening Post,* and in *True* and *The Nation* magazines, the Angels began charging money for interviews and photos. They quickly became the superstars of scum, propelled to the heights of fame.

Thompson didn't need a college degree to realize that if he wanted to write articles and books that appealed to the masses, it didn't hurt sales to create a cartoon persona for himself. He became a cult figure: the outlaw who could drink excessively, drug indulgently, shout abusively, *and* write insightfully. For Thompson, three out of four came to him naturally. "I've a lot in common with the Hell's Angels," he explains. "The main difference is that I've got a gimmick—I can write."

Thompson's appeal to the public involves his ability to live out Everyman's dream of closing the gap between "us" and "them." His style, his message, and his antics are really as much "New Mark Twain" as New Journalism. His is part of an old American tradition. He is Huck Finn, the hero as narrator, with an ethnic sidekick embarking down the highways of their time, getting sidetracked in a never-ending series of misadventures.

Thompson has taken this style to a new high by appealing to millions of Americans with too much sense to do it themselves. His demented mischief in real life and in *Doonesbury* provides the average American with his very own wind-up doll. Crank him tight, lace him with illicit substance, head him toward any social event that has a semblance of decorum and protocol, and watch the whole thing self-destruct. Thompson is a literary bull in the china shop of Western civilization.

As Thompson and I talk through the night, he loosens up but still retains a trace of shyness. As he talks, he alternates between rocking to his left like an autistic child and reaching straight overhead with both arms. His voice sounds like the distant underground testing of an atomic Gatling gun: muffled, monotonous, staccato outbursts, delivered with the ultimate stiff upper lip and punctuated by silences. He has the appearance of a thin Sean Connery who doesn't know how to smile.

As we talk about his newest project, I see over Thompson's right shoulder a black fin slicing the water twenty yards away. It is not what I feared—just a tame dolphin named Sugar who roams her inky water world undaunted by the passing of the tornado.

Fears have a habit of popping up left and right in the Keys, especially in the summer. There is something raw in the air outside. This sign of nature's cruelty to man, so visible in the Keys, is what has drawn the new Thompson to this part of the world. "I have created a new persona named Gene Skinner," he says. "I have given up Raoul Duke—he's funny. Skinner is not so funny. So I'm down here living. That's why I chose this place with a cruel, savage people—the Keys. It is decidedly not Key West, this strip of fishheads and conches.

"Around here there is a strange sense of cruelty," Thompson continues, "the kind of brainless predatory nature that comes from being ten generations of pirates. This place has thrived for hundreds of years on that kind of trade—a whole lot longer than other parts of the country—and is still going strong."

His primary purpose here, though, is to complete a novel based on his old *Rum Diary* concept. This brings him full circle to when he was in his early twenties, tramping around South America. He got an advance for it after *Shark Hunt*, padded things a bit more comfortably with a 1980 autobiographical movie, *Where the Buffalo Roam*, and now warms up for *Rum Diary*, with an occasional venture back into journalism.

The new book is taking a shape to fit the times, and the times through the eyes of Thompson are nasty. The story is about contemporary pirating. The Keys near here are covered by striking new waterfront homes with yachts alongside. They are populated by young people driving Ferraris and Jaguars—a new form of the American dream and something society will wrestle with in the 1980s. It is a high-stakes game, a life and death affair. As a reflection of all this, Thompson says of his new writing: "I'm starting to tighten the screws a little now. No more Mr. Nice Guy. I am practicing, by the attitude of the article I have written on the Pulitzer trial, for the attitude of this Gene Skinner, trying to create a new character for the Eighties. It is a brutal attitude—anti-humanist. What I'm trying to do is create a character to fit the times. It is a whole new style, and it is not as complete as I would like it to be."

For someone totally immersed in creating a new character to fit the hard edge of the 1980s, Thompson seems curiously nostalgic for past times: "The rebellion of the 1960s carried with it a kind of naive sense that since we were right, then 'right' would prevail and we would stop the war and find better ways to live.

"I think that what we have now is a loss of that sense, and people are wondering why there is no rebellion. I think there is no rebellion, not because kids are stupid or slothful, but because the dark side of America is now in charge. That's a political statement," he exclaims.

On the other part of the Key he spots a jumble of headlights from what appears to be heavy construction equipment. He suddenly jumps into action, saying, "Look! Look! Bulldozers! Over by the airstrip! Damn, I wonder if the tornado cut across there. It might have ripped up the Bat Tower." He is up on his feet now, pacing and agitated. I offer to drive out to look things over, and he says, "Yeah, yeah. Boy, it would be a damn shame if we lost the Bat Tower." We pile into my rented Chevette and head down the debris-strewn, crushed-coral road toward the Sugarloaf Key Bat Tower.

I had wandered out here earlier in the day in disbelief. The Bat Tower is an architectural piece of craziness. It is wooden, about sixty feet tall, rectangular in cross section, and pointed on the top. It sits eight feet off the ground on four pylons. It was built in the early 1900s by an Englishman who imported thousands of bats to roost in it. His idea was that the bats would leave the tower each sunset, eat ten times their weight in mosquitoes, return to roost at dawn, and make guano to be collected underneath for fertilizer. It is sort of a vertical cave, a bizarre perpetual-motion machine that failed when all the bats simply kept on flying, never to return.

We reach the unscathed tower, and Thompson is ecstatically relieved. Now we are off to see the real carnage, where several houses have been carried away, leaving clean and bare lots, side by side.

As we pull up, the blue flashing lights of the sheriffs' cars make the scene feel like a silent outdoor disco. The access road is roped off, but Thompson urges me to nose my car over where a policeman in a blue jump suit seems to be in charge.

Sometime during his senseless prattle and his mad flailing, pointing at different points of the wreckage, his full glass of Wild Turkey passes right under my nose, and the whiff of the 101-proof brings me back to reality.

I turn and look at the cop, his face stuck in the car window, six inches from mine. We go eye to eye for about five seconds, then he looks at Thompson, turns, and leaves. Maybe he knows Thompson, maybe he doesn't want to. Maybe drinking and driving is a distant second to cleaning up after a tornado.

We head back for a few last questions. Thompson seems energized by the macabre aspects of the storm. He leans back and laughs his first true let-it-all-out laugh, and he opens up so wide, I can see that all his top front teeth are not his own. His laugh is not peaceful. It is surprisingly disturbing, perhaps because it is a 180-degree turn from his behavior of a few hours before.

As one last query before calling it quits, I ask Thompson what puzzles him most about himself. His response is lightning quick. "Nothing," he says, but then adds, "my inability to be massively rich. . . . It all makes an extreme kind of mechanical, high-tension sense. I am like a weird engine that runs in a lot of different ways. And you think, 'It can't be sane. Nobody would put something like that together.' But it all makes some kind of terrible sense. I am not at all puzzled. I have all the engines harnessed; it's all working except it's just a weird machine. There is not a piece of mystery to any of this stuff.

"But writing is a hard dollar. I am a lazy bastard. I am a hillbilly. I don't see much sense in working hard all your life and being successful if you can't rest for a minute. This mania of having to work hard all the time—I would much rather be on my boat. I would like to be a fisherman. I would like to be able to con these people into letting me take them fishing. 'Gonzo Tours.' I have been missing something all this time; I could have been down here running a fifty-foot yacht doing nothing at all."

After signing my copy of *Shark Hunt*, Thompson starts his car, leans out and says, "Peter, go take your clothes off and jump in the water with that porpoise. Her name is Sugar. She'll give you a ride you'll never forget. I did it once."

So saying, he heads his rental car across the parking lot and slaloms between a land crab big enough to rip open a tire and a pile of tornado-strewn coconuts. He turns left on U.S. Highway 1 and heads into the rosy glow to the east.

Fear and Loathing in Hunter Thompson

Harold Conrad / 1986

Huge brains, small necks, weak muscles, and fat wallets—these are the dominant characteristics of the '80s—the generation of swine.

—Hunter S. Thompson

That's the way Hunter Thompson sees the pursuers of Ronald Reagan's American dream—a collage of funless, greedy little people in a dollar-bill-green world. The above is from his *San Francisco Examiner* column, soon to become nationally syndicated.

The quintessential outlaw journalist is back in hot print. His welcome was splashed all over San Francisco with eight-column, page-one plugs over the newspaper's masthead and TV blurbs in which he starred personally. Even the competition was intrigued. Peter Anderson, of the nearby *Marin County Journal*, wrote:

"The man who writes best-sellers like *Fear and Loathing in Las Vegas*, whose ideal breakfast consists of omelets stuffed with psychedelic mushrooms, a dozen beers, six Bloody Marys, and a reefer to be named later, sounds to me like, well, an ideal columnist."

The competition can make small talk about Thompson's lifestyle, but if he gets off his ass, they better shape up. He's a damn good reporter who writes in a perverse orbit of his own, leading you down weird paths strewn with fools and scamps.

His outrageous style and disdain for the establishment was "discovered" in the late '60s and his following grew as he kept turning out best-sellers and scintillating magazine articles. He started out as a tame, orthodox reporter for the *National Observer,* but the pace was too slow, and he set out to do a book on the Hell's Angels. The bike outlaws didn't just chase him off, they kicked the shit out of him first, but he did the book, and it was his first big winner.

Thompson found his niche with the new-wave publications in the mid-'60s, where his outrageous style was stamped gonzo journalism. First he wrote for *Scanlan's* and then moved over to the then budding *Rolling Stone.* Once he got in the groove, he batted out two more best-sellers, *Fear and Loathing in Las Vegas* and *Fear and Loathing on the Campaign Trail '72. The Great Shark Hunt*, a compilation of his works, was his best best-seller.

When his output slowed down, he forged a link with the new generation in the late '70s and '80s through his college lecture tours. The stories of his preposterous lifestyle became an introduction to his work for many of the uninitiated, but the legend is no longer enough for them. They're hungry for more product, and they want to know what he's been up to.

Only Hunter Thompson knows what Hunter Thompson has been up to, so if you seek the answer, you must go to the mountain, literally—outside Aspen, Colorado, where Hunter lives. But there is a slight problem here. Visitors are not welcome and he despises interviews.

I call Thompson and tell him I'd like to do a piece on him. In reply I hear heavy breathing, but no words, and it wouldn't take a psychologist to tell he isn't crazy about the idea. Finally he says, "Well . . . uh . . . I don't know." More silence, then he says, "I haven't seen you in a long while. Yeah, maybe it will be fun."

As the shuttle plane taking me from Denver to Aspen skirts the snow-crested Rockies, I wonder what the hell I'm doing up here. Thompson didn't answer any of my four calls to confirm my visit. This crazy bastard could just as well be in Mozambique or Katmandu, but when I register at the Inn of Aspen an hour later, the desk clerk tells me, "Dr. Thompson left word he'll meet you here for dinner."

I wait in the room for two hours. No Thompson. I head for the hotel lobby, and as I'm walking down the hall I see this figure coming towards me. He's solidly built, erect, square-jawed, wearing a heavy windbreaker and a baseball cap pulled down over dark shades that deny eye contact. He looks like Central Casting's version of a CIA guy on the prowl, but it's Dr. Thompson himself, the least likely candidate for such a role.

As the gap between us narrows, he starts apologizing for I don't know what, because I can't understand what the hell he's saying. Now I know the night is wasted. It's obvious that Dr. Thompson has already made his day sampling spirits and ambrosias.

It's tough enough to understand Thompson's machine-gun delivery when he's straight, but when he's on full throttle he sounds like he's talking in Morse code, and tonight he's on full throttle.

Maria Khan, Thompson's associate, joins us at dinner. She is a cool, intelligent, beautiful young lady who tries to separate sanity from chaos. Hunter keeps babbling on. Finally he realizes I'm not interpreting his high-velocity chatter and he slows up.

Now I see he has something important on his mind. He reaches into a shopping bag, pulls out a poster, unfolds it with some difficulty, then points to the photo in the center. Its' a picture of Thompson when he ran for sheriff of Pitkin County many years ago. Below the picture a caption reads, "Would you sell this man peyote?"

It's a funny picture—weird-funny. His head is completely shaved, his face has a pallor, and although he is wearing the obligatory dark shades, you know those eyes are seeing pictures in another world. He looks like a stoned alien who has been left behind by the mother ship. I laugh at the picture. Hunter bristles, then points to it again. "Has to be on the cover," he says.

"Cover? What cover?" I ask.

"The cover of *Spin*. No cover, no story."

For a second I think he's putting me on. He leans back and quaffs the Bloody Mary. He is now behind a panoply of glass and spirits in full color: a double Bloody Mary in tomato-red, two Heineken soldiers in dark green, and a margarita, opaque in the light, the glass rimmed in salty snow.

He sips the margarita, then takes three small pieces of notepaper out of his pocket and tosses them on the table. "It's all there," he says. The notepaper is marked pages 1, 2, and 3. The writing is barely legible, but I get the drift. It's instructions on how to handle the picture.

Now I know he's serious. I see I'm going to have to play the game. I say, "I don't know whether this can work. I don't have much lead time."

"Then you better get the picture to New York right away," he answers. "There's a Federal Express agency at the desk."

I see I have no other option. "OK," I lie. "It will be taken care of."

Now he's all business. He leans forward in his chair. "What have you got in mind for this story?"

"I'd like to do a piece on you up at your house, your workbench," I tell him.

He holds up his hand, palm out, like an Indian chief about to make a benediction, then says, "My good friend Harold Conrad, he may visit my house, can stay six weeks if he wants, or as long as he likes . . . Harold Conrad the journalist is barred." Then he dives into a second helping of chocolate seven-layer cake, irrigated with chartreuse.

It's several hours after dinnertime when Hunter starts back to his mountain. Maria, lagging behind, stops to say, "Don't worry, everything will work out. I'll see that he calls you around one tomorrow."

Maria calls a little after noon the next day. "Hunter's embarrassed about last night. I'm sorry about this confusion. We'll meet for breakfast at the Woody Creek Tavern around 1:30. Taxi drivers know the place."

I had been warned about renting a car. They're not safely equipped for some of the more hazardous, icy roads. A wrong slide and you're over and down a thousand-foot precipice. But the taxis have four-wheel drives and are as tenacious as mountain goats. I wondered how the hell Hunter, who drives as though he is on the Indianapolis Speedway no matter where he is, made it safely on these treacherous roads over the years. I'm sure he rides with the devil.

Thompson's mystery house is high above the hamlet of Woody Creek, which is in a gully below, some ten miles from the glitz of Aspen. It has two storefronts—a post office and the tavern—adjoining each other, and that's it for the business end of Woody Creek. There are spells when this town is Hunter's only link with the living.

Woody Creek Tavern is a comfortable place that smells of good home cooking. It has a bar, a jukebox, and a dozen tables. The walls are covered with pictures, postcards, and newspaper clippings, mostly of local interest.

I find one clipping interesting. It is a column about a Denver television crew that hung around the Tavern for two days, waiting to catch Thompson on film. In despair they searched out and found his house, but were chased off the property by Hunter, the once-almost-sheriff of Pitkin County.

It's now 2:30. He's an hour late. I call his house. The service answers. "No, Mr. Thompson is not picking up." Mike, the guy behind the bar, says, "You can't put the clock on Hunter. If he says he'll be here, he'll be here." But Mike doesn't understand about editorial deadlines.

It's now three o'clock. I call a taxi and start out for Hunter's house. Ask a native how to get to Thompson's and he'll ask how well you know him, then, no matter what you say, he'll give you the wrong directions. But I got a map from Terry McDonell, an editor and mutual friend of Hunter's and mine, before I left New York.

I have been warned that I would be under penalty of death if I revealed the directions in print, so let's say the house is way up there on the mountain. The site is called Owl Farm, and the house is a sturdy garrison of logs and glass, facing a postcard panorama with fifty wild acres behind it.

I see both cars in the snowy driveway, but there are no tracks, which means no car has left today. He has to be in there. As I approach the door I see a room that has been tacked onto the front of the house. A huge peacock is sitting on a shelf, his great tail hanging down in gorgeous colors as he peers through the glass. This anteroom is known as the Peacock Hotel.

I rap on the entrance door hard, and two female peacocks, the ugly half of the species, scramble and give me dirty looks through mean, beady eyes. I'm waiting for someone to answer the door. You'd figure that anybody who would breed and mother peacocks, tropical birds, eight thousand feet up in the Rockies can't be all bad.

No one is answering. I trudge through three feet of snow to the back entrance and rap some more. Still no answer. I'm not about to hang around up there and freeze, so I go back to the tavern to find out if there is any message.

I tell Mike I was just up at Thompson's house but couldn't rouse him. "Did he shoot at you?" Mike asks complacently.

"Shoot at me?" I ask. "Does he do that?"

"Yeah," he says. "Sometimes."

Zip . . . back to my hotel in Aspen. I'm delving into airline schedules when the phone rings. It's Hunter, the other Hunter, not the ogre of last night. It's like I just arrived. He tells me he's been in the shower for an hour, probably a cop-out for not answering my pounding on the door. "Meet me at the Tavern in an hour. We'll have dinner and go up to the house and get this thing started."

With trepidation, I take a taxi back to the Tavern. He and Maria are already there. I see a couple of cowboys at the bar and some local people at the tables. It is made plain that tourists are not welcome here.

I know Hunter takes it for granted that I understand the rigors of reentry after a tough night. I never mention the crazy cover-story pictures or any of the ultimatums presented the night before. Neither does he. It never happened.

Now he's solicitous and polite. People seem to forget that Thompson was southern, raised a God-fearing, well-mannered little Kentucky gentleman, and that's what he is when he's straight. Fortunately, he's not straight all that much. I like Hunter when he's in second gear, just a couple of double Bloody Marys on an empty stomach.

Now he's a combination of the southern gentleman, the fey, absent-minded professor, the brilliant observer of today's mores. Top this off with a tincture of his inimitable weirdness, and he's a lovable guy. His following is devoted.

After dinner we start back up the mountain, Maria driving, thank God. The front entrance to the house leads into the living room. It's a place to hibernate, big comfortable couches and a huge open fireplace.

Lining the top of the room is an array of hats, maybe thirty of them—Borsalinos, fedoras. Panamas, cowboy hats, and more hats—a hat collection, a common fetish for guys with sparse hair.

The kitchen is an all-purpose room with all the cooking equipment on one side. On the other side is a standup piano. Books are all over the place. The walls are festooned with photos, handbills, and the knickknacks a traveling man with a sense of humor accumulates.

Hunter points out his communication center, a big television set and stereo setup. He has a large satellite dish outside for reception. "How about this?" he says, patting a bulky piece of equipment, a telefax machine. "I just stick the copy for my column in here and it's reproduced at the paper in San Francisco, over the phone line."

"That saves a lot of time and bother, doesn't it?"

He gives the machine a punch. "I don't know. I still haven't figured out how to get the goddamned thing started." We sit down at the kitchen counter, and I take out my tape recorder. He claps. "Yeah, let's get started. What do you want to talk about?"

"You've upset the bus on many a political campaign. Who's got the best shot at being the next president of the United States?"

Without batting an eye he says right back, "Richard Milhous Nixon. We're talking winter book. I make him my winter-book favorite. Who's a better bet right now? Bush? You kidding? Teddy's gone. Jack Kemp? Bill Bradley? Cuomo? I see your twisted smile, but just think about this. Nixon's clawing to get back. You can almost hear the scratch marks, and he's not going to rest until he's back where he thinks he should be. I miss the bastard. That's the guy we need."

"Need for what?" I ask.

"For *Saturday Night Live*. I was talking to Laila last night. That's her department, arranging for *Saturday Night*'s hosts. Nixon's made to order. I gotta call her."

For years Thompson despised Nixon and knocked his brains out, but a change seemed to come about, and it is reflected in Hunter's piece called "Presenting the Richard Nixon Doll (Overhauled 1968 Model)." He's on the campaign trail with Nixon in New Hampshire in 1968, and he has somehow wangled a ride back to the airport in the car with the next president. Nixon is talking to him:

> "You know, the worst thing about campaigning for me is that it ruins the whole football season. If I had another career, I'd be a sportswriter or a sportscaster."
> I smiled and lit a cigarette. The scene was so unreal, I felt like laughing out loud—to find myself zipping along a New England freeway and relaxing in the back seat, talking football with my old buddy, Dick Nixon, the man who came within 100,000 votes of causing me to flee the country in 1960."

I think they became kindred spirits when Hunter discovered that Nixon was a knowledgable football nut just like him. That took some of the curse off.

"How about your friend Gary Hart?" I ask.

"Hart? There weren't enough votes in the unions to elect Fritz Mondale, and there will never be enough yuppies to elect Hart. They are fickle and greedy, prone to panic like penguins, and naked of roots or serious political convictions. Jesse Jackson can crank more energy and loyalty and action out of ten people on any street corner in East St. Louis than Gary Hart could every hope to inspire in a week of huge rallies in New York, Chicago, and Pittsburgh."

The phone rings, and he answers it briefly. "A friend of mine, a local, coming up for a few minutes . . . Hey, why don't you do Jack Nicholson? He'd be a good piece for you."

"I'd like to," I say, "but I don't know him, and he's as elusive as you are."

"I've talked to him about you. He knows who you are. I'll get him for you."

"Good," I say, "but let's get this one finished. Tell me about the drug culture."

"There's no more drug culture. It's just big business, a foul business. I grew up in the drug culture in the '60s. It was a pleasant pastime for good buddies and fellow travelers. Money had nothing to do with it. I never found that the things I did ever caused me any great grief. They did put a certain stigma on my rep, but if I did half of the stuff they say I did, I'd be dead."

He pulls up his sweater. "Look at this." He flashes a lean, washboard abdomen. He's six-foot-three, weighs 190, and is an impressive specimen at forty-seven. Now he looks at me sideways and is quiet for a few beats. Then he says, "I know you, Harold. I know what you've been doing all these years, and you look as fucking healthy for your age as anybody. Now tell me. Should we have abandoned all that great fun we had?"

He says this kind of wistfully, and I'm getting his vibrations. I'm thinking of the exotic places where our paths have crossed, like the gambling joint in Kinshasa, Zaire, a hangover from the old Belgian Congo. It was like Rick's Café, the faded joint Humphrey Bogart ran in *Casablanca,* only sleazier: CIA guys masquerading as Peace Corps workers; vamps of all colors; agents and spies from half a dozen countries; *gambling*, plotting, intrigue.

If you were a friend of the owner's, he'd send one of his boys out to the fringe of the jungle, and he'd be back in an hour with a shopping bag full of buds—pungent, green dynamite—five bucks. One night Hunter threw a whole bagful of buds into the pool at the Hilton International, then dove into the water to be with his friends.

Hunter's eyes seem far away. He takes a long draw of Chivas. When I ask him about his beef with Garry Trudeau and his *Doonesbury* comic strip, Hunter pouts. "I don't want to talk about it."

"Just fill me in. Wasn't there a character in the strip named Duke, one of your pen names, and wasn't it based on your alleged lifestyle?" He nods. "And didn't most of the people who read the strip assume the character was supposed to be you?" Thompson is nodding like a guest on *What's My Line.* "And isn't Garry Trudeau a close friend of yours?"

He breaks his silence. "Never met him, never even seen him . . . he's too small to see. He claims he made the character up himself . . . had nothing to do with me . . . it was his own invention." Hunter starts scribbling on a piece of notepaper. "Gotta make sure this is accurate. Here."

I can't make out the writing. I ask him to read it into the tape recorder. He starts off in a stentorian tone: "I have to live with these rumors. Look at that wretched little comic strip . . . that thieving, chicken-shit dwarf. I feel sorry for his parents. They worked and sacrificed to put him through Yale, and all he learned was to live like a leech and a suck-fish on other people's work. It's a shameful thing, and I know he's embarrassed by it."

"What about your new book?" I ask.

"Oh, it's a monster. I was working on it for six months around San Francisco when this column project came up. You knew I was the night manager of the O'Farrell Theatre, the Carnegie Hall of public sex in America."

"Yes, I heard. I've been wondering what the night manager does."

"Well, I prowl the catwalks . . . see that the lighting is right . . . and, uh . . ." He seems stumped. "And drool all over those sexy, naked young girls?" I add.

"No, no, nothing like that," he answers quickly. "This was serious business. Jim Silberman, who runs Summit Books for Simon and Schuster, has been immensely patient. I took a half-million-dollar advance, and don't ask me where the money is."

"When is the book due?" I ask.

"Last year," he says.

"Do you still do the college lecture tour?"

"I average about two a season. You know, when I first started out on the circuit ten years ago, I was talking to my peers, as it were, people who had shared common experiences. But with the kids today, it's different. They act like I'm from some other planet. Their first questions are, 'Is it really true?' or 'How do you get away with that stuff?'

"I feel sorry for some of those poor bastards I talk to . . . I can almost feel their frustrations. They've never had that kind of fun . . . they don't know . . . It's like me telling you about my previous life in China when I lived in Peking . . . in Shanghai . . . ah, that good old Boxer Rebellion.

"But the questions can get profound—like, 'What's your opinion of the validity of suicide?' A favorite one seems to be, 'Who are the three most important men of your time?' "

"Who are they?" I ask.

"Muhammad Ali, Fidel Castro, and Bob Dylan."

"You want to give me a rundown on that rating?"

"Ali is one of the true heroes of our time. He spoke up in the '60s and stood his ground. He also paid his dues without a whimper. Castro has been running his country for twenty-six years although everybody's tried to get him knocked off, from the Kennedy brothers to the Mafia. And no matter what you hear in this country, his people love him down there. He's a hell of a leader.

"Bobby Dylan is the purest, most intelligent voice of our time. Nobody else has a body of work over twenty years as clear and as intelligent. He always speaks for the time."

Hunter puts his drink down and goes to answer the door. He admits his friend Tex from down below, then goes to get his camera. I explain to Tex what the pictures are for, and he says he knows the game. He'll take the pictures. He shoots Hunter at the typewriter, guzzling a drink, wearing the floor-length Indian headdress—Hunter is moving around like a Ford model.

Tex asks, "How many shots did you have in here?" "Twenty-four," says Hunter. "It was a fresh roll."

"Seems like we've done more than that. I can't tell. Better have a look." He cautiously opens the camera. "Shit, man, you got no fuckin' film in this camera," Tex says eloquently.

Thompson galumphs over like a bewildered ostrich. "No film!! . . . Shit!" He looks over to me to cop a plea. I give him a sneaky smile and he knows exactly what I'm thinking—the old no-film-in-the-camera caper. "Playing games, Hunter?"

"I wouldn't do that to you. I swear I thought there was fresh film in the camera. We'll get more film and do it tomorrow night. I promise."

Return to the mountain the next night to wind this thing up, but there is a two-hour delay. In the Thompson household, only first-strike and avalanche have priority over basketball and football games. Hunter demands action wherever he is, and this is action for him because he's involved. He's betting on most of the games. The Louisiana–Memphis State game has just started and I have to wait for the whistle to blow to get a word in.

Thompson is nursing his Chivas Regal. His face is animated and there is a kid's gleam in his eye. His team is winning. It's twelve years now since he jumped into the pool that night in Kinshasa. Considering that he's galloped through those twelve years like a guy riding a wild bronco, he hasn't changed all that much.

It's still fun and games to Hunter. He seems to have friends no matter where he goes, and when he hits town, it's New Year's Eve every night while he's there.

His mountain is his sanctuary. That's where the brain and the arteries are given a chance to be restored to their normal functions. Not that he lives up there like a monk, but it's far from the lifestyle his cult likes to think it is.

But what the hell has he been doing up on the mount all this time? *The Great Shark Hunt* was published in 1979 and it was a big winner. A novel, *The Curse of Lono*, came out in '82, a best-seller for a short while, but far from his best work. He did several magazine pieces for *Rolling Stone,* where he was a pillar for many years, but it was obvious that this medium isn't much fun for him anymore. He has spent a year playing around with his new book, and has now become a newspaper columnist.

The Thompson cultists have been bemoaning the scarcity of their hero's product. They want to know why he hasn't been up there beating that typewriter and meeting those deadlines. If he were the kind of guy who could settle down and hack away at his typewriter merely because he was committed to his craft, he wouldn't be Hunter Thompson.

Strange. The followers adopted him because they discovered this wild writer, their kind of guy, a rugged individualist with a weird sense of humor and a lifestyle that so titillated the uninitiated that the stories and gossip became an introduction to his work. Now they want to reform him. That's never going to happen, but if it did it would be a shame because it would be the end of a rare species. There's only one.

Thompson paid his dues in his early years, writing for obscure publications for little money and sometimes for free, but he became a pro in a hurry when the money started to roll in. If there has been a lack of motivation in Hunter's drive to enrich and fatten his body of work, it might be that the wolves at the door aren't as hungry any more.

He's had some good touches over the past decade. A bundle from Universal Pictures for episodes of his life, made into *Where the Buffalo Roam*. It has become a cult movie, it was that bad, but Bill Murray turned in a remarkable portrayal of Thompson. There's been the income from some very profitable best-sellers, plus the hefty advance from the new, unfinished book.

The basketball game is almost over now, but Thompson doesn't budge until the final whistle. Then he gets his camera, and this time I check it for film. He goes through all the same poses as the night before, with Maria doing the shooting. When we're finished, he says he thinks this exhausting work has earned us a nightcap at the Tavern, so down the mountain we go. It's about five below, and Hunter is wearing shorts.

There are several "final" nightcaps, but I have to catch a plane in the morning. Ten minutes after they call a cab for me, a wild-looking guy walks into the place. Thompson walks over to him and starts talking. I don't know what he is saying, but whatever it is, I can see it's something intense. Then he comes back to me. "That's Weird John, your driver," he says.

"What were you just telling him off about?" I ask.

"I was merely telling him to be careful . . . that you were a good friend of mine . . . and that if anything happened to you, I would kill him."

On that warm, happy note, I took off from Woody Creek and headed back to the mundane.

The Doctor Is In

Curtis Wilkie / 1988

From the *Boston Globe Magazine*, February 7, 1988, pp. 16–17, 69–77.
Reprinted with permission of Curtis Wilkie.

**Fear and Loathing at Woody Creek . . . Notes from a Strange Time . . .
A New "Generation of Swine" . . . Gonzo Man Joins Jingo Paper . . .**

I'm older now, but still running against the wind.

—Bob Seger, "Against the Wind"

So many of the icons of our generation are in ruins, victims of time and Reagan's cultural revolution. "Just say no" are the new catchwords, and the Red Queen and White Rabbit have been replaced by King Condom. John Lennon is seven years dead, and Timothy Leary might as well be. Jerry Rubin promotes capitalism. Janis and Jimi, Duane Allman and Jim Morrison are gone. Otis Redding and Mama Cass, gone. All gone. James Brown's screams have lost their pitch. Lynyrd Skynyrd's "Free Bird" crashed in a swamp. Richard Brautigan snuffed himself. The landscape is littered with burned-out cases, children of the 1950s who spent themselves over the next two decades like Roman candles.

But there is a survivor, unrepentant and unforgiving, lurking in a log cabin high in the Colorado Rockies. Hunter S. Thompson just reached the landmark age of fifty, and after a midlife lull when it was feared he was finished, the outlaw prince of gonzo journalism is writing again with the fury of a shark in a feeding frenzy. As one of the last two-fisted drinkers, Thompson defies the legacy of Dylan Thomas, who died before forty of what the coroner called "insult to the brain." Despite years of physical abuse—best characterized by an orgy of drugs and alcohol at a law-enforcement convention he chronicled in *Fear and Loathing in Las Vegas* in the early 1970s—Thompson, amazingly, still looks healthy enough to challenge a professional athlete.

Searching through my beer-sodden notes after several days in his company on the fringes of Aspen in December, I find one of his quotes: "It only feels like one long year since I was twenty-two. I never grew up." Exactly. After a half-century, Hunter Thompson is a macho Peter Pan.

His political writing, which appears in a syndicated weekly column in the *San Francisco Examiner,* has regained the intensity of his work in *Rolling Stone* magazine nearly twenty years ago, when he was heaping scorn on Richard M. Nixon, Hubert H. Humphrey, and other officials. His chief target these days is the right-wing gang in the Republican Party. If Thompson can get his act together—and his book editor was threatening to abort the project while I was in Aspen unless he met a deadline—a collection of his recent columns will be published this year by Summit Books under the title *Generation of Swine.*

Just as he described Humphrey in 1972 as "a treacherous, gutless old ward-heeler who should be put in a goddamn bottle and sent out with the Japanese Current," Thompson is now relentlessly keelhauling another vice president, George Bush. Of Bush, Thompson wrote in a recent column: "He has the instincts of a dung beetle. No living politician can match his talent for soiling himself in public. Bush will seek out filth wherever it lives—going without sleep for days at a time if necessary—and when he finds a new heap he will fall down and wallow crazily in it, making snorting sounds out of his nose and rolling over on his back and kicking his legs up in the air like a wild hog coming to water."

Why am I repeating these things? It is all madness, these irresponsible descriptions and apocryphal stories: gonzo journalism run amok. Yet underneath the lurid gibberish it is possible to sniff out, like truffles, kernels of wisdom and truth. Thompson describes gonzo journalism—his term for his work—as "a style of reporting based on William Faulkner's idea that the best fiction is far more true than any kind of journalism."

He sprung on the world this novel approach to political journalism during the 1972 presidential campaign, as he followed Edmund S. Muskie's breakdown in the primaries, a collapse accompanied by the candidate's public tears in New Hampshire and private fits of rage. In his reports to *Rolling Stone,* which resulted in the book *Fear and Loathing on the Campaign Trail '72,* Thompson speculated that Muskie's reactions were caused by injections of the jungle drug Ibogaine, which left his "brain almost paralyzed by hallucinations at the time; he looked out at that crowd and saw gila monsters instead of people. . . ."

This year, Thompson has a new mandate to skewer the latest generation of politicians, and his pulpit, of all places, is that flagship of the Hearst empire, the *San Francisco Examiner,* a newspaper he once described as "particularly influential among those who fear King George III might still be alive in Argentina." Under the leadership of William Randolph Hearst III, the paper has hired Thompson and, among others, another '60s renegade, Warren Hinckle, in an effort to jazz up its traditionally conservative image.

The arrangement permits Thompson to write from his own lair, a cabin at Woody Creek, about ten miles outside Aspen. "I'm a hillbilly," he says, "a lazy bastard." Late one night, while Thompson and I were talking in the cluttered kitchen of his home—the erstwhile "National Affairs Desk" of *Rolling Stone*—Will Hearst telephoned to inquire about the whereabouts of an overdue column. Thompson put me on the line and disappeared. An awkward conversation ensued. I observed that the *Examiner* seemed a strange outlet for Hunter Thompson. Hearst replied that publishing Thompson was in the "libertarian" tradition of a newspaper chain that once carried iconoclasts such as Mark Twain and Ambrose Bierce. "It is slow getting copy out of him," Will Hearst admitted. Thompson had still not reappeared. "Tell him we demand his copy tonight," Hearst said. "He has got to call back in two hours."

Under pressure, and using an old-fashioned typewriter, Thompson cobbled together two thoughts he had already put down on tattered paper. As the supply of Molson dwindled in an auxiliary beer refrigerator outside the kitchen where he writes, Hunter Thompson met another deadline.

The Doctor Is In . . . Brainrapers and Greedheads . . . Reagan on the Gibbet . . . The Secret Service Is Watching . . .

Whether he is writing the exact truth—or has raised it a few notches to make a point about hypocrisy and greed in modern America—is not the point. The point is that he is writing well, and with humor, an acid-head Mencken reincarnated. . . .

—William Zinsser
On Writing Well

In person, Thompson is as wild and undisciplined, entertaining and irreverent, as his writing. If he sleeps, it is like a vampire—by day. An avowed speed freak, he can go for several days without rest. The night does not belong to Michelob; it belongs to Hunter Stockton Thompson.

Dr. Thompson, if you will. He insists upon the title, saying that he is a doctor
of "philosophy, chemotherapy, and divinity."

He is from Louisville, Kentucky, but vague about his educational
background, mumbling something about attending Columbia University and
other institutions of higher learning. In a piece on "The Nonstudent Left" he
wrote for *The Nation* in 1965, Thompson said, "In 1958, I drifted north from
Kentucky and became a nonstudent at Columbia. I signed up for two courses
and am still getting bills for the tuition." No matter. How many prophets do
you know with a college education?

For a while, he toiled as a straight journalist. As a young man, he applied
for a job on the *San Juan Star* in Puerto Rico, but the managing editor, a
fellow named William Kennedy, turned him down. (All is forgiven.
Thompson hopes Kennedy, who became a prize-winning novelist in Albany,
New York, will write an introduction for *Generation of Swine*.) Thompson's
first job in journalism was at *Time* magazine. He was a copy boy. He later
wrote for a daily newspaper in Middletown, New York, but was fired after
attacking a vending machine with a hammer. He finally gained employment
at a respectable weekly newspaper, the *National Observer,* but it went out of
business. At the time, he was reporting the news conventionally. All that
would change.

Living in California's Big Sur country, he wrote a book, *Hell's Angels*,
which culminated with his own stomping by the motorcycle gang. But the
real catharsis would come in Chicago, just as it did for so many of his
contemporaries. In an essay about the episode that turned an age of idealists
into cynics, Thompson wrote:

"Probably it was Chicago—that brainraping week in August of '68. I went
to the Democratic convention as a journalist, and returned a raving beast.
For me, that week in Chicago was far worse than the worst bad acid trip I'd
even heard rumors about. It permanently altered my brain chemistry, and my
first new idea—when I finally calmed down—was an absolute conviction
there was no possibility for any personal truce, for me, in a nation that could
hatch and be proud of a malignant monster like Chicago."

He moved to Aspen and helped lead an insurgent political movement
against "a mean bunch of rednecks" who ruled the county. The "Freak
Power" ticket had its headquarters in the bar of the Hotel Jerome, a gathering
spot at the time for "freaks, heads, fun-hogs, and weird night-people of every
description." Thompson ran for sheriff in 1970, mocking the law-and-order

crowd by shaving his head and wearing sinister sunglasses in campaign posters. His platform called for ripping the streets with jackhammers and planting sod in place of asphalt, renaming Aspen "Fat City" in order to "prevent greedheads, landrapers, and other human jackals from capitalizing" on the town's name, and installing a "bastinado platform and a set of stocks" on the courthouse lawn to punish drug dealers who cheated customers.

He lost, but the political complexion of Aspen was changed irrevocably. Today the little town, with a population of eight thousand people and an altitude of eight thousand feet, is both precious and radicalized. It serves as the winter home of Jack Nicholson, Goldie Hawn, and other celebrities as well as hundreds of sybaritic visitors. Aspen's streets are lined with chic boutiques and bars with names like The Red Onion.

The town has become so trendy that Thompson rarely goes beyond the Woody Creek Tavern, a rustic watering spot located a couple of switchbacks down the mountain from Owl Farm, where he lives. Cigarette smoke hangs low in the tavern, where cowboys and construction workers wear ragged sheepskin jackets, denims, and frayed ten-gallon hats. The food is cheap but sustaining, and the jukebox does not carry Barry Manilow. Jill, the cook, points out that it may be the only bar in the world without a mirror. The clientele at the Woody Creek Tavern is not narcissistic.

One night we met there for dinner, and Thompson burst through the door carrying a hideous, rubber facsimile of a sickly grinning Ronald Reagan he had bought at an airport. The cowboys cheered, but one table was occupied by stylishly dressed apres-skiers who had apparently decided to visit this "quaint little place" for dinner. The tourists watched in horror as Thompson puffed the Reagan device to life-size. He cursed loudly after discovering it was not the sort of steel-based toy he could use as a punching bag. A cry of "String him up!" arose from the bar.

Thompson and Gaylord Guenin, the majordomo of Woody Creek Tavern, disappeared into the attic and returned with a coil of rope. As he worked on a goblet of Chivas Regal and a Molson on the side, Thompson constructed a hangman's noose, fitted it over the rubberized neck, and left the ersatz president dangling in effigy from a rafter. "I always thought he was an elderly dingbat," he declared, "a silly old fool."

The Secret Service would not have been amused. The agency's travails with Thompson date back to the time in Florida in 1972 when he loaned his press credentials during a Muskie whistle-stop trip to "The Boohoo," a bartender-desperado named Peter Sheridan who would eventually kill himself in a motorcycle wreck. While Muskie, then an august senator and the leading candidate for the Democratic nomination, attempted to deliver a speech from the caboose at the Miami train station, "The Boohoo" used his place in the press area to claw at Muskie's pants, demanding more gin.

This past year, Thompson says, the Secret Service has investigated his vicious comments about George Bush, whom Thompson claims is "doomed." As the Iran-contra affair unfolded, Thompson wrote that the "hallways in the White House basement were slick with human scum. Even the Gipper was bleeding and George Bush was walking around like a man with both wrists slit and trying to ignore the blood." Blaming Bush for the contra connection, Thompson continued his screed: "Before this thing is over, George will know agonies far worse than simple gout, or leech fever, or even the heartbreak of psoriasis. There is already talk among his neighbors up there in Kennebunkport about strapping him onto one of those old-timey dunking stools and letting the local boys have a go at him."

In a Subsequent column, he depicted a scene in which Bush learns he is linked to Lt. Col. Oliver North, a man Thompson described as "the Charles Manson figure in this hideous scandal that crawls like a plague of maggots. . . ." At a White House meeting, Thompson reported, "George went stiff, then dropped to his knees like a wino and wept openly in front of his staff people. . . . The shrewd and treacherous vice president was no longer clean."

Thompson prides himself on his own "outlaw" status. Last year, golfing with his friend Ed Bradley of *60 Minutes,* he was charged with firing a shotgun on the Aspen municipal course. My sources say he fired two "warning shots" near a man on a lawn-mower tractor who was disrupting their game. Thompson showed me how he stuffs the shotgun, like a three-wood, into his golf bag for "protection." He insisted he simply shot it once into the air for fun. Bradley testified he heard a mysterious shot, but saw nothing. Thompson was fined a hundred dollars.

There is a pickle jar on the shelf of the Woody Creek Tavern devoted to the "Hunter S. Thompson Defense Fund." A sign on the jar says, "Help Save This Pathetic Victim of Police Brutality, FREE THE DOCTOR." Contributions have included small change, dollar bills, condoms, a piece of beef jerky, and some hamster droppings.

Flight to the Unknown . . . The Phoenix Also Rises . . . Remembrance of Things Past . . . Revenge in Orlando . . .

O lost, and by the wind grieved, ghost, come back again.

—Thomas Wolfe
Look Homeward, Angel

The inspiration to track down Thompson came after a Boston cabdriver, who admired his reporting, asked me what ever happened to the wizard of gonzo journalism. After falling out with Jann Wenner, the editor and publisher of *Rolling Stone,* Thompson seemed to have disappeared from the scene. But I knew he was now writing a column for the *Examiner,* and after placing calls to his answering service, his editor, and the Woody Creek Tavern, I got a collect call late one night from "Dr. Thompson."

We agreed to meet in Aspen in early December. He urged me not to fly Continental Airlines, which had just suffered a crash in the snow at Denver that cost a number of lives. In that week's column, Thompson savaged Continental for earning "what is beginning to look like the ugliest reputation in the American business community since the Edsel, thalidomide, or the economic wisdom of Herbert Hoover." So I took United. En route to Denver, rereading *The Great Shark Hunt,* an anthology of Thompson's work, I came across this paragraph from 1970: "Flying United, to me, is like crossing the Andes in a prison bus. There is no question in my mind that somebody like Pat Nixon personally approves every United stewardess. Nowhere in the Western world is there anything to equal the collection of self-righteous shrews who staff the 'friendly skies' of United."

By the time I got to Aspen, the author had vanished. At the Woody Creek Tavern there were reports of a "sighting" in Phoenix. The next day, Thompson called the Hotel Jerome to assure me he was on his way home after dealing with an "emergency." He related a strange tale of how his travels had been diverted to Phoenix in order for him to see Maria—who may or may not be his wife. After returning to Colorado, he showed me her photograph. She is young and lovely and, according to Thompson, the daughter of a wealthy Pakistani who is not amused by their relationship. The father, he swears, put out a contract on his life. "When we met, he asked me, 'Just what kind of doctor are you?' He didn't have the vaguest idea who I was. Now he knows. It gets me in a lot of trouble." Thompson's voice trailed off, "If my daughter ran off with a freak when she was twenty-two . . ."

I first encountered Hunter Thompson during the McGovern campaign in 1972. We met one night covering the Ohio primary. J. Edgar Hoover had just died, and we celebrated the end of his despotic rule of the FBI through a long night's journey into morning, while corrupt politicians delayed the count of the primary vote in an attempt to steal the election for Humphrey.

I was witness to Thompson's aberrant behavior later that year as a trainload of journalists followed George McGovern through the San Joaquin Valley during the California primary. A European camera crew had been particularly obnoxious, pushing and shoving us to obtain a better angle. Thompson produced a hunting knife and threatened to cut the cord that bound the soundman to the cameraman—indeed, to relieve them of certain vital organs if they did not desist. They fled in terror.

Four years later, we were having dinner at the Sheraton Wayfarer near Manchester as the New Hampshire primary approached. The management had informed Thompson there was no room for him at the inn. He was seething because he felt he had helped immortalize the hotel in his book about the last campaign. He took matters into his own hands, literally. Grabbing a fork, he marched to the desk and vowed to gouge out the eardrum of the night clerk. A room was found for him.

Thompson was partially responsible for the rise of Jimmy Carter that year, "turning on" the readers of *Rolling Stone* to this obscure governor of Georgia. He lavishly praised a Law Day speech Carter had delivered in 1974, a performance Thompson ranked with Gen. Douglas MacArthur's "old soldiers never die" address to Congress as a Great American Speech. Carter was grateful, and over the course of the early 1976 campaign, Thompson felt he had a special franchise with the candidate. He expected an interview with Carter as they flew from Orlando to Chicago on the morning after Carter's triumph in the Florida primary, but Carter stiffed him. The future Democratic nominee said he was too tired and wanted to sleep. Muttering and glowering upon arrival at O'Hare Airport, Thompson caught the next plane back to Orlando to beseige the hotel room where Hamilton Jordan— Carter's campaign manager—was still sleeping. When Jordan refused to respond to Thompson's screeching, the national affairs correspondent for *Rolling Stone* soaked the base of Jordan's door with lighter fluid and set it ablaze.

Over the course of his career, Thompson has pillaged many hotels. One correspondent who attended the cataclysmic events in Vietnam in 1975 remembers that the sound of Thompson crashing down the steps of Saigon's Continental Hotel was louder than the artillery of the approaching North Vietnamese Army.

The Duke of Doonesbury . . . Bimbos and Bomb-shells . . . Giving Odds in an Odd Time . . . The Doctor of Philosophy . . .

By sundown on Friday the banshee had screamed for more stiffs than the morgues could hold, and the jails were filling up like cheap hotels in Calcutta.

—Hunter S. Thompson
San Francisco Examiner

Thompson has been cultivating an outlandish persona for years—the drunken, raving, dope fiend who narrated *Fear and Loathing in Las Vegas*. The book first appeared in *Rolling Stone* and was allegedly written by "Raoul Duke," a psuedonym that Thompson says he picked "off the wall." Raoul Duke is still listed as "Contributing Editor (Sports)" on the *Rolling Stone* masthead. Thompson, for that matter, has the title of "Health & Fitness Editor" for a publication named *Bathroom Journal*.

Duke, of course, was transmogrified by Garry Trudeau into a durable cartoon-strip character in *Doonesbury*. Trudeau's Duke resembles Thompson: the balding head, the sunglasses, the cigarette holder, the reckless talk of drug deals and scams. Oddly enough, Thompson and Trudeau, the two high priests of American satire who both harass Bush unmercifully, have never met. It is just as well.

After Duke first appeared in the cartoon more than a decade ago, Thompson sent Trudeau several menacing letters in which the subject of the artist's dismemberment was raised. At the time, Thompson's marriage to his first wife, Sandy, was crumbling, and he resented the inclusion of her name in the comic strip. Thompson says he no longer looks at *Doonesbury*, where Duke has degenerated to zombie status.

Even today, Thompson will not discuss his divorce. He gestured as if to slit my throat, brandishing a steak knife from the Woody Creek Tavern, if I brought it up. But he is proud of a product of that union, his twenty-two-year-old son, Juan, a student at the University of Colorado.

There may not be a sober side to Hunter Thompson, but there is a generous one. It turns out that one of his running mates is Semmes Luckett, who was my college roommate in 1959. Like half of the residents of Aspen, it seems, Luckett got turned in to the Feds by an informer a few years ago. He copped a plea for moving massive shipments of what he calls "herbs," did some time in a halfway house, and is now in the midst of a five-year probation period. Things have not always been easy for him, but when he was down-and-out, he says, Thompson sent him a large, unsolicited check.

While I was in Aspen, another of Thompson's friends was badly hurt in a car wreck. He immediately began making arrangements to take care of the victim's sixteen-year-old son.

And for all of the nihilistic language he uses, Thompson cares about the American political process. When he accepts speaking engagements on campuses, he says, "I preach to the college students that politics is the art to control your environment. . . . In a democracy, you've got to believe you can make a difference."

His problem is that he distrusts most of the politicians involved. We didn't know it the last night we talked politics, but Gary Hart would be back in the race the next day. Even though Hart was supposedly gone at that moment, he was not forgotten. In fact, he was the butt of much derision, even though Thompson and Hart are old Colorado friends. (I remember Thompson arriving at a low moment during the Hart effort in 1984 with heavy-duty cables to "jump-start" the campaign.) There is a bogus letter signed "Gary," written on U.S. Senate stationery, that adorns one wall of the Woody Creek Tavern. Written in a style suspiciously similar to Thompson's prose, the letter refers to the Donna Rice affair and concludes, "Thank God I got rid of her before she got her rotten little teeth into me."

Thompson says that as a reporter, he would never stake out a candidate's home "unless he was suspected of selling cocaine to little children. There we might draw the line. We all know these candidates are womanizers. Sex never hurt anybody. In the meantime we lose track of what matters. The press becomes obsessed with the *National Enquirer* syndrome. There are more ominous things happening in politics than a bimbo from Miami. They've been around all the time."

Thompson predicts Sen. Edward M. Kennedy will get into the race and hopes he will win the presidency this year, though he adds, "I like Gary Hart better than Kennedy." Thompson is not bothered by what tarnishes both men. "So Kennedy ran off a bridge. Hell, Bush killed 243 Marines and another 69 at the embassy," he says in reference to the administration's policy in Lebanon.

Handicapping the presidential field, Thompson sounds like a police sergeant reading out a rap sheet on each candidate:

Gov. Michael Dukakis. "His wife spent twenty-six years as a speed freak. She is more interesting than her husband. She makes Rosalynn Carter look like a charwoman. She should be running."

Sen. Albert Gore. "I have no interest in Gore, and I'd be surprised if anybody else does."

Rep. Richard Gephardt. "He won't be around by Super Tuesday."

Former governor Bruce Babbitt. "Are you kidding? Really?"

Sen, Paul Simon. "I like Simon. I think he's honest in a simple way. But you don't run for president as a simpleton. Look at him. He couldn't win an election for sheriff in most places."

Rev. Jesse Jackson. "My inclination is to vote for Jesse. I like Jesse. He makes politics what it should be." Then, and stressing that he means the words to be complimentary, like a soul brother, he calls Jackson "a wild nigger."

Gorbachev, he says, "could win in Iowa."

No Republicans need apply:

Bush he dismisses as an obsequious geek. "Electing him would be the continuation of Nixon." In one diatribe in the *Examiner,* Thompson wrote that Bush's "face has become swollen and he is said to be plagued by a growth of dead fatty tissue on his back, which is gathering in a lump in the area between his shoulder blades and prevents him from walking normally."

Sen. Robert Dole. "Against Bush, I'd make him 3-to-1. Electing Dole would be like electing Jim Wright (the Speaker of the House). It's the Peter Principle at work."

Former governor Pierre S. du Pont. "A dilettante."

Al Haig. "I enjoy Haig. He's crazy as a loon. I like him like I like Pat Buchanan." In one column, Thompson wrote of "Cruel Crazy Patrick and Big Al, the Wild Boys, roaming around Washington like a pair of Foam Frogs in heat, laying 3,000 eggs every night and cranking up a genuinely mean ticket—Haig & Buchanan, Buchanan & Haig. What does it matter? 'We will kill the ones who eat us, and eat the ones we kill. . . .'"

Rep. Jack Kemp. "An airhead stuck with that 'trickle-down' crap."

Rev. Pat Robertson. "He's in it to sell his revival tapes."

Thompson confesses, "My great fear is that it'll go by default to Bush. If Bush wins, we all might as well give up on this country until the year 3000."

Thompson has no apologies for his treatment of Bush, or for his verbal manhandling of Humphrey. Nearly ten years after Humphrey died of cancer, Thompson was excoriating another old New Deal Democrat in a recent column in which he said, "Even Hubert Humphrey was shamed, all alone in his unquiet grave down in the depths of the River Styx." Humphrey, he says, "cost us control of the country for ten years." Thompson's only regret is that once he wrote that Humphrey should have been castrated, then later learned that Humphrey had a handicapped grandchild. "I felt bad about that."

It was five below zero outside Thompson's cabin, and the dawn sky was gray as slate. The cabdriver from Mellow Yellow Taxi Co., who had been waiting outside for me, came inside to warm up and pop a Molson for himself.

We were talking about books and, flushed with drink, mortality. Thompson has completed a novel he calls *The Night Manager,* which he hopes will be published someday. Thompson has had no fiction published, although critics might say that the body of his work should be considered fiction. He particularly admires Joseph Conrad. "He's a gloomy bastard."

I reminded Thompson of his own introduction to *The Great Shark Hunt,* a despondent author's note written on another winter night ten years before when he was contemplating suicide: "I have already lived and finished the life I planned to live (thirteen years longer, in fact) and everything from now on will be A New Life, a different thing. . . ."

Thompson replied that he had been unnecessarily morbid at the time; the words were a cryptic reference to his marriage that was failing. He may have been troubled about being forty years old then, but he insisted he doesn't mind being fifty today. There are new politicians to gore, new pomposities to puncture. He is back in command of his career. There is another presidential campaign to cover, and there is no one who can spare the candidates from the wrath of Hunter Thompson.

Gonzo's Last Stand? The New Aspen Takes Aim at Hunter S. Thompson

Geoffrey Stokes and Kevin Simonson / 1990

From *Village Voice*, May 15, 1990, pp. 35–39. Reprinted with permission of the Geoffrey Stokes Estate.

For my part, I had lived about 10 miles out of town for two years, doing everything possible to avoid Aspen's feverish reality. My lifestyle, I felt, was not entirely suited for doing battle with any small town political establishment. . . . In my very limited congress with the local authorities, I was treated like some kind of half-mad cross between a hermit and a wolverine, a thing best let alone as long as possible.

—Hunter S. Thompson, 1970

At about 6:30 on Wednesday evening, February 21, thirty-five-year-old Gail Palmer got into the cab she'd called to the inn where she and her husband, Michigan ophthalmologist Charles Slater, were spending their Aspen ski vacation. Leaving the expensively manicured confines of Snowmass Village, the cab carried Palmer west on Route 82— away from Aspen and toward the less fashionable "downvalley" regions where those who cater to its wealthy visitors can still afford to live. Across 82, about a half-mile past the cluster of trailers that flank the frame building shared by Woody Creek's post office and the Woody Creek Tavern, the cab made a hairpin turn to the right, starting the long climb toward Owl Ranch, the longtime residence of Hunter S. Thompson.

Palmer was excited; well before coming to Aspen, she'd written Thompson to set up a meeting. A "self-employed writer" (as she later described herself to investigators), she thought of Thompson, the snarling founding father of Gonzo journalism, as "a hero." This was by no means an entirely unreasonable judgment; though Thompson, now in his fifties, has lost a foot or so off his fastball over the years, both *Fear and Loathing in Las Vegas* and *Fear and Loathing on the Campaign Trail* are journalistic classics, and the lead

80

of the former— "We were somewhere around Barstow on the edge of the desert when the drugs began to take hold"—was a generation's answer to "Call me Ishmael."

But Palmer's evening was not a success. "When I first got there it was really wonderful," she says, but by 10:30, a time when Thompson's usual cocktail hour has scarcely begun, the night was a shambles. According to her, Thompson and some friends who were also present had first done some coke, and then Thompson had invited her (though "not directly") to share his hot tub. Shortly after that, in a rage the cause of which Palmer still can't pinpoint ("My husband says, 'Stop trying to rationalize an irrational person'"), he began screaming, "Get that lesbian bitch out of here," pushing at her, grabbing and twisting her left breast, finally threatening, "Get out of here or I'll blow your head off." Since Thompson's house was full of firearms, this was not a remark she took lightly, and she fled to the front porch, where she was soon joined by Thompson's assistant, Catherine ("Cat") Sabonis-Chaffee, who sat with her until a cab arrived to bring her back to her hotel.

Thompson, who believes Palmer was trying to pull off a publicity stunt, tells a different story: "The broad was sloppy drunk," he says, sitting at a typewriter in a corner of his paper-festooned kitchen. "She might have been a *little* drunk when she got here, but I mean drooling, reeling and bumping into things. And then *she* came on to *me*, backed me into this corner right here. I was saying, 'No, dammit. Get away,' but she kept on lurching at me, and I finally stiff-armed her—Poom! Like this, both arms at her shoulders," he spins on his stool and gestures with considerable force. "*Could* I have hit her in the tit? I suppose so. But *if* I did, neither one of us noticed it at the time. All I wanted was for her to get the fuck away from me, but *this*,"—he gestures toward an imaginary circle enclosing him—"this is a fucking *nightmare*."

No, it's not. It's real. As a result of Palmer's complaint, Thompson faces misdemeanor charges of both simple and sexual assault. More seriously, as a result of a search warrant based on that complaint, he's also been charged with misdemeanor marijuana possession, four counts of felony drug possession and use, and one of possessing illegal explosives. Under Colorado's stiff laws, some of these charges could bring sentences of up to sixteen very real years in the state penitentiary. Trial, after some preliminary hearings, is now scheduled for early September.

"It's settled down now, and it's almost hard to remember what it was like," says Tim Mooney, "but a few years ago, *everybody* in this restaurant would have been carrying some coke. People would have been banging in and out of the bathroom all the time."

Though this seems unlikely—ski season is over and the lunchtime crowd of local businessfolk at the Wieserstube shares a certain heavy seriousness with its German cuisine—it is no fantasy. According not merely to Mooney but to Aspenites ranging from law-enforcement officials to longtime bartenders, Aspen was a *wide open* town. "There was always the feeling," said one, "that laws were something made in Denver." Local enforcement was what counted, and in 1970, for instance, Thompson himself came perilously close to being elected sheriff, capturing 38 percent of the vote in a three-way contest.

But times have changed since Mooney—now forty-two, and preternaturally boyish, as long as a cap hides his bald head—came out here twenty years ago. He headed west after graduating from college in Pennsylvania, eventually hooking on as a ski instructor at the famous Aspen Mountain Ski School. Though still associated with the school, by now most of his teaching—of film and music people plus the occasional corporate mogul—is by appointment only, and his friends jokingly refer to him as "Ski Instructor to the Stars."

Mooney's access to the rich and famous is one of the reasons Thompson has asked him to chair his legal defense fund, but Mooney is also a friend, and his admiration for Thompson is transparent. "Hunter is a genius as a writer," he says, "but he's also special in Aspen—and becoming more special—because he really has *fun*. I remember one night we were out at his house, probably a little doped up, and we went on a 'strafing mission.' We were all over the ranch in his jeep, firing weapons into the hillsides, watching these blue streaks, when we got back, he looked around and said with this big grin, "Who *didn't* have fun tonight?' And nobody said a word, because we all had. Underneath all that talent, Hunter's like a mischievous little kid."

Aspen, however, has grown less tolerant of mischief. In the Reagan '80s, a truly unthinkable mass of disposable wealth was created at the high end of the economic scale, but the supply of prime Aspen real estate was limited, for the legacy of Thompson's sheriff campaign was a political movement that seized control of Aspen's government, passing a series of laws that sharply limited the growth of new housing. Meanwhile, Aspen became fashionable, and with too much money chasing too few toys, housing prices rocketed, bending the local economy out of shape. As recently as 1985, the average Aspen home sold for $450,000; in the first quarter of 1990, the figure had more than tripled, reaching $1,442,000.

Clearly, most people who work in Aspen can no longer afford to live there, and development is pushing downvalley. Even Thompson's Woody Creek neighborhood is feeling the pressure. As Pitkin County sherrif Bob Braudis put it, discussing Floyd Watkins's troubled arrival in the area, "Our millionaires are being replaced by billionaires." The change is not without friction; last year, Watkins, whose ranch is upstream from Thompson's, accused him of firing automatic weapons at his house (Thompson admits the gunfire but claims he was shooting in self-defense because he was being attacked by a giant porcupine.)

Those who've been pushed out of Aspen are particularly frustrated, because the people who can afford the houses don't live in them. Mike Solheim, a twenty-three-year resident, was active in the campaign to limit growth. "In our naïveté, we thought we were doing something good," he says, "but a couple of years ago, I took my daughter into town to go trick-or-treating on Halloween. *There was nobody there!* House after house in the West End was dark, and everyone was in Hollywood or Manhattan."

People who've spent millions for houses they use perhaps two or three weeks a year are unlikely to be amused by Thompson's boho antics—or, indeed, by any vestiges of Aspen's cowboy mentality. Pulling his battered red pickup truck out of Jack Nicholson's permanently reserved parking spot ("A perk," Mooney says), Mooney provides a real-estate House-of-Horror tour. Here, he says, is the ski-in, ski-out house that department store heir Ted Field bought (together with condo space for servants and pilots) for $22 million; there, ringed by construction cranes, the foundation for a new Ritz-Carlton Hotel and convention center that will effectively end Aspen's off-season. Here, the small log home in the East End he rents for the "bargain" price of $1200 a month; there a tiny West End frame house that is being sold—"as a teardown"—for $950,000. Here is a spec house sold two years ago for $1.8 million, now back on the market for $3.2 million; there are the town's elementary and middle schools, not overcrowded, but sitting on land so valuable that developers are pressuring the school board to bus Aspen's inconvenient children to a new "education center" downvalley.

"What all this brings in," he says, "are citified people, people who are accustomed to having things done *their* way, and the rest of us just don't matter. All they want—unless they need their house cleaned or their car pulled out of a ditch—is for us to stay out of their sight."

Sometime on the night of February 21, Dr. Charles Slater called the sheriff's office to complain that Thompson had assaulted his wife—the precise time of his call is very much at issue, for the Aspen *Times Daily* has reported that the tape which automatically records all incoming police calls is missing Dr. Slater's. Later on that night (sometime between 2 and 5 a.m. on February 22, actually), Palmer's former boyfriend and business partner, Marco DiMercurio, also called. Saying that he was speaking from Los Angeles, DiMercurio claimed that Thompson had in the course of the evening held a gun to Palmer's head. He insisted that there be an investigation, but warned that Palmer couldn't be interviewed until after 2 p.m.

By then, Sheriff Braudis had withdrawn from the case; a close friend of Thompson's, he'd been criticized for not being sufficiently aggressive in investigating the dispute between Thompson and Floyd Watkins. Seeking to ensure the appearance of fairness, Braudis transferred the complaint to Chip McCrory, the deputy district attorney for Aspen. McCrory, formerly a prosecutor from a Denver suburb, was appointed to the Aspen office in 1985, becoming chief deputy after his predecessor resigned in 1988.

Though McCrory is neither well-liked nor regarded as politically ambitious, the man who appointed him—a pleasant, conservative downvalley Republican named Milton Blakey—is affectionately called "Judge Blakey" by those who like him well enough to tease him about his much desired judicial appointment. Based in Glenwood Springs, a community markedly more conservative than Aspen, Blakey—like all lawyers, whether prosecution or defense—is barred by Colorado law from discussing a case once a charge has been filed, but he does say that with regard to the somewhat laxer standards long prevalent in Aspen, I've "not been misled."

With Blakey's encouragement, McCrory has moved sharply away from the path marked out by his predecessors, who'd tempered the prosecutorial urge with a healthy dose of what the Supreme Court has called "community standards." McCrory, for instance, recently brought—and lost, after less than an hour of jury deliberation—a felony case for the alleged sale of some twenty-five dollars worth of cocaine. Even more problematic was his decision to seek a felony conviction against a well-regarded young woman who, while being booked for DUI, pushed a recovered-alcoholic jailer who was pressuring her about the virtues of AA. Even members of the jury that had just convicted her were horrified to discover that the law McCrory chose to invoke—which was designed to discourage incarcerated prisoners from assaulting their guards during riots—carried an inescapable, mandatory prison sentence ("old Aspen," including the mayor, has contributed generously to her appeal fund). For the zealous McCrory, who'd been prominent among those criticizing the sheriff's allegedly laissez-faire attitude toward Thompson, Palmer's tale of sex, violence, drugs, and weaponry must have seemed a dream come true.

Whatever the cause, McCrory seems to have reacted to Palmer's complaint with more speed than prudence. Without interviewing any of the other people who'd been at Thompson's, McCrory drew up charges for assault and sexual assault, and then—after a local judge had passed on signing a search warrant—had it signed by a judge based some sixty miles downvalley. While one certainly doesn't want to encourage any prosecutor to downplay a woman's charges of violence, in this case a delay might have caused McCrory to rethink his choice, for to put it as charitably as possible, Palmer, as she tried to warn him, is not an ideal complainant. "I tried to explain to them that I wouldn't work out for them as much as they would like to use me to get at Hunter," she says, referring to her career as a director and producer of porn films.

Palmer grew up middle-class and Catholic in East Detroit. In high school, she played basketball, was a cheerleader and, she says, was a member of the National Honor Society. She got into the porn biz when she was a nineteen-year-old college student, doing a live show for bookstore/peepshow mogul Harry Mohney. A year later, *Playboy* gave her a thousand dollars to take her clothes off for one of its "Girls of the Big Ten" features ("Spartan Gail Palmer is a student film maker who wrote, produced, and directed an X-rated movie").

With Mohney as patron, she began directing her own films, ultimately making nine, the best-known of which is probably *The Erotic Adventures of Candy*. In most, she says, she played only "cameo" roles, but this is still the stuff that should have given a district attorney pause. I mean, do you want to be up there trying to convince a jury that a defendant should get whacked for touching a woman's breast and then have his lawyer start showing the jury pictures of her smiling during some extremely gymnastic exercises involving well-endowed gentlemen, a trapeze, and, perhaps, a pony?

Reached by phone at her home in Michigan, Palmer says that when the district attorney's investigator, Michael Kelly, first called her hotel room to "get the whole story," she told him, "I'm not interested." Kelly, however, persisted, telling Slater that his wife should talk for Thompson's own good: "He said, 'She should do this. We have problems. Someday he's going to kill someone. Someday he is going to hurt someone.' "

Even then, however, Palmer did not want to press charges. But Kelly told her "Sometimes it's not up to you," and, "It's for me to decide if there was a crime committed." Palmer says she responded, "I can tell you right now that a crime didn't take place," but she finally agreed to talk. Despite extensive pressure from Kelly, however, she repeatedly denied DiMercurio's report that Thompson had held a gun to her head and insisted that Thompson had never come on to her sexually (Thompson, who has seen the D.A.'s transcript of the interview, also says that it was Kelly, not Palmer, who first suggested that her breast had been "twisted"). "I felt they were using me and I even told them that," she says, and it appears that she was right.

Certainly what happened next was unusual police work. With the "victim" both strongly denying the only possible felony charge (DiMercurio's long-distance gun-to-head claim) and dismissing any sexual context, what Kelly and McCrory had was the equivalent of a drunken bar fight—albeit one that allegedly involves drugs as well as drinking. This is the sort of thing that happens a dozen times a week in resort towns, and if the complainant doesn't actively insist on pressing charges—and if the assailant doesn't have a record of violence—that's usually the end of the story.

But what had (or had not) happened to Palmer seemed to be irrelevant to McCrory. What mattered, apparently, was that her story gave him a rationale to go after Thompson, whose writings made him a bone in Aspen's throat. Though Thompson's courthouse contacts with Aspen law enforcement included nothing more serious than a speeding ticket, McCrory prepared formal charges for misdemeanor sexual and simple assault—and at the same time, sought a search warrant.

Thus, three days later, McCrory and Kelly, a tame judge's warrant in hand, met with the sheriff to discuss serving it. When it was suggested at that meeting that a single-source search warrant might not stand up, McCrory is said to have pounded his fist on the table and said, "If we go out and interview other people who were there, we're going to blow this warrant out of the water." In fairness to McCrory, this didn't *have* to mean that further interviews would so discredit the complaint that not even the most acquiescent judge would issue a warrant; he might simply have meant it would give Thompson time to do a little frantic housecleaning (but since neither he nor Kelly is talking, there's no way to know).

The weird thing about the meeting, however, was McCrory's insistence that because Thompson was armed and violent, the sheriff should put together a SWAT team to go out to Woody Creek and bring him in. The sheriff suggested that a phone call might do just as well, and indeed, when Kelly called to say there was an arrest warrant and ask Thompson downtown for "a chat," Thompson promptly appeared.

Shortly after that, based on no more evidence than Palmer's uncorroborated and uninvestigated statement, the authorities began a search of Thompson's house. It involved six officers for eleven hours; a sixty-six-hour effort that yielded the sort of leftovers one might have imagined from reading any of Thompson's books: ballpoint pen shells with traces of "white powder," rolled bills, a mirror, a hookah, two pipes, a metal can with "green leafy residue," several pharmacist's vials of unidentified pills, a scale . . . thirty-five items in all, including something described as "video tape child porn" with which the press had a field day (and which eventually proved to be a BBC show on the subject that *Inside Edition* had broadcast). Sixty-six hours of extensive searching turned up only enough (even if all the items were illegal, and most of them proved to be prescription or over-the-counter medicines) to suggest that Thompson is a private, recreational drug user. This is not what you'd call a surprise.

But there's another way of describing what they found in the pockets of his jackets and corners of his bureau drawers: They found enough to send him to jail until well into the twenty-first century.

As Dr. Johnson said of the knowledge that one is about to be hanged, the prospect of jail concentrates the mind wonderfully, and Thompson has been laboring hard on his own behalf, making calls, planning strategies, and faxing notes of thanks or instruction to local, national, and international supporters. Buoyed by a successful working visit from the editor of his already announced *Songs of the Doomed,* Thompson is keeping his customary eccentric schedule: seventy-hour bursts of energy followed by a day or so of uninterrupted sleep.

These periods of collapse make it a little hard to get hold of him on a regular schedule, but after two lunches at the Woody Creek Tavern go by the

board ("You're waiting for Hunter? Good luck"), we eventually get together at his house. Thompson's home, a multilevel structure that seems to have been designed by Ludwig of Bavaria on a tight budget, stands perhaps a hundred yards back from Woody Creek Road, behind a locked gate whose posts are topped with carved vultures. Peacocks scream angrily as visitors near the door, and a *serious* hunting knife plunged into the doorframe holds a note in place. The door is locked, but Thompson's friend Michael Solheim lets us in. There are more knives inside, and guns, and virtually every surface but that of the projection-size television is covered with Scotch-taped notes. "Moths," reads the Magic-Marker scrawl on one, "Millions of hungry moths. They will destroy all of our wool clothes by labor day if we give them free reign. We must kill moths
   —get bug lights
   —moth balls
   —screens
   —Raid, many cans."
Thompson, wearing a blue terrycloth robe over a striped polo shirt, emerges from the bedroom and heads for a stool near the partition/counter that divides the kitchen from the living room. Walking with the controlled speed of a sick teenager who wants to convince his parents he's well enough to go out at night, he pours himself a cup of coffee and begins planning a defense committee meeting with Solheim. He seems genuinely touched by the amount of local support he's getting. (That morning, a local excavating contractor, one of the conservative Democrats the "no-growth" faction had chased from power, told me, "You can quote me on only one thing: Hunter Thompson is an A-number-one asshole. No, make that two: There's too many goddamn liberals in Aspen. *Off* the record, the assholes had no right to search the other asshole's house.")

"I have more public support now than I did when I ran for sheriff," Thompson laughs, and he's almost certainly right; there are a lot of houses in Aspen where sixty-six hours of searching could produce *something* incriminating. As a supportive ad in the *Times Daily* read, "Today, the Doctor. Tomorrow, you." But beyond that, there is something about the D.A.'s invasion of Thompson's house that seems to grate against the Western sensibility of even Aspen's conservatives. Finally, of course, there is the matter of the Fourth Amendment of the United States Constitution.

A few years ago, McCrory's warrant would have been worth as little legally as it is morally, but the Nixon/Reagan legacy on the Supreme Court means that it has a better than even chance of standing up against the challenge Thompson's lawyers plan to bring. And what that means is that on the basis of someone's unsupported word that you used drugs (burned a flag/plotted insurrection/planned a possibly illegal demonstration/committed sodomy/possessed pornography/arranged an abortion) in the privacy of your own home, the cops can break down your door.

Over the course of a long and energized evening, Thompson does all the predictably Gonzo things—sets huge logs blazing in his fireplace with some sort of fierce chemical, barks to startled acquaintances on the phone, drinks countless water tumblers full of whiskey, plays music at a volume well beyond the pain threshold—but keeps returning to the question of police invasiveness. "Why don't they get it in New York?" he asks almost plaintively. "They understand *here*, they understand in *Europe*. Why don't they understand in New York?"

I remember, but do not mention, part of my conversation with Mooney. Early on in forming the defense committee, he'd talked with Jann Wenner at *Rolling Stone*. Wenner would be helpful, said Mooney, but wouldn't agree to publish Thompson's own story of what was happening: "What he said was, 'Hunter doesn't have enough of the journalist left in him.' "

Maybe not; though Wenner says he'd be delighted to publish Thompson's story, the sense that Thompson is past it is widespread. He is yesterday's hero. But this is not, I think, sufficient cause for imprisonment.

"Hunter's problem," says George Stranahan, "is that when Braudis pulled out—as he had good reason to do—that opened the door for a district attorney who's lusted after Hunter's hide for a long time." Stranahan, a monied and handsome fifty-eight-year-old physicist turned rancher, runs the Flying Dog Ranch, a mile or so up Woody Creek Road from Thompson. A thirty-year resident of Woody Creek, he's guardedly optimistic about the case ("Aspen juries have a habit that possessors of small amounts of drugs are acquitted"), but somewhat less optimistic about Aspen.

"It's not so much that there's a change in the community values that have always prevailed here, but an influx of people with new values. They're very wealthy, very glitzy, but even *that's* not new. After all, Gary Cooper was here when I used to come skiing in 1947. But he bought his own six-packs, his own broom at the hardware store where he knew the kids' names; these people send their chauffeurs.

"All over the place now, you see fences with Westec Security signs on them, no trespassing, no hiking trails near my property, no dropping in on a neighbor—because you have nothing in common with that neighbor."

"It doesn't take much to turn a community like ours around. One or two of those people buy in, and you suddenly find yourself with no neighbors to speak of, and your $40,000 equity in your house is worth $2 million. People can only withstand that pressure if they can see a dream—a community—and in a lot of places right now, they're not feeling that dream. So you take the money, go downvalley to Carbondale, buy a nice house for $300,000, put $1.7 million into treasury bonds, and try to forget what you've lost. A Floyd Watkins doesn't just poison the community by bringing in earth-movers and shifting the course of the river."

Watkins, a burly, bald fifty-year-old who seems to wear a perpetual scowl, moved in on Woody Creek almost six years ago. It is fair to say that he doesn't get on with Thompson, Stranahan, or, in his phrase, with any of the "cuckoos and long-haired weirdos" that hang out at the Woody Creek Tavern. In general, indeed, his effect on Woody Creek seems to be not unlike the effect of a baleful giant on Happy Valley in a Disney cartoon: As the shadow slowly darkens the meadow, birds stop their singing, cute little bunnies dive into their holes . . . He has withdrawn the armed guard he'd set to patrolling his new, fenced-in home last year, but he still keeps a couple of caged Bengal tigers near the gate.

He and Thompson have had a couple of set-tos over the years, but Watkins dismisses Thompson as a minor problem; the real villain, he thinks, is Stranahan. "My problem," he says, "is that coming from the big city, I didn't realize when I moved into Woody Creek that you didn't do anything without George Stranahan's permission."

Beyond the overall question of what ties a fragile community together, Watkins and Stranahan are divided by the only thing that unites them: the narrow, twisting, and undeniably dangerous dirt road that is gouged from the side of their mountain. Watkins wants it paved, so that visitors can come to his ranch more easily. Stranahan is willing to have safety improvements, but doesn't want a highway running up to Watkins's house. "That's a *community* road and a *community* decision," says Stranahan; "I'm not accustomed to losing to some hick who grows cows," says Watkins.

"Either I'm going to have the road fixed," he continues, "or I'm going to have every county commissioner voted out. I not only have enough ties in this community, I have enough time, money, and energy to do just that.

"I just brought them in a petition to improve the road, 130-plus signatures. And when they tell me petitions don't make any difference, like Wayne Ethridge did last week, that makes me mad. Did you hear him? Stood up there and said, 'If we did things automatically by petition, we wouldn't *need* county commissioners.'"

"I'm gonna stick it right up his ass. Look at those clowns. There's an electrician there who lives in a county housing project, and none of the others have two nickels to rub together. You turn them upside down and shake them, you wouldn't get a nickel to drop to the ground. They fuck with me and they're *gone*."

Watkins is the voice of the new Aspen carried to its logical conclusion. Rich beyond any useful purpose from a debt-collection empire he began in Chicago, he is almost a caricature. He is, in fact, a Gonzo Donald Trump, and on a face-to-face basis, he and Thompson almost like each other. But he is, I'm afraid, the future—almost as surely as Hunter Thompson is the past.

And because Thompson *is* the past, there is a tendency to dismiss his legal troubles. Clearly, if he beat up Palmer, he should be punished. Bullies— whether they use their money or their fists—shouldn't get away with it. But the idea that Thompson should be packed off to prison for possessing drugs, when the *real* probable cause for the search could only have been his *writing*, ought to be unthinkable. Which may be why so few people seem to be thinking about it.

Interview with
Hunter S. Thompson
William McKeen / 1990

From *Hunter S. Thompson*, Twayne's United States Author Series (Boston: Twayne Publishers, 1991), pp. 105–9. Reprinted with the permission of William McKeen.

William McKeen: Your North American articles for the *National Observer* in 1963 seem so much more sedate than your dispatches from South America in 1962 and early 1963. Were there some problems in dealing with the *Observer* when you were closer to the editors?

Hunter S. Thompson: When I came back from South America to the *National Observer,* I came as a man who'd been a star—off the plane, all the editors met me and treated me as such. There I was—wild drunk in fatigues and a Panama hat. I said I wouldn't work in Washington. *National Observer* is a Dow Jones company so I continued to write good stories—just without political context. I drifted West. *National Observer* became my road gig out of San Francisco. I was too much for them. I would wander in on off hours drunk and obviously on drugs asking for my messages. Essentially, they were working for me. They liked me, but I was the bull in the china shop—the more I wrote about politics the more they realized who they had on their hands. They knew I wouldn't change and neither would they.

Berkeley, Hell's Angels, Kesey, blacks, hippies . . . I had these *connections.* Rock and roll. I was a crossroads for everything, and they weren't making use of it. I was withdrawn from my news position and began writing book reviews—mainly for money. The final blow was the Wolfe review. I left to write *Hell's Angels* in 1965.

WM: What was the nature of the conflict with the *Observer* over the coverage of the Free Speech Movement at Berkeley?

HST: The Free Speech Movement was virtually nonexistent at the time, but I saw it coming. There was a great rumbling—you could feel it everywhere.

92

It was wild, but Dow Jones was just too far away. I wanted to cover the Free Speech Movement, but they didn't want me to.

My final reason for leaving was because I wrote this strongly positive review of Wolfe's *Kandy-Kolored Tangerine Flake Streamline Baby*. The feature editor killed it because of a grudge. I took the *Observer's* letter and a copy of the review with a brutal letter about it all to Wolfe. I then copied that letter and sent it to the *Observer*. I had told Wolfe that the review had been killed for bitchy, personal reasons.

WM: You spent some of your time at Time, Inc., typing the works of Faulkner, Fitzgerald, and other great writers in an effort to understand their style. What writers have had the greatest influence on you?
HST: I would type things. I'm very much into rhythm—writing in a musical sense. I like gibberish, if it sings. Every author is different—short sentences, long, no commas, many commas. It helps a lot to understand what you're doing. You're writing, and so were they. It won't fit often—that is, *your* hands don't want to do *their* words—but you're *learning*. Writers of greatest influence? Conrad, Hemingway, Twain, Faulkner, Fitzgerald . . . Mailer, Kerouac in the political sense—they were allies. Dos Passos, Henry Miller, Isak Dinesen, Edmund Wilson, Thomas Jefferson.

WM: Did writing sports have an effect on your writing that writing news might not have had? I'm curious, because some of the best American writers (Lardner, Hemingway, even Updike) covered sports in one way or another.
HST: Huge. Look at the action verbs and the freedom to make up words—as a sports editor, you'll have twenty-two headlines and not that many appropriate words. At the Air Force base, I'd have my section: flogs, bashes, edges, nips, whips—after a while you run out of available words. You really get those action verbs flowing.

I put it all together once with my farewell to sports writing, but I always come back to it under odd circumstances: Ali, the Kentucky Derby, even the Mint 400.

WM: What caused the rift with *Rolling Stone?* Was it something that was building for a while, or was it directly related to the "Great Leap of Faith" article?

HST: Wenner folded Straight Arrow Books shortly before the Saigon piece. I had to write that piece because the war had been such a player in my life for ten years. I needed to see the end of it and be a part of it somehow. Wenner folded Straight Arrow at a time when they owed me $75,000. I was enraged to find that out. It had been an advance for *Shark Hunt*. I wrote a seriously vicious letter—finally saying all I was thinking as I was taking off for Saigon. While in Saigon, I found I'd been fired when Wenner flew into a rage upon receiving the letter. Getting fired didn't mean much to me. I was in Saigon, I was writing—except that I lost health insurance. Here I was in a war zone, and no health insurance.

So, essentially, I refused to write anything once I found out. I found out when I tried to use my Telex card and it was refused. I called *Rolling Stone* to find out why (*perfect* phone system right to the end of the war). I talked to [managing editor] Paul Scanlon, who was sitting in for Wenner (off skiing). He told me I was fired, but fixed my telex card, etc. The business department had ignored the memo to fire me because it'd happened too many times before. They didn't want to be bothered with the paperwork, so Wenner's attempt had been derailed.

Anyone who would fire a correspondent on his way to disaster. . . . I vowed not to work for them. It was the end of our working relationship except for special circumstances. About that time, they moved to New York. *Rolling Stone* began to be run by the advertising and business departments and not by the editorial department. It was a financial leap forward for Wenner and *Rolling Stone*, but the editorial department lost any real importance.

You shouldn't work for someone who would fire you en route to a war zone.

I got off the plane greeted by a huge sign that said, "Anyone caught with more than $100 U.S. currency will go immediately to prison." Imagine how I felt with $30,000 taped to my body. I was a pigeon to carry the *Newsweek* payroll and communication to those in Saigon. I thought we'd all be executed. It was total curfew when we got off the plane so we were herded into this small room with all these men holding machine guns. There I was with three hundred times the maximum money allowance. We got out and I leapt on a motor scooter and told the kid to run like hell. I told Loren I wouldn't give him the money until he got me a suite in a hotel. Not an easy task, but he came through.

"The Leap of Faith": I had already picked up on Carter in '74. It was a special assignment as everything was after Saigon. I was still on the masthead: it was an honor roll of journalists, but the people on it—well, all of them were no longer with *Rolling Stone*. I didn't like that they put on the cover that I *endorsed* Carter. I picked him as a gambler. Endorsing isn't something a journalist should do.

Essentially, the fun factor had gone out of *Rolling Stone*. It was an outlaw magazine in California. In New York it became an establishment magazine and I have never worked well with people like that.

Today at *Rolling Stone* there are rows and rows of white cubicles, each with its own computer. That's how I began to hate computers. They represented all that was wrong with *Rolling Stone*. It became like an insurance office with people communicating cubicle to cubicle.

But my relationship had ended with the firing. The *attempt* was enough.

WM: Your use of drugs is one of the more controversial things about you and your writing. Do you think the use of drugs has been exaggerated by the media? How have drugs affected your perception of the world and/or your writing? Does the media portrayal of you as a "crazy" amuse, inflame, or bore you?

HST: Obviously, my drug use is exaggerated or I would be long since dead. I've already outlived the most brutal abuser of our time—Neal Cassady. Me and William Burroughs are the only other ones left. We're the only unrepentant public dope fiends around, and he's seventy years old and claiming to be clean. But he hasn't turned on drugs, like [Timothy] Leary.

As for my perception of the world and my writing, drugs usually enhance or strengthen my perceptions and reactions, for good or ill. They've given me the resilience to withstand repeated shocks to my innocence gland. The brutal reality of politics alone would probably be intolerable without drugs. They've given me the strength to deal with those shocking realities guaranteed to shatter *anyone's* beliefs in the higher idealistic shibboleths of our time and the "American Century." Anyone who covers his beat for twenty years, and that beat is "The Death of the American Dream," needs every goddamned crutch he can find.

Besides, I *enjoy* drugs. The only trouble they've given me is the people who try to keep me from using them. *Res ipsa loquitur*. I was, after all, a literary lion last year.

The media perception of me has always been pretty broad. As broad as the media itself. As a journalist, I somehow managed to break most of the rules and still succeed. It's a hard thing for most of today's journeyman journalists to understand, but only because they can't do it. The smart ones understood immediately. The best people in journalism I've never had any quarrel with. I *am* a journalist and I've never met, as a group, any tribe I'd rather be a part of or that are more fun to be with—in spite of the various punks and sycophants of the press. I'm proud to be a part of the tribe.

It hasn't helped a lot to be a savage comic-book character for the last fifteen years—a drunken screwball who should've been castrated a long time ago. The smart people in the media knew it was a weird exaggeration. The dumb ones took it seriously and warned their children to stay way from me at all costs. The *really* smart ones understood it was only a censored, kind of toned-down children's-book version of the real thing.

Now we are being herded into the nineties, which looks like it is going to be a *true* generation of swine, a decade run by cops with no humor, with dead heroes, and diminished expectations, a decade that will go down in history as The Gray Area. At the end of the decade no one will be sure of anything except that you *must* obey the rules, sex will kill you, politicians lie, rain is poison, and the world is run by whores. These are terrible things to have to know in your life, even if you're rich.

Since that's become the mode, that sort of thinking has taken over the media as it has business and politics: "I'm going to turn you in, son—not only for your own good but because you were the bastard who turned *me* in last year."

This vilification by Nazi elements within the media has not only given me a fierce joy to continue my work—more and more alone out here, as darkness falls on the barricades—but has also made me profoundly orgasmic, mysteriously rich, and constantly at war with those vengeful retro-fascist elements of the Establishment that have hounded me all my life. It has also made me wise, shrewd and crazy on a level that can only be known by those who have been there.

WM: Some libraries classify *Fear and Loathing in Las Vegas* as a travelogue, some classify it as non-fiction, and some classify it as a novel. How much of this book is true? How would you characterize this book (beyond the jacket copy info in *The Great Shark Hunt*)? You refer to it as a failed experiment in

Gonzo journalism, yet many critics consider it a masterwork. How would you rate it?

HST: *Fear and Loathing in Las Vegas* is a masterwork. However, true gonzo journalism as I conceive it shouldn't be rewritten.

I would classify it, in Truman Capote's words, as a non-fiction novel in that almost all of it was true or did happen. I warped a few things, but it was a pretty accurate picture. It was an incredible feat of balance more than literature. That's why I called it *Fear and Loathing*. It was a pretty pure experience that turned into a very pure piece of writing. It's as good as *The Great Gatsby* and better than *The Sun Also Rises*.

WM: For years your readers have heard about *The Rum Diary*. Are you working on it, or on any other novel? Do you have an ambition to write fiction? Your stint as a newspaper columnist was successful, but do you have further ambitions within journalism?

HST: I've always had and still do have an ambition to write fiction. I've never had any real ambition within journalism, but events and fate and my own sense of fun keep taking me back for money, political reasons, and because I'm a warrior. I haven't found a drug yet that can get you anywhere near as high as sitting at a desk writing, trying to imagine a story no matter how bizarre it is as much as going out and getting into the weirdness of reality and doing a little time on The Proud Highway.

The Rum Diary is currently under cannibalization and transmogrification into a very strange movie.

I am now working on my final statement—*Polo Is My Life,* which is a finely muted saga of sex, treachery and violence in the 1990s, which also solves the murder of John F. Kennedy.

Exclusive Interview with Hunter S. Thompson

Kevin Simonson / 1993

Ever since Hunter S. Thompson was thrust into the international spotlight after the release of his comic masterpiece, *Fear and Loathing in Las Vegas,* myriads of observers have attempted to capture the essence of the creator of gonzo journalism. Oddly enough though, it wasn't an educator, a reporter, or even a historian who best described Thompson, but fellow Aspenite Jack Nicholson, who put it so succinctly when he called Thompson "the most baffling human iceberg of our time."

Thompson's career began in Jersey Shore, Pennsylvania, where he served as a sports writer for the local paper. From there, Thompson took to the road as a correspondent for such diversified publications as *Time, Cock-Fight Journal,* the New York *Herald Tribune, Rolling Stone,* and a bowling tabloid in Puerto Rico. It was a magazine article in the *Nation,* at a time when Thompson "couldn't even get wino's work," that prompted the initial book offers. In 1966, Thompson published his first book, *Hell's Angels,* and his role as demented observer of American's seedy underbelly was cast.

Thompson calls his creation of gonzo journalism "an almost accidental breakthrough," yet it seems to have evolved quite naturally from Thompson's chosen life-style. The best-selling author's aberrant behavior and sinister spirit are no myth. Gonzo journalism—part fact, part fiction, part controlled substance—is the perfect vehicle for Thompson.

I knew that the Doctor would have some sort of initiation that I would be required to pass before earning the right to click on my recorder—kind of like a barbarous fraternity for big boys. My rite of passage lay in a tiny

98

ceramic saucer, directly in front of me and a few inches from Thompson's smoldering Dunhill. A shriveled, pale red globule, resembling a pickled schnauzer's tongue, glistened in the harsh fluorescent lighting. A crowd had gathered around us at the Woody Creek Tavern. It was some type of exotic hot pepper—probably illegal in this country.

To my great relief, I saw that Thompson, who may be masochistic but certainly not suicidal, was going to consume one with me. Thompson downed his, and I followed suit. Within seconds, both of our foreheads were glistening with pea-size beads of sweat. I walked to the wall where a Thompson-scrawled memo hung and struggled valiantly to keep from projectile vomiting in front of our wide-eyed audience. The memo was one Thompson had penned a few years ago promising the proprietors that he would never, ever light another smoke bomb in the tavern. As I turned, the bar was filling with smoke, people were running for the exit, and a waitress was shrieking at Thompson. Though Thompson claimed the smoke bomb lighting was accidentally caused by a stray ash from a nearby patron's cigarette, we were asked to get the hell out of the bar and not come back for a couple of days.

The tape recorder was turned on at 4:10 A.M. in Thomspon's dark kitchen.

SPIN: Are you anybody's target?
Hunter S. Thompson: I'm in a weird position—I'm seeing films about me on television and people writing books about me. It's very eerie to live like that. I try to ignore it.

SPIN: Tell me about your next book, *Polo Is My Life: Memoir of a Brutal Southern Gentleman.*
HST: *Polo Is My Life* will be my final statement. It's a love story much in the manner of *Blue Velvet* or *Psycho.*

It is a bizarre story about a doomed and dangerous love affair between a journalist who also works for the CIA and a beautiful pure blond, polo-crazy heiress from Palm Beach who is hiding out in the Rockies because her "family" was somehow involved in the murder of John Kennedy. She had written a bad check to buy a chic nightclub in Aspen—so her younger brother, a failed priest, can play the jazz piano every night in public, like Eddie Duchin.

It's a doom-struck tale for our time. A hopeless maze of sex, violence, and treachery that can only end in death.

SPIN: For years I've been hearing about your book, *The Rum Diary*. Are you working on it and what are your ambitions toward fiction writing?
HST: I've always had and still do have an ambition to write fiction. I've never had any real ambition within journalism, but events and fate and my own sense of fun keep taking me back for money, political reasons, and because I'm a warrior. I haven't found a drug yet that can get you anywhere near as high as doing a little time on the Proud Highway.
   The Rum Diary is currently under cannibalization and transmogrification into a very strange movie.

SPIN: Any other movie projects in the future?
HST: I got *Fear and Loathing in Las Vegas* sold and launched into a movie project.

SPIN: Are you doing the screenplay?
HST: Probably. We're still arguing about the ending. They say it's weird and not fulfilling for today's "escapist" movie audience . . . which may be true. The script ends with the hero snorting amyls and going crazy in a gift shop at the Denver airport, while trying to purchase stolen dobermans. I told them I'd rewrite it to have a bomb explode at the end—the whole airport will explode—like in *Terminator*.

SPIN: You once said that if the movie was ever made, you wanted Dennis Hopper to play you.
HST: He might direct it. I wanted James Woods and Anthony Perkins. I still think Dennis might be good playing my role.

SPIN: Sounds like a good project for David Lynch.
HST: We talked about that. He wanted to do that, as a matter of fact, and then he got onto that *Twin Peaks* thing.

SPIN: Do you think the book's heavy drug and alcohol content would have to be toned down to appeal to today's audience?
HST: No. Times have changed, the pendulum is swinging back. There are millions of boozers and hopheads out there, but they *lie* about it. It's dangerous these days to whoop it up in public. You can get locked up for having *fun*. TWA and Pan Am go broke, but new jails are a growth industry.

It's like Germany in 1937. The Nazis were all dope fiends. They just refused to admit it.

SPIN: Were you disappointed with *Where the Buffalo Roam*?
HST: Yeah. Yeah. It's weird, you turn on the TV set about every three months and there it is. I've never seen the theater version, but I've got all the different versions here. Different beginnings, different endings . . . scenes that I wrote. They paid me to write new beginnings and endings. But it was a bad script, you couldn't cure it.

SPIN: Do you still drive a red Chevy convertible—"the Great Red Shark"—like you did in the Vegas book?
HST: You bet. Let's go to the garage, I'll show you my convertibles. This is all trouble waiting to happen—two red cars, one a gift from the Mitchell brothers, a new BMW motorcycle, the newest one, that will go 140 miles per hour.

SPIN: What was your role as executive consultant on *Where the Buffalo Roam*?
HST: I was staying with Bill Murray that summer. We had a big house in the Hollywood Hills, and I had a red 450 Mercedes. We've been friends a long time. It's a tribute to some kind of friendship that it can survive that movie. He did a good job. I refer to it as impersonation. But it's a silly film . . . it's a cartoon. Bill and I did all kinds of rude scenes. I had pretty much free reign.

SPIN: Some libraries classify *Fear and Loathing in Las Vegas* as a travelogue, some classify it as nonfiction, and some classify it as a novel. You refer to it as "a failed experiment" in gonzo journalism, yet many critics consider it a masterpiece. How much of this book is true and how would you rate it?
HST: *Fear and Loathing in Las Vegas* is a masterpiece. However, true gonzo journalism as I conceive it shouldn't be rewritten.

I would classify it, in Truman Capote's words, as a "nonfiction novel" in that almost all of it was true or did happen. I warped a few things, but it was a pretty accurate picture. It was an incredible feat of balance more than literature. That's why I called it *Fear and Loathing*. It was a pretty pure experience that turned into a very pure piece of writing. It's as good as *The Great Gatsby* and better than *The Sun Also Rises*, but it is not a novel. It is a very strange piece of reporting, at least it seems very strange now. Almost crazy [*smiles dreamily*] and of course I would never do that kind of thing now. We are Nazis. . . .

SPIN: A while ago, the spotlight shifted from your writing to your personal life when you were accused of sexual assault and several other felonies. [After being accused of third-degree sexual assault, six D.A. investigators showed up at Thompson's home and conducted a search, finding large quantities of drugs and illegal dynamite.] Did the experience change you?
HST: I couldn't have told you what the Fourth Amendment said until I got rolled over by that gang of white trash pigs that came out here to the house. You pay more attention to it when they come to get you. The "Victory or Death" stance that I took is really a difficult one for most people to take. [Thompson refused a plea bargain for two years of court supervision and chose to face a possible sixteen-year prison term. All charges were dropped.] Everybody is rolling over. This is an age of cowardice, fear, greed. You can fight city hall, you beat the system. People are getting afraid to try.

SPIN: Did the end result overcome the bad publicity you received?
HST: It was about as much fun as I've had in my life. I thought it was a huge, positive thing. A great victory, and I don't think it's a personal one-shot victory.
    I think it's something people should do and be able to do. If more people could say: "Fuck you. You're the ones who broke the law. You came into my house." However, the law is changing so rapidly now that, boy, you really have to have the best lawyers to fight now.

SPIN: Since the trial, have you had any more encounters with law enforcement agencies?
HST: I had a little problem at the Durango Red Lion Inn. I fell in love with a table that was sitting in the middle of the presidential suite, so I told the management that I wanted to buy it from them, but nobody had the authority to sell it to me. So I went down to the office and had a friendly talk with them. Finally I said, "Shit, I should have just stolen the table. Here I am down here trying to be honest and asking you just to put it on my bill and you won't." And the catering manager said, "Yeah, you should have." And then I said, "Yeah, I'll do that." I had a chartered plane and I was picking up four peacocks so we just loaded the table on the plane. About two days later

one of the deputy sheriffs from here called and said, "There is a sergeant calling from Durango saying they are going to have to arrest you for grand theft unless you make some arrangements to pay for that table." So I had a buddy go down and pay for it—$509—I could have bought the same thing in Denver for $150. Evidently the maid had reported a big egg-shaped indentation in the rug and the manager turned me in to the police.

SPIN: Don't you have a pretty impressive collection of robes you've stolen from hotels around the country?
HST: I pay for those robes! They always go on the bill. They put them on there for $75 a piece.

SPIN: Your use of drugs is one of the more controversial elements about you and your writing. Do drugs and alcohol play as big a role in your life now as they did in your earlier work?
HST: Obviously, my drug use is exaggerated or I would be long since dead. I've already outlived the most brutal abuser of our time—Neal Cassady. Me and William Burroughs are the only ones left. We're the only unrepentant public dope fiends around, and he's seventy-eight years old and claiming to be clean. But he hasn't turned on drugs, like Timothy Leary—that big phony.

SPIN: How have drugs affected your perception of the world and/or your writing?
HST: Drugs usually enhance or strengthen my perceptions and reactions, for good or ill. They've given me the resilience to withstand repeated shocks to my innocence gland. The brutal reality of politics alone would probably be intolerable without drugs. They've given me the strength to deal with those shocking realities guaranteed to shatter anyone's beliefs in the higher idealistic shibboleths of our time and the "American Century." Anyone who covers his beat for twenty years, and that beat is "The Death of the American Dream," needs every goddamned crutch he can find.

Besides, I enjoy drugs. The only trouble they've given me is the people who try to keep me from using them. *Res ipsa loquitur.* I was, after all, a Literary Lion last year.

SPIN: How is your physical health?
HST: I am like a *fawn.*

SPIN: Does the media portrayal of you as a "crazy" amuse, inflame, or bore you?
HST: The media perception of me has always been pretty broad. As broad as the media itself. As a journalist, I somehow managed to break all the rules and still succeed. It's a hard thing for most of today's gentleman journalists to understand, but only because they can't do it. The smart ones understood immediately. The best people in journalism I've never had any quarrel with. I am a journalist and I've never met, as a group, any tribe I'd rather be a part of or that are more fun to be with—in spite of the various punks and sycophants of the press. I'm proud to be part of the tribe.

It hasn't helped a lot to be a savage comic-book character for the last fifteen years—a drunken screwball who should've been castrated a long time ago. The smart people in the media knew it was a weird exaggeration. The dumb ones took it seriously and warned their children to stay away from me at all costs. The really smart ones understood it was only a censored, kind of a toned-down children's book version of the real thing.

Now we are being herded into the '90s, which looks like it is going to be a truer generation of swine, a decade run by cops and wardens—a generation without humor, without mercy; dead heroes and diminished expectations, a decade that will go down in history as the Gray Area.

At the end of this decade no one will be sure of anything except that you must obey the rules, sex will kill you, politicians lie, rain is poison, and the world is run by whores. These are terrible things to have to know in your life, even if you're rich.

A doomsday kind of thinking has taken over the media, as it has business and politics: *"I'm going to turn you in, son—not only for your own good, but because you were the bastard who turned me in last year."*

SPIN: How do you react when you see others mimicking or plagiarizing your individual gonzo style?
HST: What others? Only a madman would want to be labeled a "gonzo journalist" in these wretched times. I have not pioneered a growth industry. I never looked for gangs, or crowds or followers . . . in the Tim Leary tradition. But it's nice to have friends. Nobody needs mimics.

SPIN: Do you consider P.J. O'Rourke a worthy gonzo associate?
HST: P.J. is an old friend. He is a monster. We have fought back to back with iron bars against people who wanted to *kill* us. We have spilled blood together. We have walked with the King. Shit, P.J. would stab you just for fun.

SPIN: Sweet Jesus, why?

HST: Who knows? P.J. is a warrior. He stabs for his own reasons, and he's usually right. Any enemy of P.J.'s is an enemy of mine. So be warned. If he stabs you, so will I.

SPIN: Did O'Rourke get his style from you?

HST: No. P.J. has a style all his own and an attitude of his own. P.J. doesn't need to imitate my style. He isn't trying to be a gonzo writer. I first ran into P.J. when he was testing new cars for *Car and Driver*. He came out here and we did some driving. I performed some serious road tests on a new Chrysler—one that he'd rented for Jimmy Buffett's wedding. I ran it full bore on twisting roads with him in the backseat. Anytime you're in the backseat and somebody is really screwing it on it is totally terrifying. The driver has to think about what he's going to do next, but the passenger becomes increasingly fearful about what the driver is going to do next—or he's still weeping about what happened last time. But P.J. handled it well. He is very cool under fire and he's also a good driver.

SPIN: Do you worry about plagiarism, Doc?

HST: No, I pride myself with having the wisdom and the taste to steal from the right people: Conrad, Fitzgerald, the Marquis de Sade, Prescott, Isak Dinesen, Coleridge, Twain, Pee Wee Herman—that swine. Yeah, there's also Ed Bradley, Anne Rice, Ralph Steadman—these are all my friends. I learn from these people. Especially the dead ones.

SPIN: Are there other authors you're partial to?

HST: Jim Harrison is one of the really good writers in this country. I like everything Harrison's done.

SPIN: What does your writing routine consist of?

HST: It's very unusual that you arrive here on the same day as my box [of X-rated tapes]. I use these things for mood-setters to get in the rhythm of working. *Caligula's* one of my all-time favorites.

I think I've suffered a general dip in adrenaline production, and I'm addicted to my own adrenaline usually.

SPIN: Do you still crank everything out on your typewriter or have you started using a computer?
HST: I don't like the little screen. It's good for short stuff, but I think in terms of tangible weight. If I could get a big screen and show ten pages at once, but that kind of defeats the purpose. I suppose if I really got into it, it would help, or if I thought Harrison worked on a computer or he persuaded me I should, maybe I'd try it. I really think computers are only as smart as the person who programs it, and I'd have to program the damn thing myself in order for it to meet my needs.

SPIN: I understand you have a difficult time keeping your editorial assistants around.
HST: It's my eternal quest for an editorial assistant or assistants. I need a staff of about six. I need a staff and apparently it has become too onerous for people in this country. I've been interviewing people out here for I don't know how long.

I'm looking for a girl who is fast and vicious, she must be fun and smart. The real question is, of course: Can she type? We can narrow this down pretty quick.

I've got a catalog of mail-order brides here I'm currently considering bringing over. Right now English isn't so important—I just need an assistant. It's a dating service, of sorts.

SPIN: Why was your last David Letterman appearance canceled?
HST: Well, I've been on there two or three times. I hate to go over there to the studio and hang around for two or three hours. I get drunk and mean, pacing around for that long.

The producer called me up the day before I was scheduled and said, "Hunter, you're going to be a *good* boy? You're going to be *nice* this time?" And I said, "Yeah, Frank, don't worry about it, as long as I can go on first. That way you don't have to worry about my behavior later on." He said he'd try to do it, but I was scheduled for third. I replied, "Well Frank, if that happens, you know I'll get drunk and mean. I'll bring four huge thugs over there and they're going to hold Letterman down while I shave his head on camera."

Letterman has never liked me—he loses control of the show. Letterman's kind of a chickenshit. I never even thought he was really that funny; he's just sort of a punk.

The next day I was informed nothing could be done so I said, "You know what's going to happen. I've been up all night and I'm nuts already. If I come over there and drink heavily, you know shaving the head might be all the humor I can find that afternoon." Later, Letterman abruptly canceled it, and he had to talk, shovel smoke for twenty minutes, rather than have me on there.

SPIN: The *New York Times* called you a "bitterly disillusioned idealist." Do you agree with this assessment?
HST: Yeah. But so what? That comes with the territory, and it's not bad company. They could have called me a "rich and joyful cynic"—like Ivan Boesky or George Bush. I take a certain pleasure in being a bitterly disillusioned idealist. It's not as bad as it sounds. Maybe I'm just a romance junkie born addicted to the love and adventure ethic—cursed and burdened and stooped all my life from carrying the albatross of the "Romantic Sensibility"—like Shelley and Keats and Lord Byron and Big Sam Coleridge and Keith Richards and Bob Dylan.

SPIN: All those people went nuts, Doc. Is that what you're trying to say? That you're going insane?
HST: Not *me*, Jocko. I am a brutal Southern gentleman who somehow got into politics. There was no avoiding it, then or now. They are backing us out of our holes—and you know what happens then.

Still Gonzo after All These Years

Richard Keil / 1996

From *American Journalism Review,* 18 (April 1, 1996): pp. 30–36.
Reprinted with permission of *American Journalism Review.*

For years Dr. Hunter S. Thompson's twisted, unflinching journalism has cut through the babble of America's popular and political culture like a chainsaw being dragged through a vat of Jell-O. And time has hardly mellowed the gonzo guru. Here's what happened when a longtime Thompson admirer ventured into Thompson's Colorado redoubt.

> *"In the whole eastern dark wall of the divide this night there was silence and the whisper of the wind, except in the ravine where we roared. . . . All in darkness now as we fumed and screamed in our mountain nook, mad drunken Americans in the mighty land. We were on the roof of America, and all we could do was yell, I guess."*
>
> —Jack Kerouac, *On The Road*

I had that passage on my mind, and a beer resting on the seat between my legs, as I made the hard left turn into the rutted gravel driveway of Hunter S. Thompson's home outside of Aspen.

Suddenly, a peacock darted into my path; I cursed and swerved my rental car to the left, narrowly missing the little bastard. Not a good way to begin an interview with a man whose cynically warped take on American culture in the '60s and '70s influenced as many budding journalists as Kerouac created mad backpackers.

I killed the engine and flicked off the headlights. Twilight was giving way to darkness—evening for the rest of the world, morning for Thompson. I sat there a moment, finishing my beer, trying to decide how to approach a man who was like Muhammad Ali at the end of his career: Someone trying, without much success, to match his earlier triumphs, but someone still capable, on a good night, of throwing a more brutal punch than anyone in the business.

His business being politics, it seemed important, somehow, to try to get inside his head. The gaggle of talking heads that so dominate political coverage these days take themselves–and the candidates—so seriously that no one ever thinks to ask whether any of the current crop of presidential aspirants have any legitimate claim to representing the nation's political hopes.

I figured that a man who described Richard Nixon, well before Watergate, as representing "that dark, venal, and incurably violent side of the American character" might think to ask why lawmakers who helped push the nation to the brink of financial ruin in the 1980s thought they deserved a chance to lead America into the twenty-first century.

I grabbed the six-pack of my home brewed beer I had brought along and approached the screen door of Thompson's log cabin home.

No one answered, although the TV was audible from inside. I stepped back, took a deep breath and surveyed the yard: Scattered over the grounds were an old Volvo 244, a Jeep Wagoneer, a 1976 Cadillac Fleetwood convertible and a behemoth of a John Deere 770 tractor.

I stepped toward the garage and peeked in, noticing what I had missed before: a '71 Chevy Caprice convertible, with white leather interior and a hood the length of an aircraft carrier. This would be the same model in which Thompson roared across the desert in *Fear and Loathing in Las Vegas,* a seminal work that both established his literary genius and served as an instruction manual on drug use, expense-account fraud and rental car abuse for a generation of Americans.

I banged harder on the door this time, and within moments Thompson's personal secretary, Deborah, welcomed me in.

"Hunter's in the shower," she said, leading me through an impossibly cluttered side room into the kitchen. "Still doing the wake-up thing. You want something to drink?"

I asked for a beer and settled onto a stool, turning my attention to the big-screen TV across the room that was blaring an exhibition game between the Jets and the Bengals.

"I told Hunter that you were coming at eight and that since this was just an exhibition game, he had no excuse to sit there and watch it," Deborah told me by way of apology. "That's why he's running late."

"Nonsense," I corrected her. "The regular season starts next week. These things count now." She shook her head as she handed me a beer. "That's what Hunter said. You want me to show you around?"

I nodded, although I had been trying to take in as much as I could just sitting there, trying not to get too wild-eyed. Tacked to a lampshade was a warning from the Palm Beach police department; the human skull sitting atop the television was pretty hard to miss, as was the Colombian marshal's badge mounted beside it.

And just below that, taped to the side of the TV, was this motivational warning: No Music + Bad TV = Bad Mood and No Pages. "That's where he writes," Deborah said, pointing to the far end of the kitchen counter at which I was sitting. The stools faced the TV and a massive sound system.

A low-hung couch, perfect for collapsing on and musing, scribbling or creating, sat beneath the counter. "He just sits here," she said.

"Amid general chaos and confusion," I interrupted.

"Right. Typing away."

That seemed to make sense; Thompson's best stuff had always come together in hotel bars, noisy convention halls and speeding cars, where he was able, through chemical assistance, to step up and out and make a twisted kind of sense of everything around him.

I looked around more carefully now, since I had been invited to do so. Every square inch of space, it seemed, was covered with old post cards, press clippings, speeding tickets from here and there, reminder notes, summonses, addresses, phone numbers—a private, chemically altered universe of political memorabilia.

A long bulletin board sat next to the entertainment complex, jammed chock-full of material for his book-in-progress, "Polo Is My Life." All sorts of intriguing plot developments were set off on index cards, one after another, with summaries like "Incident With Stolen Rental Car."

"He's got a drop-dead deadline with *Rolling Stone,* which is publishing this," Deborah said, suddenly sounding tired. "They really mean it this time. They need it by Monday."

"It must be difficult, working like this," I told her.

"You get used to Hunter's schedule," she said. "It's getting back on a normal schedule, when you go away, that can be difficult."

We stood for a second, looking out at the gathering gloom. She flicked on a light switch, and the peacock shelter was suddenly illuminated. "Out around the back there is where Hunter fires his guns," she said, knowing that I would be familiar with this element of the Thompson M. O. "He just fires off into the hills back there."

I asked her whether there were problems with the neighbors. She shook her head ruefully.

"They're used to Hunter."

"I saw some pretty impressive weaponry when I came in," I told her.

"Oh, yeah, let's go back there," Deborah said. "That's where Hunter does his artwork."

She led me back through the kitchen, and I noticed for the first time that the stove was unusable, since boxes and papers were stacked across all four burners.

In the side room where I had come in, four guns were mounted on the rough-hewn walls. I glanced over at Deborah, who was simply pointing to a two-by-three-foot gilt-edged frame propped up against a table.

Behind the glass was what was left of Mickey Mouse, superimposed over a silhouette of Disneyland. Huge, ragged holes—from a. 12-gauge shotgun, it appeared—had been blown through the lower half of Mickey's face, tearing his silly smile right in half.

"He does these things as the mood strikes him," Deborah said mysteriously. "Then he sells them for big money."

A few feet away was a framed Warren Zevon publicity poster, pockmarked with neater, smaller-bore holes. This didn't make sense; Thompson, it seemed, would probably identify with a man who wrote songs with titles like "Roland the Headless Thompson Gunner"; and memorialized psychotic violence in "Excitable Boy."

"What's the deal with that one?" I asked, pointing at the poster.

"Oh, Warren and Hunter are good friends. He was up here a while back, and he and Hunter did some shooting. Warren thought this was a great idea."

He must have; peering closer, I could see that it had been signed by both Thompson and Zevon.

"So, there you have it," Deborah said, with the practiced, prideful air of someone who knew that her various duties included serving as a de facto tour guide in what amounted to one of the world's most bizarre museums.

I peered in a little alcove just off the kitchen; a huge refrigerator sat there. "That's the beer fridge," Deborah told me.

I went over and opened the door. The shelves had been removed, and several cases of Molson were stacked one atop another, turned sideways to allow quicker, easier access to the brew.

We went back into the kitchen, and I positioned myself on the stool, intent on finishing my beer. I was getting nervous now; I couldn't help it.

My tensions increased a moment later when Thompson padded into the room with his trademark bouncing stride, extended his hand, and gave me the piercing, searching look for which he is so famous.

"New York is winning," I told him cautiously. "Thought you might want to know."

He allowed himself a tight smile, and told me he had money on the Jets. "Or was it the Bengals?" he asked, filling a glass with Chivas Regal. "I don't know. Maybe I'm drunk."

He glanced sharply at me, looking for a reaction. This was beginning to feel like some sort of test. "I wouldn't know if you were," I told him. "I'm getting there myself."

Thompson chuckled, his cheeks glowing like Santa Claus, as he poured another four jiggers-worth of Chivas into his glass.

"Sit down," he commanded, then gestured expansively to a counter covered with bowls of salsa, oranges, apples and freshly cut mint. "Help yourself."

We settled in and felt each other out for a few minutes, talking football; each of us offered the other a quick summary of our predictions for the upcoming season, Thompson's punctuated by several pauses to light Dunhills, which he was chain-smoking in his trademark cigarette holder.

"You find the place OK?" he asked.

"Deborah's directions were fine," I assured him. "I guess a lot of people find their way up here, though, right?" I had guessed, correctly, that thousands of drug-addled acolytes made their way to Woody Creek; such was the price of Thompson's fame.

"It's a problem," Deborah said simply as she settled in on the couch.

"How do you get rid of them?" I asked.

Thompson smiled, and rubbed his bald head. "Sometimes I've got to wave a gun around," he chuckled.

The Jets game ended and segued into the ten o'clock news back in New York, where a breathless, blow-dried TV reporter was describing from a police headquarters somewhere in the middle of Long Island the wildfires raging out in The Hamptons.

Our bonding, of sorts, occurred a moment later, when the screen switched to a shot of the angry orange flames licking the sky, edging ever closer to pricey vacation homes in that pricey Eastern version of paradise.

"Jesus Christ!" I shouted.

Thompson paused from lighting up another cigarette to ask me what was wrong.

"Well, it seems odd for Armageddon to begin in The Hamptons," I began, pausing to take a sip. "But the more I think about it, the more appropriate it seems." A vicious smile spread across his face, and his eyes gleamed behind his eyeglasses as a maniacal chuckle emanated from his throat.

"That's exactly what I was saying to Deborah here an hour ago," he said. "Those greedheads."

I glanced over at Deborah, who was rolling her eyes. Thompson then looked expectantly over my shoulder, toward the refrigerator.

"You about ready for one of my beers?"

I had offered to bring my own beer, mostly as a means of keeping my interview request as low-key as possible. I had hoped it might set me apart from the usual dim-eyed types who try to hang out with him: Here I was offering to bring my own beer, beer I made at that, instead of just trying to glom off of his generosity.

Thompson nodded. He took a sip and pronounced it good. We had several more beers sitting there and I became momentarily worried.

I had serious business to conduct, of course, and I could see that my temptation to simply get savagely drunk with Thompson might be unavoidable anyhow, and that it was better to just plunge ahead, become one with my environment, as it were, boring questions about presidential politics be damned. The Experience, I convinced myself, was The Story.

"I don't often let people up here to the house," Thompson said after a moment, his voice softer than it had been all evening. "But I figured if you were willing to bring your own beer, beer you made, you were probably all right."

I glanced at a stack of books on the counter in front of me: some of Thompson's own works, a book on Leonard Cohen, something on Genghis Khan and a whole sheaf of legal-sized paper. The top sheet was blank, but headed with a drawing of what looked like one of the Four Horsemen of the Apocalypse wielding a polo mallet. "Kill" was inscribed on its saddle blanket.

"Ah, you've found the galley sheets," he said, bounding over in front of me and sifting through the pile. "Here. Read this out loud, will you, and tell me what you think."

This almost shocked me back into sobriety: Thompson wanted me to read his own work, and offer comments? I took a stack of papers he had thrust in front of me.

"This how you work?" I asked.

He nodded sagely. "Sometimes, when you hear it," he said, muttering something else into his scotch glass.

I read three or four pages that went on at some length about a baroness traveling in the polo circuit, who told Thompson that she was flogged by Clinton every evening.

"The public doesn't give a hoot in hell if Clinton flogs foreign women at night, just as long as he doesn't deny it. Many admire his attitude, in fact, and they secretly vote accordingly," one passage began. "This is what big-time politicians call 'the adulterers' vote,' and it is huge. They are linked by a chain of guilt and perjuries too foul to admit."

I paused and looked up; Thompson was nodding his head contentedly; but his eyes remained fierce and wary, evaluating every word.

"'Adulterers' vote'—I started that with Gary Hart, which you know, if you're familiar with my work," he mumbled. "Continue."

"Bill Clinton is a natural magnet for these people," I read. "He is clearly guilty, but it doesn't bother him, and that gives the others new hope. They envy him, because he has dropped his veil of shame and they haven't. They can't. They feel guilty like rats in the walls of a cheese factory."

Thompson held his hand up and nodded, satisfied. "What do you think?"

"Well," I began, opening a fresh beer, "I think the bit about Clinton being a magnet for adulterers: You miss a fairly obvious Nixon comparison."

"Nixon wasn't an adulterer!"

"That we know of," I said quickly. "But on a thematic point he just oozed the kind of human ugliness that others couldn't admit in their own souls, and this guy had the audacity to run for president and govern the free world! God, no wonder they admired him. That total absence of shame."

Thompson nodded thoughtfully, jotted something in the margin, and then heaved them back onto the pile.

We sat and drank for another couple of hours, our disjointed conversation flowing from his efforts to restrict expansion of the local airport—a battle against "greedheads" he seemed to be enjoying—to whatever his relentless channel-surfing picked up. We stopped for a minute on a CNN update on the Simpson trial, which prompted Thompson to cackle with glee.

"Fuhrman is going down," he predicted, "like the low-rent piece of garbage he is. Total scum."

I wondered out loud whether Fuhrman could be forced to take the stand, a subject then in much debate after the discovery of the most famous tapes since Watergate.

"Let's find out," Thompson yelled, stabbing his index finger at the phone.

Moments later, his attorney was on the line, guiding us through the intricacies of the California penal code and whether witnesses could be compelled to testify, or take the Fifth, in the presence of the jury. In California, they couldn't.

As we listened to this, I took note of the cassette tapes scattered throughout the room—various Bob Dylan offerings, something by Los Lobos, and an Austin band called Arc Angels. I made a note to ask Thompson what was going on with some homemade tape called "Kidnap" and then promptly forgot.

The Fuhrman issue resolved, I proposed we get some dinner. Glancing at my watch, I was stunned to see that it was almost midnight. "Shit," Thompson said. "We should have done this sooner."

After Deborah announced she was going off to take a nap and commanded Thompson to be done with me by 4 A.M., the Doctor squinted at the phone and punched up some numbers.

"Woody Creek Tavern," we heard after a couple of minutes.

"Uh, hi," Thompson said.

"Uh, hi Doc," said the voice, sounding less chipper than a minute before. "You want to eat?"

"We need to eat," Thompson corrected him. "You still open?"

"We can be."

Orders for fish and enchiladas were quickly placed, and Thompson jumped out of his chair. I scrambled to my feet, thinking we were about to leave, but the good doctor was bent double, coughing violently into his hand.

"Deborah," he rasped. "Deborah!"

His assistant, who had not yet left, jumped from the couch and yanked a bottle from the collection of liquor atop the refrigerator. Thompson, his face as red as a tomato, took a bottle of Chartreuse and gargled noisily with it for a second or two before finally swallowing and sighing.

"You maybe should have that looked at," I suggested politely.

"Nah," he said, waving his hand dismissively. "I had my lungs X-rayed recently. Clean as a baby's."

After another admonition from Deborah about being ready to work at 4 A.M., we stepped outside into a night that had grown quite chilly.

"I'll drive," he growled. He smiled slightly when I told him I'd be happy to drive my paltry little rental car.

"Grab these," he said, tossing a couple of pint glasses in my direction. "I'm on the revolving plan with these guys. Gotta take their glasses back."

I slid into the Caprice, a bigger, more solid piece of machinery than anything Detroit pumps out today. Moments later we were out on the main road. Thompson thrust the pedal down, and the engine roared to life. My head snapped back, and as I looked up at a blanket of stars blurring past me, I guessed the wind-chill factor was probably about 40 below.

Moments later we were lurching to a stop outside the Woody Creek Tavern, which is to Thompson what the Algonquin Hotel was to the early *New Yorker* crowd.

"Wait," he commanded, as I was nearing the door. He reached into the back seat and turned on a little tape machine; the shrill squealing of a pig pierced the solitude. "Gotta let them know we're here," Thompson said with a shrug.

The next three hours were a blur. Our food sat, getting cold, as Thompson got his daily fill of local politics. The airport issue was hot, and the developers and ski barons were eager to finish killing off Aspen, he told me.

We were alone in the place, except for the chef, a waitress and an affable bartender who bore a disturbing resemblance to Jerry Garcia.

After Thompson disappeared into the back with the waitress and emerged ten minutes later looking more relaxed than I'd seen him all night, I tried to bring up politics again. He dismissed the current crop of presidential candidates with a derisive snicker.

"Would you want to have a beer with any of those people?" I thought about knocking back a Rolling Rock with Bob Dole, or sucking down some Lone Stars with Phil Gramm.

"I see your point," I told him.

"Exactly," he said. "Empty suits, padded resumés and, like we talked about with Clinton, evil the only natural human tendencies present."

Finally, it was almost 3 A.M., time to go.

Out in the Caprice, with a final pint of draught beer in hand, I took a tumbler of scotch from Thompson as he fumbled in both pockets for his keys. Once he had backed up and successfully negotiated two speed bumps, I handed him his drink just as he jammed the accelerator again, heading toward the hairpin turn that lay about a hundred yards down the road.

As we came up to the corner, Thompson swerved left and slammed on the brakes, taking his foot off the pedal and flooring the accelerator as soon as the Shark had skidded to the point where it was aiming back uphill. The gravel underneath sounded like a machine gun erupting; the speedometer never went below sixty. Neither one of us spilled a drop.

"You're a good driver, Hunter," I said.

"Racing suspension," he said proudly, taking a sip of scotch. "Racing suspension."

We ate our dinner quickly, once we had reheated the food in the microwave. My ride was about over, and I knew it. He was brooding as he chomped on his fish, staring at a blinking light on the answering machine. He played the message, and it was from an agitated Deborah warning that 4 A.M. was approaching.

I went to the bathroom and came out to find Thompson standing there, clad only in a terry-cloth robe, holding a towel in his hand. "Time for a swim," was all he told me. "I gotta go and get back, or there's going to be hell to pay."

He lit up another Dunhill and took his tumbler of scotch outside. "Don't let the fucking bastards get you down," he said as he climbed into the Jeep. "And watch your back."

I heard nothing more from Thompson after that bizarre evening. I had only one snapshot of the Red Shark serving as confirmation that I had actually been to Woody Creek.

On the day after the November elections, I read a news article from Colorado saying that the battle against the airport expansion had been successful; I chuckled thinking of Thompson, tumbler of scotch in hand, cackling about having defeated the greedheads.

When I got home that night, the light from a full moon was streaming in the window, providing the only light besides the blinking of the answering machine.

I pressed the playback button. It was Thompson offering me a scoop: He had been busted for DWI the night before while in the midst of some election-night celebrating. "It's a political setup," he muttered angrily. "All these ski Nazis are out to get me." (The case has not yet gone to trial.)

The message drifted to an end, and the disembodied voice inside the machine told me what time the call had come in. I realized that he probably called as soon as he got sprung from jail.

I dialed his number, and got the answering machine. "Politics is an ugly business," I reminded him, after expressing interest in hearing his end of the story. "Watch your back."

Writing on the Wall: An Interview with Hunter S. Thompson

Matthew Hahn / 1997

From the *Atlantic Online*, August 26, 1997, pp. 1–18. Reprinted with the permission of Matthew Hahn.

"The aim of every artist is to arrest motion, which is life, by artificial means and hold it fixed so that a hundred years later, when a stranger looks at it, it moves again since it is life. . . . This is the artist's way of scribbling 'Kilroy was here' on the wall of the final and irrevocable oblivion through which he must someday pass."

—William Faulkner, interview with *Paris Review*, 1956

What would you do? You're sitting in Hunter S. Thompson's kitchen conducting an interview and he wants you to drink. So you drink.

I'd been directed to read aloud Thompson's farewell to Richard M. Nixon, "He Was a Crook" (*Rolling Stone*, June 16, 1994), an obituary fired off in a burst of rage. The author insisted it be read aloud to capture the right effect, and apparently I hadn't been reading with proper and resounding emphasis.

"No. No! Again. Start over. Clip your words!"

A glass of Wild Turkey and ice was placed in front of me—for elocution purposes, of course—and the reading proceeded, this time with the benefit of Thompson's coaching.

Earlier that day I'd stopped at the Woody Creek Tavern, in Woody Creek, Colorado, to order a drink and steady my nerves before heading up the hill to the house of the Gonzo Journalist and self-proclaimed King of Fun. I'd heard the last reporter who went up the hill looking for a story had to mow the lawn before the man would talk to him. I guess my luck was better. Before the night was over I heard the famous peacocks screaming in the dark. I held the Lono club. A shade before two o'clock in the morning I saw my copy of Thompson's latest book, *The Proud Highway: Saga of a Desperate Southern Gentleman*, shot through with a .45 ("It's never too late to shoot guns," an assistant whispered to me). And I heard Thompson hold forth for three hours about the state of politics, journalism, and the American Dream.

118

This year marks not only the twenty-fifth anniversary of Watergate and the beginning of Nixon's downfall but also twenty-five years since the publication of Thompson's *Fear and Loathing: On the Campaign Trail,* the volume that collected his coverage of the 1972 presidential race for *Rolling Stone.* Last year *Fear and Loathing in Las Vegas* (1971), his bad dream of a novel based on a shred of fact, was reissued by the Modern Library. The movie director Terry Gilliam's vision of that book started production this July, with Johnny Depp starring as Thompson's alter ego, Raoul Duke. This is a time Thompson has obviously dreamed about. Read through *The Proud Highway,* especially the early letters, and it seems he's been waiting most of his life for someone to play him in a movie. (He doesn't count *Where the Buffalo Roam.*)

You could spend hours poring over all the memorabilia on display in Thompson's house. The front room (red walls, red carpet) is full of mounted animal heads. There's a human skeleton in there. A four-foot-long pair of bolt cutters rests on a counter top; you expect locks to pop open out of respect when the thing comes near. "What are these for?" I asked when I first entered the house. "You don't want to know," came the answer.

Thompson speaks in a low rumble, but not as unintelligibly as I'd been led to believe. You keep your eyes and ears open when he's talking, looking around the room for objects that might hum in sympathetic vibration.

The interview took place at Thompson's home on the evening of July 15, extending into the early hours of July 16, 1997. Both the transcript and audio excerpts have been edited for clarity and length. At times they do not correspond.

MH: The Internet has been touted as a new mode of journalism—some even go so far as to say it might democratize journalism. Do you see a future for the Internet as a journalistic medium?

HST: Well, I don't know. There is a line somewhere between democratizing journalism and every man a journalist. You can't really believe what you read in the papers anyway, but there is at least some spectrum of reliability. Maybe it's becoming like the TV talk shows or the tabloids where anything's acceptable as long as it's interesting.

I believe that the major operating ethic in American society right now, the most universal want and need is to be on TV. I've been on TV. I could be on TV all the time if I wanted to. But most people will never get on TV. It has to be a real breakthrough for them. And trouble is, people will do almost anything to get on it. You know, confess to crimes they haven't committed. You don't exist unless you're on TV. Yeah, it's a validation process. Faulkner said that American troops wrote "Kilroy was here" on the walls of Europe in World War II in order to prove that somebody had been there—"I was here"—and that the whole history of man is just an effort by people, writers, to just write your name on the great wall.

You can get on [the Internet] and all of a sudden you can write a story about me, or you can put it on top of my name. You can have your picture on there too. I don't know the percentage of the Internet that's valid, do you? Jesus, it's scary. I don't surf the Internet. I did for a while. I thought I'd have a little fun and learn something. I have an e-mail address. No one knows it. But I wouldn't check it anyway, because it's just too fucking much. You know, it's the volume. The Internet is probably the first wave of people who have figured out a different way to catch up with TV—if you can't be on TV, well at least you can reach 45 million people [on the Internet].

MH: Let's talk about your inclusion in the Modern Library. You are now sandwiched in between Thackeray and Tolstoy. What does that mean to you? *Fear and Loathing in Las Vegas*, twenty-five years after it was published, is in the Modern Library.

HST: That's a little faster than you'd normally think it could occur. You know, most of those people in [the Modern Library] are dead. No, I'm not surprised to be there. I guess it's a little surprising to be here still walking around and shaking people's hands.

It tells me the Modern Library's catching up. But everything has sped up now. Instant communication. Instant news.

MH: When you were starting out, when you were eighteen and you started writing these letters in *The Proud Highway*, did you think your work would ever be considered classic?

HST: I never sat down and thought about it and stared at it. Obviously, if you read *The Proud Highway*, I was thinking somewhere along those lines. I never lobbied the Modern Library to include more living writers. I've always assumed it was for dead writers. But what I did assume at that time, early on and, shit, every year forever after that, was that I would be dead very soon. The fact that I'm not dead is sort of puzzling to me. It's sort of an awkward thing to deal with.

MH: You wrote in 1977, in the introduction to *The Great Shark Hunt* [a collection of HST's journalism], "I have already lived and finished the life I planned to live—(thirteen years longer, in fact). . . ." Thirteen years earlier would have been around the time you wrote *Hell's Angels*. Now it's twenty years since you wrote that introduction. Do you still feel the same way? What was behind writing that?

HST: Oh, sitting alone in an office in New York, the day before Christmas Eve, editing my own life's work—the selection, the order—because I couldn't get anybody else to edit it. Somebody pulled out because he wouldn't publish that poem, "Collect Telegram from a Mad Dog." I guess he was using that as an excuse. So I ended up having to do it myself. It was a little depressing, sitting up there having to do it myself. One of the advantages of being dead, I guess, is that somebody else can edit all this.

For quite a while there I had to assume that I would never be in anything, much less the Modern Library.

MH: How is your health? How are you feeling now?

HST: I haven't started any savings accounts. . . . I tell you, you'd act differently if you thought you were going to die at noon tomorrow. You probably wouldn't be here doing this. I just figured, "Bye, bye, Miss American Pie, good old boys drinkin' whiskey and rye, singin' this'll be the day that I die." Yeah, I just felt that all along.

MH: Live every day like your last, because you don't know what tomorrow's going to be like?

HST: Well, there's no plan for it. It's like going into the twenty-seventh inning in a baseball game. You're like, what the fuck am I doing here, man?

MH: There's a lot happening for you these days: *Fear and Loathing*, the movie; the Modern Library; twenty-five years of *Fear and Loathing: On the Campaign Trail*. Can you compare this time with anything prior—the excitement, maybe, of running for sheriff, or covering Nixon—now that you are sitting here looking back on it all?

HST: I got more of a kick out of running Nixon out of office than I have with these author parties.

You know, Gonzo Journalism is a term that I've come to dislike because of the way it's been cast: inaccurate, crazy. And in a way it might sound like,

What am I complaining about? But there's a big difference. What I called Nixon is *true*—just a little harsh.

MH: If you were doing it again today, do you think you would go at it the way you did?
HST: Would I do it again, is that what you mean? I'm talking about the word "gonzo." Yeah, I'd do it again. And that's the test of everything in life. You know, the way you look back on it. I use this a lot, a great measuring stick. I'd like a good war, a good fight. I get lazy when there's not one.

In journalism, one of the reasons I think I get the pleasure I do is the political factor. It's the effect you can have, with journalism. It's like writing a poem in the woods . . . you know that old thing about if a tree falls in the woods—

MH: If nobody heard it, did it happen?
HST: Yeah. Technically, no, there's no sound unless it's heard. [With journalism,] it's the effect, it's the sound, you know, when it's heard.

MH: It's the effect? And in that context you would call yourself—
HST: Successful. I don't need any prizes or parties to shore up my self esteem. When I see Nixon getting on a plane, then I'm there. And he's headed west and I'm not.

MH: So that was it? Nixon getting on the plane?
HST: Yeah. That might have been the peak of effectiveness.

MH: What were you doing that day? Do you remember?
HST: Absolutely, man. I was in the White House Rose Garden. I was at the end of a red carpet that stretched from the stairs to the helicopter which landed on the lawn. There were some Marines to my left, but I was the last human being in the line. Annie Leibovitz was right beside me. And yeah, just being there and watching him get on, it was—not total victory, but it gave me a sense of being very much a part of not just my reality but everybody else's. There's big difference between railing against some oppressor for twenty years and then ending up in the Bastille, or fighting a twenty-year war and watching the enemy vanquished.

MH: What were your thoughts when you saw him getting on the helicopter?
HST: I felt sorry for him. He hit his head. Right after he did this thing [*makes the v-for-victory sign*] at the helicopter door, he turned and lashed his head on

the top of the rounded door, staggered sideways, and he was so—in some jurisdictions we might have called it "luded out"—he was tranquilized. There's a civilized word for it: sedated. He was almost led up the stairs. Yeah, I felt sorry for him. Can you imagine that ride west? Jesus Christ, they flew to Andrews Air Force Base, I guess, on the helicopter, and then they had like a six-hour flight to San Clemente. Whew. That must have been a really dark flight.

MH: Did you have a relationship or correspondence with him after that?
HST: No. I was urged to, and I thought about it, but no, I didn't. I guess that's a political technique: the war's over, the game's over. I don't want to make it into a game, although I guess it is in the same sense that getting elected President can be seen as a game. It's a deadly serious game. It's a very mean thing.

I don't know why people think that the Mafia is merciless and badder than you know—and yet they don't assume that the President of the United States is in a position of such power, and that of course he's going to use the same fucking tools as the Mafia.

MH: The last we heard from you on politics was in *Better Than Sex*, and that was a couple years back. What do you think about the state of politics today?
HST: I would say that I am more into politics now than I was in '92. Yeah, I was mesmerized a little bit by the access [Clinton] offered me—like *total* access. "Come on down," you know? "Go out drinkin' with Hillary." Yeah, they did a good job on me. But I was set on beating Bush. I thought we were going to beat Bush at the Iran-Contra hearings, and I worked overtime. He was guilty as fifteen hyenas, and he got off, and it really bothered me. So I would have been for anybody in '92, just to beat Bush. And that's a dangerous trap to fall into—you know, the lesser of two evils.

MH: There's a lot of apathy today. People don't want to go out and vote.
HST: And why should they? I felt that way, and I didn't vote for Clinton in '96. I voted for Ralph Nader. There's a terrible danger in voting for the lesser of two evils because the parties can set it up that way.

MH: What do you think about the current two-party system here?
HST: I don't think it is a two-party system. And I think the reason Clinton was re-elected is that he understands the same thing. He took the crime issue

away from the Republicans, and now he's taking the tax issue away. He's proposing a lower capital-gains tax than the Republicans already had. So now the Democrats are champions of big business. He's an extremely skilled fucking politician.

The Clinton people all had e-mail, beepers . . .

MH: They were wired in.
HST: Yeah, as opposed to the [Bush] White House. [The Clintons] moved into the White House, and it was like they moved into a cave. [A good friend] called me—a photographer, very close to the Clintons—telling me, ye gods, we move in here, and they still have a phone system that Abraham Lincoln would have appreciated.

MH: Clinton had wanted to be JFK. That's who he talked about in his campaigns.
HST: You tell Mr. Bill there's a reason that Jack Kennedy was shot, and he hasn't been. There's a very good reason that Jack Kennedy was shot, and Clinton hasn't been.

MH: What's that?
HST: There's no reason to shoot Clinton. They didn't hesitate when Kennedy seemed to be going against them. They shot him. And they shot Bobby.

MH: *They?*
HST: They. If you are going to shoot the President of the United States, plan it and do it, you must be extremely well-connected and smart and organized. Anybody who can organize a three-position, triangulated shooting at the President of the United States is very good.

MH: Your theory on the JFK assassination is what?
HST: That it was carried out by the Mob but organized and effectuated by J. Edgar Hoover.

MH: If popular culture holds up JFK as something good that could have been—and Nixon is seen as the opposite extreme—where does Clinton fall on the spectrum between JFK and Nixon?
HST: Well, Clinton will be lucky if he rates above Ulysses Grant or Warren Harding on the great scale. And he will, as long as the economy's good.

Carville was right—it's the economy, stupid. And Clinton finally took that to heart. I think there are only three occasions in the history of American presidential elections when people have not voted obviously with their wallets.

MH: What are those?
HST: Oh, boy. I walked into that one, didn't I? I believe one was the JFK election, in '60. I can't scan it back that fast now. But in every case there was—Woodrow Wilson may have been one—there was an instant, passionate issue. How the fuck Kennedy ever made Nixon a bad guy in 1960 is beyond me. That was real politics. A crazed Catholic playboy from Massachusetts, rich father supported the Nazis in 1940—I was against [JFK] at first.

MH: *The Proud Highway* contains some letters you wrote on November 22, 1963 [the day JFK was shot], to your friends Paul Semonin and William Kennedy. In the one to Kennedy you wrote, "There is no human being within 500 miles to whom I can communicate anything—much less the fear and loathing that is on me after today's murder. . . . No matter what, today is the end of an era. No more fair play. From now on it is dirty pool and judo in the clinches. The savage nuts have shattered the great myth of American decency." According to the book it was the first time you wrote the words "fear and loathing."
HST: I was amazed that it went back that far. I was not aware that I was accused of stealing it from Kierkegaard. People accused me of stealing "fear and loathing"—fuck no, that came straight out of what I felt. If I had seen it, I probably *would* have stolen it. Yeah, I just remember thinking about Kennedy, that this is so bad I need new words for it. And "fear and loathing"—yeah, it defines a certain state, an attitude.

MH: Clinton had a vision for a Great Society when he was elected. What do you think has happened since then?
HST: Well, the things that Clinton has been accused of are prima facie worse than what Nixon was run out of office for. Nixon was never even accused of things like Clinton is being accused of now. Bringing the Chinese into the political process, selling out to the Indonesians, selling the Lincoln bedroom at night, dropping his pants, trying to hustle little girls in Little Rock. God, what a degenerate town that is. Phew.

MH: How will history remember Bill Clinton?
HST: I don't know about history. I don't get any satisfaction out of the old traditional journalist's view—"I just covered the story. I just gave it a balanced view." Objective journalism is one of the main reasons American politics has been allowed to be so corrupt for so long. You can't be objective about Nixon. How can you be objective about Clinton?

MH: Objective journalism is why politics have been corrupt for so long?
HST: If you consider the great journalists in history, you don't see too many objective journalists on that list. H. L. Mencken was not objective. Mike Royko, who just died. I. F. Stone was not objective. Mark Twain was not objective. I don't quite understand this worship of objectivity in journalism. Now, just flat-out lying is different from being *subjective.*

MH: If you found yourself teaching a journalism course—Dr. Thompson's Journalism 101—what would you tell students who were looking to go about covering stories?
HST: You offering me a job? Shit. Well, I wouldn't do it, I guess. It's not important to me that I teach journalism classes.

MH: But if you did, what would your reading list be?
HST: Oh, I'd start off with Henry Fielding. I would read writers. You know, I would read Conrad, Hemingway, people who use words. That's really what it's about. It's about using words to achieve an end. And the Book of Revelation. I still read the Book of Revelation when I need to get cranked up about language. I would teach Harrison Salisbury of the *New York Times.* All the journalists who are known, really, have been that way because they were subjective.

I think the trick is that you have to use words well enough so that these nickle-and-dimers who come around bitching about being objective or the advertisers don't like it are rendered helpless by the fact that it's good. That's the way people have triumphed over conventional wisdom in journalism.

MH: Who's writing that way today?
HST: Oh, boy. Let's just say, who's been arrested recently? That's usually the way. Like in the sixties you look for Paul Krassner, I. F. Stone. I don't think that my kind of journalism has ever been universally popular. It's lonely out here.

A lot of times I recognize quality in the enemy. I have, from the very beginning, admired Pat Buchanan, who's not even a writer. He knows how to use words. I read something the other day, and I totally disagreed with him. But you know, I was about to send him a note saying, "Good!"

MH: If you were going to start a paper, and you were editor, who would you hire on? Who'd be on your writing staff? Living or dead.
HST: Whew! That would be fun. We're thinking of starting a paper here. These are not abstract questions.

If I were to surround myself with experts, I'd hire P. J. [O'Rourke], Tom Wolfe, Tim Ferris. I'd hire Jann Wenner, put him to work.

MH: For this publication you're thinking about putting together now, what would be your mission?
HST: I can't think in terms of journalism without thinking in terms of political ends. Unless there's been a reaction, there's been no journalism. It's cause and effect.

[*A bottle of Wild Turkey is introduced.*]

HST: Aw, man. I drank this like some sort of sacrament for—I mean, constantly—for I think fifteen years. No wonder people looked at me funny. No offense. This is what I drank, and I insisted on it and I drank it constantly and I liked it. Jesus. I laid off it for six months and went back to it—an accident one night, in a bar—and it almost knocked me off the stool. It's like drinking gasoline. I thought, what the fuck. . . ?

[*At HST's request, a cardboard placard is brought into the room, bearing HST's obituary of Richard Nixon for* Rolling Stone, *dated May 1, 1994, and entitled, "He Was a Crook."*]

HST: Here's one of the things I'm proudest of. It's about time you read something. Why don't you read that for us? This will be a lesson for you. Start at the beginning. If you haven't read this, it might explain a little more. Take it from the top. Headline and all.

[*MH proceeds to read aloud the entire scathing obituary.*]

MH: " 'He Was a Crook.' By Hunter S. Thompson. Memo from the National Affairs Desk. Date: May 1, 1994. Subject: The Death of Richard Nixon: Notes on the passing of an American monster. . . . He was a liar and a quitter, and he should have been buried at sea. . . . But he was, after all, the President.

"Richard Nixon is gone now, and I am poorer for it. He was the real thing—a political monster straight out of Grendel"—
HST: Slow down, slow down. I've learned this the hard way. You gotta read slower, bite the words off.

MH: Okay. Okay. [*Slowly*] "Richard Nixon is gone now."
HST: Good.

MH: "And I am poorer for it."
HST: Good.

MH: "He was the real thing—a political monster straight out of Grendel and a very dangerous enemy. He could shake your hand and stab you in the back at the same time."
HST: That's good.

[*The reading continues. HST stops MH numerous times, telling him to re-read lines that MH hasn't delivered to the author's satisfaction. Several times HST laughs out loud, clearly enjoying the sound of his own words. HST soon becomes distracted and digresses, and MH puts the placard down on the couch.*]

HST: Don't put that away! All the way to the end!

MH: All the way to the end?
HST: You bet. It's a lesson for you. You'll learn from this. I guarantee it. You're going to be happy at the end.

MH: A happy ending?
HST: Have a drink here, first, since you've already fucked up. You may as well have a drink.

[*A glass of Wild Turkey and ice is placed before MH, and he continues reading to the end.*]

MH: What inspired you to write this?

HST: I don't know if inspired is the right word. It's like tapping into a vein, I guess. But the history of this is instructive.

As it happens I was sitting in a house in New Orleans with Nixon's biographer, Steve Ambrose. He's a friend. And we were watching the last hours of Nixon. And Ambrose in his wickedness, in his self-serving skill, got me into one of these weepy, you know, "Well, he really was a nice guy . . ." Yeah, the death of Nixon: I either had to die or write it. I was staying at the Pontchartrain Hotel at the time in New Orleans. And I tried to react to it there. And after maybe two days, total failure. I couldn't. I was not up to the majesty of the event. I set such a high standard—H. L. Mencken's obituary for William Jennings Bryan, which then ranked as the most savage and unnatural thing ever said on the death of a famous or any other person. Mencken is a person I'd hire. But, with that being the standard, the target being so high, it was like being asked to run the three-minute mile.

And, fuck, I tried for like two weeks. I failed in New Orleans, and I got back here, and I failed again. I despaired several times. I had Jann and Tobias frantic on the other end [at *Rolling Stone*]. But I wouldn't let it go unless it was right, and it was nowhere near right.

MH: What was it that gelled it for you?

HST: Ah ha, thank you. It was watching his funeral on TV. It enraged me so much. It was such a maudlin, truthless affair. I was thinking about going, but I wouldn't have seen the clarity of it as I did watching it on TV here. It was such a classically—You're talking about your objective journalism?—it was one of those things . . . speak no evil of the dead. Well, why not? What the fuck? Nixon goes out as a champion of the American dream and a hero. It enraged me. So it was the rage that tapped the vein.

But it's cold-blooded accurate.

I felt that same way—not really quite the same way, but in the same direction—about Allen [Ginsberg], since I was billed as a major speaker at his funeral. And due to very legitimate reasons it would have been crazy for me, with my back, to go down there. But I said, all right, I can't be there but I will write a funeral statement and Johnny Depp will deliver it. And then started a week of horrible nights. Hideous nights. Failure. It got worse and worse instead of better. I was trying to say nice things about him. And I gave up totally. I actually gave up physically. Set Depp up. He had no idea. He was very nervous about having to deliver my statement. I was so depressed that I was impossible to be around. I could not do it. And I wanted to a lot. It was nine or ten in the morning, and I sent Depp a short fax saying, "You're on your own. I failed. I can't do it. Say whatever you want." Luckily he was off somewhere, and he didn't get it.

And I went to bed and ate a Halcion, which usually knocks me out—you know, a sleeping pill. I had already been up for two or three nights. Two hours later I woke up, like at noon, and came out here like a zombie and sat down and wrote it. So I was writing out of desperation, out of fear and hatred of failure. I hate to think that, but God almighty, that's the thing.

MH: You say "Gonzo Journalism" is a term that you're not so fond of anymore, because it's been cast as inaccurate, crazy. Has anyone written Gonzo besides you?
HST: Is that [the Nixon obituary] Gonzo in your mind?

MH: No. I guess when I think of Gonzo, I'm thinking of your story "The Kentucky Derby Is Decadent and Depraved" [*Scanlan's Monthly*, June, 1970]. You throw yourself into the middle of a story and write your way out of it. Has anybody else done that?
HST: Oh, yeah, there are some good ones. Very few, but there was a novel called *Snow Blind*, in the seventies, about the cocaine trade.

MH: Why has the term "gonzo" fallen out of favor with you?
HST: Well, maybe because of what I just asked you. Since the Random House Dictionary defines "gonzo" as sort of whatever I write or do, and I ask you, Does that Nixon obit seem like Gonzo Journalism to you? And you say no, then I have to wonder, right?

MH: How do you compare Gonzo to the New Journalism? Do you see them as separate or intertwined?
HST: Intertwined, in that it is no accident that Gonzo is in Tom Wolfe's book *The New Journalism* [1973].

MH: When you were writing in this way, did you feel that you were part of a movement, the New Journalism, or did you feel like you were just doing your own thing?
HST: No, I felt like I was just a journalist on assignment, really.

MH: In an early letter to William Kennedy you spoke of the "dry rot" of American journalism. Tell me what you think. What's the state of the American press currently?

HST: The press today is like the rest of the country. Maybe you need a war. Wars tend to bring out out the best in them. War was everywhere you looked in the sixties, extending into the seventies. Now there are no wars to fight. You know, it's the old argument about why doesn't the press report the good news? Well, now the press is reporting the good news, and it's not as much fun.

The press has been taken in by Clinton. And by the amalgamation of politics. Nobody denies that the parties are more alike than they are different. No, the press has failed, failed utterly—they've turned into slovenly rotters. Particularly the *New York Times*, which has come to be a bastion of political correctness. I think my place in history as defined by the PC people would be pretty radically wrong. Maybe I could be set up as a target at the other end of the spectrum. I feel more out of place now than I did under Nixon. Yeah, that's weird. There's something going on here, Mr. Jones, and you don't know what it is, do you?

Yeah, Clinton has been a much more successfully deviant president than Nixon was. You can bet if the stock market fell to 4,000 and if four million people lost their jobs there'd be a lot of hell to pay, but so what? He's already re-elected. Democracy as a system has evolved into something that Thomas Jefferson didn't anticipate. Or maybe he did, at the end of his life. He got very bitter about the press. And what is it he said? "I tremble for my nation when I reflect that God is just"? That's a guy who's seen the darker side. Yeah, we've become a nation of swine.

MH: In *Fear and Loathing in Las Vegas* you were looking for the American Dream. What is there for people to find in 1997?

HST: Do you think we were surprised [in *Fear and Loathing*] to find that the American Dream was a nightclub that had burned down five years earlier? That we were surprised to find when we tracked it down that it had been the old Psychiatrist's Club? Prior to that its name had been the American Dream. Do you think that we were surprised to find that? No. I went out there looking to reaffirm Horatio Alger. I knew what was happening. That's what the book is all about.

MH: From what I've read and from people I've talked to, the thing that people find most impressive about *The Proud Highway* is that from the age of seventeen or eighteen, you knew what you were going to do—
HST: Fifteen.

MH: People are impressed with your sense of destiny. I know that you say you got in trouble and journalism or writing was the only thing that was there for you, but at seventeen, eighteen—or even fifteen—plenty of things were open to you.
HST: Right, the world is your oyster. I guess I found out early on that writing was a means of being effective. Well, you can see the beginnings of that in *The Proud Highway*. I grew up thinking that despite the obstacles presented by the swine, I would be successful no matter what I did. I guess that's one of the things about growing up in the fifties, it never occurred to me that you wouldn't be at least as successful as your parents. Now it's minority position to believe that you might be even as successful as your parents.

MH: There's a letter in *The Proud Highway* [from 1965] in which you said, "I should have quit journalism . . . and hit the fiction for all I was worth. And if I'm ever going to be worth anything I honestly think it will have to be in the realm of fiction." What if you had stuck to straight journalism? What do you think would have been the outcome?
HST: It might have all hinged on Phil Graham's suicide in 1963, I guess. He was the publisher of the *Washington Post*. [HST had struck up a correspondence with Graham.] It's a wild thought—we'll have to wrap this up before I get really wild and start thinking out loud—but by now I could have been the editor of the *Washington Post*.

Fear and Loathing in Hollywood: A Strange and Terrible Saga of Guns, Drugs, and Hunter S. Thompson

Kevin Simonson / 1998

From *Hustler* magazine, August 1998, pp.58–60, 70–72. Reprinted with the permission of LFP Publishing Group.

In 1971, Hunter S. Thompson set off for Las Vegas armed with a keen sense of the absurd and a plentiful cache of drugs. The resultant book, *Fear and Loathing in Las Vegas*, is a classic in the literature of depravity. Nearly three decades after publication, Thompson's demented masterwork is finally making it to the big screen. Join the doctor of gonzo journalism as he ponders movie-biz ironies with explosions and cautionary words at his Aspen, Colorado, fortress.

Hunter S. Thompson lives in a hidden fortress several miles outside Aspen, Colorado. Beyond the bumpy, rock-strewn driveway is a pair of giant, gnarled poles flanked by demon vultures crafted of rusting metal. At night the eyes glow red as Tabasco, following a visitor's every move. A bowie knife the size of a meat loaf protrudes from the rustic frame of the house's side door. A few inches away, a bullet hole pierces a thick windowpane.

"I had a couple of handymen doing some work on the porch," explains Thompson, the man credited with forming gonzo journalism—a style of reporting in which the writer becomes a part of the story. "I snuck up behind them and shot off a couple of rounds between them and through the window. Scared the bejesus out of them."

Inside the main house of Owl Farm—as Thompson calls his property—the kitchen walls are covered with thirty years' of gonzo memorabilia: an uncashed ten-dollar check from Bob Woodward, a rubber Nixon mask, dozens of newspaper articles and Scotch-taped notes. A machine gun sits against the side of a large-screen TV. Thompson, a self-described news junkie, usually has the set turned to CNN or a sporting event.

Thompson's refrigerator is adorned with black-and-white photos of him and Bill Murray riding in a high-power motor boat. In the photos, Murray is pasty, bloated and barely recognizable.

Murray and Thompson were roommates for a brief period prior to the filming of 1980's *Where the Buffalo Roam*, a fictionalized film version of Thompson's life as a gonzo journalist. Murray, who played the self-titled Good Doctor, signed on for gonzo boot camp, and Thompson became the actor's mentor and drill sergeant. Many lesser revelers who fall under Thompson's spell feel compelled to keep up with him toke for toke, drink for drink and line for line.

The time spent with Thompson took its toll on both Murray and *Where the Buffalo Roam*. Murray's new persona reportedly alienated him from his cohorts on *Saturday Night Live*, and the movie was universally panned—even by Thompson.

"He did a good job," Thompson says of Murray's acting, "but it's a silly film—a cartoon. The studio paid me to write new beginnings and endings, but it was a bad script. You couldn't cure it."

Perhaps this summer the pictures of Murray and Thompson will be replaced by new ones. Hunter's perennial cigarette holder has been passed on to Johnny Depp, who will play Raoul Duke, Thompson's alter ego, in the upcoming film version of *Fear and Loathing in Las Vegas*.

The movie also stars *The Usual Suspects*' Benicio Del Toro as Thompson's partner in crime, mammoth Samoan lawyer Oscar Zeta Acosta. The remainder of the cast includes Gary Busey, Christina Ricci and Tobey Maguire. The film is slated for an early-summer release.

For the uninitiated, *Fear and Loathing in Las Vegas* details Thompson's drunken, drug-addled adventures in Las Vegas while covering an off-road motorcycle race and concurrent law-enforcement convention. The book is on many reading lists in college classrooms throughout the country. Signed first editions can fetch up to $2,500.

Random House marked the novel's twenty-fifth anniversary with a Modern Library Edition, the literary equivalent of an Academy Award. Hunter S. Thompson can now boast that his peers include fellow hard-drinking scholars William Faulkner and Ernest Hemingway.

The twenty-fifth anniversary of *Fear and Loathing's* release was celebrated in a different manner by the author himself. Thompson invited his professional sidekick, artist Ralph Steadman, and a few select others to Owl Farm. There, in Thompson's sprawling backyard, the revelers strapped a propane tank and exploding target to an idling John Deere tractor. Straddling the tractor was a voluptuous blow-up doll.

"Hunter took aim and shot it," recalls Steadman, a well-mannered Brit who has illustrated many of Thompson's books in his scrawling, nightmarish style. "*Boom!* The whole lot went up like an H bomb. We got it all on film.

"It's wonderful to watch in slow motion—the screen goes white when this propelling gas goes up. The explosion was an amazing thing, and this was his celebration party piece."

Life hasn't always been a cabaret with guns and explosions for Thompson. In the early '70s, he lived on the road and traveled the Western hemisphere as a correspondent for such diverse publications as *Time, Scanlan's Monthly*, the *New York Herald Tribune* and a bowling tabloid in Puerto Rico. On the rare occasions he found himself at home, Thompson served as night manager for the infamous Mitchell Brothers' O'Farrell Theatre, a porn emporium in San Francisco.

Thompson and Steadman were first paired to cover the Kentucky Derby for *Scanlan's*, a doomed sports magazine. From that point on, things got weird.

"I think the whole thing with the friendship is that there's a certain chemistry—it's like chalk and cheese," says Steadman. "He has a way of inspiring loyalty in me, even though I sometimes hate him for it."

The odd couple were next sent to Newport, Rhode Island, to cover the America's Cup. At the world's most prestigious regatta, Thompson and Steadman made an ill-fated attempt to spray-paint the words FUCK THE POPE on the side of one of the competing yachts. They were run from the event when a security guard heard the *clack* of the spray-paint can as the two rowed between the multimillion-dollar boats.

Steadman calls the trip a dress rehearsal for the Vegas book: "It's how *Fear and Loathing* came about. I've hated boats ever since."

Several years later, *Hell's Angels*, a candid examination of America's infamous motorcycle gang, hit bookstores, and Thompson's role as demented observer of America's seedy underbelly was cast. He next set his sights on another corrupt and blighted institution: Las Vegas.

"So we have a parcel of drugs in the trunk of the car and take off for Las Vegas," says Steadman in his best Thompson imitation—an octave or two below Tom Waits.

Fear and Loathing in Las Vegas, first serialized in *Rolling Stone*, became an overnight success. Talk of adapting Thompson's twisted comic masterpiece began soon after and continued for more than twenty-five years.

Martin Scorsese, who wanted to direct Jack Nicholson in the main role, was the first to tackle *Fear and Loathing*. He failed. John Belushi and Dan Aykroyd were also unable to get anywhere with the project in 1975. According to Thompson, others who have expressed interest include Larry McMurtry, David Lynch and Dennis Hopper.

The copious drug use and nefarious business in the book have always been sticking points for the successful production of a film version. Picture Jerry Lewis and Dean Martin wearing tan polyester, inhaling ether and harassing tourists. Today, $5.99 all-you-can-eat prime-rib dinners are in abundance on Vegas's main drags. In Thompson's world, buffets consisted of cocaine, grapefruits and Wild Turkey.

"There was a time when you couldn't do anything in movies about drugs," says Thompson. "This is the time in Hollywood to do just that—because it's been so repressive.

"Besides, I enjoy drugs. Coffee's a drug. Coffee's a drug, aspirin's a drug. . . . It's all a matter of how much. Too much of any drug can make you act like a beast."

Six years ago, producer Steve Nemeth made it his mission to battle Hollywood's censors and bring *Fear and Loathing in Las Vegas* to the screen. Allied with Rhino Records' fledgling film division, the producer a acquired the book's film rights from *Blade Runner* director Ridley Scott's production company after Scott gave the movie the ax.

An unforeseen problem developed. It was determined that one of Thompson's ex-girlfriends, Laila Nabulsi, actually owned the movie rights. According to one of Thompson's former assistants (Thompson's life is plagued with ex's of one sort or another), the writer had granted Nabulsi the rights scribbled on a cocktail napkin.

Legalities were eventually settled. Nemeth is producing the film along with Nabulsi and Patrick Cassavetti. Their first challenge was marketing the project in a form that would convince talent to sign on and, eventually, fill theaters.

"Because *Fear and Loathing* has been one of the bestsellers on college campuses, people who were in school twenty-five years ago up through today will come and see it," says Nemeth. "It can be viewed as a horror movie because it's so creepy and scary. The film's also a satire on American culture; so it's a comedy."

Like any good Hunter S. Thompson story, the saga of bringing *Fear and Loathing* to the screen is a convoluted and twisted tale.

A film script of the book has floated around Hollywood for many years, and dozens of screenwriters have taken a crack at the adaptation. According to director Terry Gilliam, who cowrote the final draft of the script with Tony Grisoni, the most challenging aspect of penning the screenplay was "trying to get an admission from the Writers Guild of America that we had adapted it." It is still the subject of a heated debate among several writers over who will be credited with authorship.

The practice of rewriting scripts over and over, a golden rule in the film industry, doesn't sit well with Thompson. "*Fear and Loathing* is a masterwork," Hunter says. "True gonzo journalism, as I conceive it, shouldn't be rewritten.

"Take the ending, for instance. There was no ending in the book. I had to get the second half of the magazine thing in. The deadline came; I had to wind it up in the Denver airport."

The next ordeal came with the selection of a director. Alex Cox, of *Sid and Nancy* fame, was originally slated to bring the nightmare commentary on American culture to the screen. However, a few months before filming began, Cox and his version of the script were unceremoniously dumped, and former Monty Python star Terry Gilliam took over.

Rumors vary, but insiders say leading man Depp and Cox butted heads over the director's script and his take on Raoul Duke. Before Cox left, he made ominous comments on the potential success of the film: "[*Fear and Loathing*] can't be a mainstream movie because it's so countercultural and demented."

New director Gilliam seems the perfect replacement. His own legacy of dementia includes *Time Bandits, Brazil, The Fisher King* and *12 Monkeys*. His revamped vision proved more in sync with the assembled cast, especially the man hired to portray Thompson.

"Johnny Depp held a loaded gun to my head and threatened my children," recounts Gilliam. "He said that he would not shoot me if I didn't do the film. He was never very good when it came to issuing threats."

Gilliam's screenplay even drew grudging acceptance from *Fear and Loathing's* author. "The new script isn't bad," admits Thompson.

With shaved head, Depp is a spitting image of a young Hunter S. Thompson. Prior to filming, the thirty-four-year-old actor spent several weeks with Raoul Duke, studying his mannerisms. They relaxed at Owl Farm and were spotted at several of Thompson's book signings.

Principal photography for *Fear and Loathing in Las Vegas* began last August 2 in Los Angeles. The cast soon moved to Las Vegas for three weeks of filming at the Stardust, Riviera and Binion's Casino. During the Vegas shoot and the following five-week stint back in L.A., a strict closed-set policy was enforced.

While a closed set is not uncommon for Hollywood productions, Gilliam made it clear that the film's producers were also unwelcome.

"Isn't it amazing?" questions producer Nemeth. "It's a movie about a gonzo journalist who wouldn't take no for an answer, and who'll infiltrate anything to get his story. In the true spirit of Hunter Thompson, you'd have thought we'd bend over backward to make it work for the people who care."

Despite the secrecy and a budget that ballooned from an originally estimated $6 million to more than $20 million, Nemeth is excited about the end result: "[*Fear and Loathing*] is going to be one of those anomalies that will have crossover appeal because it's recognized as one of the great pieces of American literature in the twentieth century."

Despite *Fear and Loathing's* imminent release, legal problems—including a recent drunk-driving incident and a distant sexual-harassment suit—and drunken, incomprehensible book readings have prompted whispers of Thompson's demise.

"A lot of people say he's finished," says Ralph Steadman. "But some of these naysayers have never been anywhere near as good as Thompson. They use his phrases and adapt his style—the *Fear and Loathing* language. There's still a lot there, it just comes in bursts."

Thompson is accustomed to negative press. He was the inspiration for Gary Trudeau's perpetually stoned Duke in *Doonesbury*, and David Letterman banned him from the *Late Show* because Thompson threatened "to bring four huge thugs over there" and shave Letterman's head on camera after being bumped from a taping.

"This vilification by Nazi elements within the media has not only given me a fierce joy to continue my work, but has also made me profoundly orgasmic, mysteriously rich and constantly at war with those vengeful, retro-fascist elements of the Establishment that have hounded me all my life," Thompson babbles with paranoid optimism. "It has made me wise, shrewd and crazy on a level understood by those who have been there."

Back at Owl Farm, Thompson will continue to raise peacocks and dobermans. He will continue to bike down the road to the Woody Creek Tavern for his meals. He will rarely answer his phone and continue to terrorize visitors to his home.

A contented recluse, Thompson's privacy will be invaded with a barrage of requests for magazine and television interviews because of the long-awaited release of *Fear and Loathing in Las Vegas* on the big screen.

He will grant only a few: "I guess *Hustler*'s okay for an article. Who knows? Not me—I'm just a country boy."

The Art of Journalism:
An Interview with
Hunter S. Thompson

Douglas Brinkley / 2000

Additional materials provided by Terry McDonell and George Plimpton. From "The Art of Journalism I: An Interview with Hunter S. Thompson and his journal notes from Vietnam" © 2000 by *The Paris Review*. Originally published in *The Paris Review,* No. 156 (Fall 2000). Reprinted with the permission of The Wylie Agency, Inc.

In an October 1957 letter to a friend who had recommended he read Ayn Rand's *The Fountainhead,* Hunter S. Thompson wrote, "Although I don't feel that it's at all necessary to tell you how I feel about the principle of individuality, I know that I'm going to have to spend the rest of my life expressing it one way or another, and I think that I'll accomplish more by expressing it on the keys of a typewriter than by letting it express itself in sudden outbursts of frustrated violence. . . ."

Thompson carved out his niche early. He was born in 1937, in Louisville, Kentucky, where his fiction and poetry earned him induction into the local Athenaeum Literary Association while he was still in high school. Thompson continued his literary pursuits in the United States Air Force, writing a weekly sports column for the base newspaper. After two years of service, Thompson endured a series of newspaper jobs—all of which ended badly— before he took to freelancing from Puerto Rico and South America for a variety of publications. The vocation quickly developed into a compulsion.

Thompson completed *The Rum Diary,* his only novel to date, before he turned twenty-five; bought by Ballantine Books, it finally was published—to glowing reviews—in 1998. In 1967, Thompson published his first nonfiction book, *Hell's Angels,* a harsh and incisive firsthand investigation into the infamous motorcycle gang then making the heartland of America nervous.

Fear and Loathing in Las Vegas, which first appeared in *Rolling Stone* in November 1971, sealed Thompson's reputation as an outlandish stylist

successfully straddling the line between journalism and fiction writing. As
the subtitle warns, the book tells of "a savage journey to the heart of the
American Dream" in full-tilt gonzo style—Thompson's hilarious first-person
approach—and is accented by British illustrator Ralph Steadman's
appropriate drawings.

His next book, *Fear and Loathing: On the Campaign Trail '72*, was a
brutally perceptive take on the 1972 Nixon-McGovern presidential
campaign. A self-confessed political junkie, Thompson chronicled the 1992
presidential campaign in *Better than Sex* (1994). Thompson's other books
include *The Curse of Lono* (1983), a bizarre South Seas tale, and three
collections of Gonzo Papers: *The Great Shark Hunt* (1979), *Generation of
Swine* (1988) and *Songs of the Doomed* (1990).

In 1997, *The Proud Highway: Saga of a Desperate Southern Gentleman,
1955–1967*, the first volume of Thompson's correspondence with everyone
from his mother to Lyndon Johnson, was published. The second volume of
letters, *Fear and Loathing in America: The Brutal Odyssey of an Outlaw
Journalist, 1968–1976*, has just been released.

Located in the mostly posh neighborhood of western Colorado's Woody
Creek Canyon, ten miles or so down-valley from Aspen, Owl Farm is a rustic
ranch with an old-fashioned Wild West charm. Although Thompson's
beloved peacocks roam his property freely, it's the flowers blooming around
the ranch house that provide an unexpected high-country tranquility. Jimmy
Carter, George McGovern and Keith Richards, among dozens of others, have
shot clay pigeons and stationary targets on the property, which is a
designated Rod and Gun Club and shares a border with the White River
National Forest. Almost daily, Thompson leaves Owl Farm in either his Great
Red Shark Convertible or Jeep Grand Cherokee to mingle at the nearby
Woody Creek Tavern.

Visitors to Thompson's house are greeted by a variety of sculptures,
weapons, boxes of books and a bicycle before entering the nerve center of
Owl Farm, Thompson's obvious command post on the kitchen side of a
peninsula counter that separates him from a lounge area dominated by an
always-on Panasonic TV, always tuned to news or sports. An antique upright
piano is piled high and deep enough with books to engulf any reader for a
decade. Above the piano hangs a large Ralph Steadman portrait of
"Belinda"—the Slut Goddess of Polo. On another wall covered with political
buttons hangs a Che Guevara banner acquired on Thompson's last tour of

Cuba. On the counter sits an IBM Selectric typewriter—a Macintosh computer is set up in an office in the back wing of the house.

The most striking thing about Thompson's house is that it isn't the *weirdness* one notices first: it's the *words.* They're everywhere—handwritten in his elegant lettering, mostly in fading red Sharpie on the blizzard of bits of paper festooning every wall and surface: stuck to the sleek black leather refrigerator, taped to the giant TV, tacked up on the lampshades; inscribed by others on framed photos with lines like, "For Hunter, who saw not only fear and loathing, but hope and joy in '72—George McGovern"; typed in IBM Selectric on reams of originals and copies in fat manila folders that slide in piles off every counter and table top; and noted in many hands and inks across the endless flurry of pages.

Thompson extricates his large frame from his ergonomically correct office chair facing the TV and lumbers over graciously to administer a hearty handshake or kiss to each caller according to gender, all with an easy effortlessness and unexpectedly old-world way that somehow underscores just who is in charge.

We talked with Thompson for twelve hours straight. This was nothing out of the ordinary for the host: Owl Farm operates like an eighteenth-century salon, where people from all walks of life congregate in the wee hours for free exchanges about everything from theoretical physics to local water rights, depending on who's there. Walter Isaacson, managing editor of *Time,* was present during parts of this interview, as were a steady stream of friends. Given the very late hours Thompson keeps, it is fitting that the most prominently posted quote in the room, in Thompson's hand, twists the last line of Dylan Thomas's poem "Do Not Go Gentle into That Good Night": "Rage, rage against the coming of the light."

For most of the half-day that we talked, Thompson sat at his command post, chain-smoking red Dunhills through a German-made gold-tipped cigarette filter and rocking back and forth in his swivel chair. Behind Thompson's sui generis personality lurks a trenchant humorist with a sharp moral sensibility. His exaggerated style may defy easy categorization, but his career-long autopsy on the death of the American dream places him among the twentieth century's most exciting writers. The comic savagery of his best work will continue to electrify readers for generations to come.

> . . . *I have stolen more quotes and thoughts and purely elegant little starbursts of writing from the Book of Revelation than from anything else in the English Language—and it is not because*

I am a biblical scholar, or because of any religious faith, but because I love the wild power of the language and the purity of the madness that governs it and makes it music.

—Generation of Swine

Interviewer: Reading *The Proud Highway,* I got the impression you always wanted to be a writer.

Hunter S. Thompson: Well, wanting to and having to are two different things. Originally I hadn't thought about writing as a solution to my problems. But I had a good grounding in literature in high school. We'd cut school and go down to a café on Birdstown Road where we would drink beer and read and discuss Plato's parable of the cave. We had a literary society in town, the Athenaeum; we met in coat and tie on Saturday nights. I hadn't adjusted too well to society—I was in jail for the night of my high school graduation—but I learned at the age of fifteen that to get by you had to find the one thing you can do better than anybody else . . . at least this was so in my case. I figured that out early. It was writing. It was the rock in my sock. Easier than algebra. It was always work, but it was always worthwhile work. I was fascinated early by seeing my byline in print. It was a rush. Still is.

When I got to the Air Force, writing got me out of trouble. I was assigned to pilot training at Eglin Air Force Base near Pensacola in northwest Florida, but I was shifted to electronics . . . advanced, very intense, eight-month school with bright guys . . . I enjoyed it but I wanted to get back to pilot training. Besides, I'm afraid of electricity. So I went up there to the base education office one day and signed up for some classes at Florida State. I got along well with a guy named Ed and I asked him about literary possibilities. He asked me if I knew anything about sports, and I said that I had been the editor of my high-school paper. He said, "Well, we might be in luck." It turned out that the sports editor of the base newspaper, a staff sergeant, had been arrested in Pensacola and put in jail for public drunkenness, pissing against the side of a building; it was the third time and they wouldn't let him out.

So I went to the base library and found three books on journalism. I stayed there reading them until it closed. Basic journalism. I learned about headlines, leads: who, when, what, where, that sort of thing. I barely slept that night. This was my ticket to ride, my ticket to get out of that damn place. So I started as an editor. Boy, what a joy. I wrote long Grantland Rice–type stories. The sports editor of my hometown *Louisville Courier Journal* always had a column, left-hand side of the page. So I started a column.

By the second week I had the whole thing down. I could work at night. I wore civilian clothes, worked off base, had no hours, but I worked constantly. I wrote not only for the base paper, *The Command Courier,* but also the local paper, *The Playground News.* I'd put things in the local paper that I couldn't put in the base paper. Really inflammatory shit. I wrote for a professional wrestling newsletter. The Air Force got very angry about it. I was constantly doing things that violated regulations. I wrote a critical column about how Arthur Godfrey, who'd been invited to the base to be the master of ceremonies at a firepower demonstration, had been busted for shooting animals from the air in Alaska. The base commander told me: "Goddamn it, son, why did you have to write about Arthur Godfrey that way?"

When I left the Air Force I knew I could get by as a journalist. So I went to apply for a job at *Sports Illustrated.* I had my clippings, my bylines, and I thought that was magic . . . my passport. The personnel director just laughed at me. I said, "Wait a minute. I've been sports editor for *two* papers." He told me that their writers were judged not by the work they'd done, but where they'd done it. He said, "Our writers are all Pulitzer Prize winners from the *New York Times.* This is a helluva place for you to *start.* Go out into the boondocks and improve yourself."

I was shocked. After all, I'd broken the Bart Starr story.

Interviewer: What was that?

Thompson: At Eglin Air Force Base we always had these great football teams. The Eagles. Championship teams. We could beat up on the University of Virginia. Our bird-colonel Sparks wasn't just any yo-yo coach. We recruited. We had these great players serving their military time in ROTC. We had Zeke Bratkowski, the Green Bay quarterback. We had Max McGee of the Packers. Violent, wild, wonderful drunk. At the start of the season McGee went AWOL, appeared at the Green Bay camp and he never came back. I was somehow blamed for his leaving. The sun fell out of the firmament. Then the word came that we were getting Bart Starr, the All-American from Alabama. The Eagles were going to roll! But then the staff sergeant across the street came in and said, "I've got a terrible story for you. Bart Starr's not coming." I managed to break into an office and get out his files. I printed the order that showed he was being discharged medically. Very serious leak.

Interviewer: The Bart Starr story was not enough to impress *Sports Illustrated?*

Thompson: The personnel guy there said, "Well, we do have this trainee program." So I became a kind of copy boy.

Interviewer: You eventually ended up in San Francisco. With the publication in 1967 of *Hell's Angels*, your life must have taken an upward spin.

Thompson: All of a sudden I had a book out. At the time I was twenty-nine years old and I couldn't even get a job driving a cab in San Francisco, much less writing. Sure, I had written important articles for the *Nation* and the *Observer,* but only a few good journalists really knew my byline. The book enabled me to buy a brand new BSA 650 Lightning, the fastest motorcycle ever tested by *Hot Rod* magazine. It validated everything I had been working toward. If *Hell's Angels* hadn't happened I never would have been able to write *Fear and Loathing in Las Vegas* or anything else. To be able to earn a living as a freelance writer in this country is damned hard; there are very few people who can do that. *Hell's Angels* all of a sudden proved to me that, Holy Jesus, maybe I can do this. I knew I was a good journalist. I knew I was a good writer, but I felt like I got through a door just as it was closing.

Interviewer: With the swell of creative energy flowing throughout the San Francisco scene at the time, did you interact with or were you influenced by any other writers?

Thompson: Ken Kesey for one. His novels *One Flew Over the Cuckoo's Nest* and *Sometimes a Great Notion* had quite an impact on me. I looked up to him hugely. One day I went down to the television station to do a roundtable show with other writers, like Kay Boyle, and Kesey was there. Afterwards we went across the street to a local tavern and had several beers together. I told him about the Angels, who I planned to meet later that day, and I said, "Well, why don't you come along?" He said, "Whoa, I'd *like* to meet these guys." Then I got second thoughts, because it's never a good idea to take strangers along to meet the Angels. But I figured that this was Ken Kesey, so I'd try. By the end of the night Kesey has invited them all down to La Honda, his woodsy retreat outside of San Francisco. It was a time of extreme turbulence—riots in Berkeley. He was always under assault by the police— day in and day out, so La Honda was like a war zone. But he had a lot of the literary, intellectual crowd down there, Stanford people also, visiting editors, and Hell's Angels. Kesey's place was a real cultural vortex.

Interviewer: Did you ever entertain the idea of writing a novel about the whole Bay area during this period, the sixties, in the vein of Tom Wolfe's *Electric Acid Kool-Aid Test*?
Thompson: Well, I had thought about writing it up. It was obvious to me at the time that the Kesey action was on a continuum with the *Hell's Angels* book. It seemed to me for a while that I should write a book, probably the same one that Wolfe wrote, but at the time I wasn't really into it. I couldn't do another piece of journalism.

Interviewer: Did you connect at all with Tom Wolfe during the San Francisco heyday?
Thompson: It's interesting. I wanted to review Wolfe's book, *The Kandy-Kolored Tangerine-Flake Streamline Baby.* I'd read some of it in *Esquire*, got a copy, had a look at it and was very, very impressed. the *National Observer* had taken me off politics by then, so book reviews were about the only thing I could do that they didn't think controversial. I had wanted to cover Berkeley and acid, and all that, but they didn't want any of it. So I picked up Wolfe's book and wrote a glowing review and sent it in to the *Observer,* and my editor, Clifford Ridley, was pleased with it. About a week went by and I hadn't heard anything. Then my editor called me up and said, "We're not going to run the review." It was the first one they ever said no to; up until that point my reviews had been full-page lead pieces, like in the *Times Book Review,* and I was shocked that they would turn it down. I asked, "Why are you turning it down? What's wrong with you?" The guy obviously felt guilty, so he let me know there was an editor at the *Observer* who had worked with Wolfe somewhere else and didn't like him, so he had killed my review. So I took the review and sent it to Tom Wolfe with a letter saying, "the *Observer* won't run this because somebody there has a grudge against you, but I wanted you to get it anyway since I worked real hard on it, and your book was brilliant. I thought you should have it even though they won't print it." Then I took my carbons of that letter and sent them to the *Observer.* They said I'd been disloyal. That's when I was terminated. I just felt it was important not only that Wolfe knew about it, but that the *Observer* editors knew that I had turned them in. It sounds kind of perverse, but I'd do it again. But that's how

Tom and I got to know each other. He would call me for directions or advice when he was working on the *Acid* book.

Interviewer: Did that friendship and Wolfe's journalism have much of an impact on your writing?
Thompson: Wolfe proved that you could kind of get away with it. I saw myself as having a tendency to cut loose—like Kesey—and Wolfe seemed to embrace that as well. We were a new kind of writer, so I felt it was like a gang. We were each doing different things, but it was a natural kind of hook-up.

Interviewer: Wolfe later included you in his book, *The New Journalism.*
Thompson: I was the only one with two entries, in fact. He appreciated my writing and I appreciated his.

Interviewer: As you explored the acid scene did you ever develop a feel for Timothy Leary?
Thompson: I knew the bastard quite well. I ran into him a lot in those days. As a matter of fact I got a postcard invitation from something called the Futique Trust in Aptos, California, inviting me to attend the fourth annual Timothy Leary Memorial Celebration and Potluck Picnic. The invitation was printed in happy letters, with a peace symbol in the background, and I felt a burst of hate in my heart when I saw it. Every time I think about Tim Leary I get angry. He was a liar and a quack and a worse human being than Richard Nicon. For the last twenty-six years of his life he worked as an informant for the FBI and turned his friends into the police and betrayed the peace symbol he hid behind.

Interviewer: The San Francisco scene brought together many unlikely pairs—you and Allen Ginsberg, for instance. How did you come to know Allen during this period?
Thompson: I met Allen in San Francisco when I went to see a marijuana dealer who sold by the lid. I remember it was ten dollars when I started going to that apartment and then it was up to fifteen. I ended up going there pretty often, and Ginsberg—this was in Haight-Ashbury—was always there looking for weed too. I went over and introduced myself and we ended up talking a lot. I told him about the book I was writing and asked if he would help with it. He helped me with it for several months; that's how he got to know the

Hell's Angels. We would also go down to Kesey's in La Honda together. One Saturday, I drove down the coast highway from San Francisco to La Honda and I took Juan, my two-year-old son, with me. There was this magnificent crossbreeding of people there. Allen was there, the Hell's Angels—and the cops were there too, to prevent a Hell's Angels riot. Seven or eight cop cars. Kesey's house was across the creek from the road, sort of a two-lane blacktop country compound, which was a weird place. For one thing, huge amplifiers were mounted everywhere in all the trees and some were mounted across the road on wires, so to be on the road was to be in this horrible vortex of sound, this pounding, you could barely hear yourself think—rock'n'roll at the highest amps. That day, even before the Angels got there, the cops began arresting anyone who left the compound. I was by the house; Juan was sleeping peacefully in the backseat of the car. It got to be outrageous: the cops were popping people. You could see them about a hundred yards away, but then they would bust somebody very flagrantly, so Allen said, "You know, we've got to do something about this." I agreed, so with Allen in the passenger's seat, Juan in the back sleeping, and me driving, we took off after the cops that had just busted another person we knew, who was leaving just to go up to the restaurant on the corner. Then the cops got after *us*. Allen at the very sight of the cops went into his hum, his *om,* trying to hum them off. I was talking to them like a journalist would: "What's going on here, Officer?" Allen's humming was supposed to be a Buddhist barrier against the bad vibes the cops were producing and he was doing it very loudly, refusing to speak to them, just "*Om! Om! Om!*" I had to explain to the cops who he was and why he was doing this. The cops looked into the backseat and said, "What is that back there? A child?" And I said, "Oh, yeah, yeah. That's my son." With Allen still going, "*Om,*" we were let go. He was a reasonable cop, I guess—checking out a poet, a journalist and a child. Never did figure Ginsberg out, though. It was like the humming of a bee. It was one of the weirdest scenes I've ever been through, but almost every scene with Allen was weird in some way or another.

Interviewer: Did any other Beat Generation authors influence your writing?
Thompson: Jack Kerouac influenced me quite a bit as a writer . . . in the Arab sense that the enemy of my enemy was my friend. Kerouac taught me that you could get away with writing about drugs and get published. It was *possible,* and in a symbolic way I expected Kerouac to turn up in Haight-Ashbury for

the cause. Ginsberg was there, so it was kind of natural to expect that Kerouac would show up too. But, no. That's when Kerouac went back to his mother and voted for Barry Goldwater in 1964. That's when my break with him happened. I wasn't trying to write like him, but I could see that I could get published like him and make the breakthrough, break through the Eastern establishment ice. That's the same way I felt about Hemingway when I first learned about him and his writing. I thought, Jesus, some people can *do* this. Of course Lawrence Ferlinghetti influenced me—both his wonderful poetry and the earnestness of his City Lights bookstore in North Beach.

Interviewer: You left California and the San Francisco scene near its apex. What motivated you to return to Colorado?
Thompson: I still feel needles in my back when I think about all the horrible disasters that would have befallen me if I had permanently moved to San Francisco and rented a big house, joined the company dole, become national-affairs editor for some upstart magazine—that was the plan around 1967. But that would have meant going to work on a regular basis, like nine to five, with an office—I had to pull out.

Interviewer: Warren Hinckle was the first editor who allowed you to write and pursue gonzo journalism—how did you two become acquainted?
Thompson: I met him through his magazine, *Ramparts.* I met him even before *Rolling Stone* ever existed. *Ramparts* was a crossroads of my world in San Francisco, a slicker version of the *Nation*—with glossy covers and such. Warren had a genius for getting stories that could get placed on the front page of the *New York Times.* He had a beautiful eye for what story had a high, weird look to it. You know, busting the Defense Department—*Ramparts* was real left, radical. I paid a lot of attention to them and ended up being a columnist. *Ramparts* was the scene until some geek withdrew the funding and it collapsed. Jann Wenner, who founded *Rolling Stone,* actually worked there in the library—he was a copy boy or something.

Interviewer: What's the appeal of the "outlaw" writer, such as yourself?
Thompson: I just usually go with my own taste. If I like something, and it happens to be against the law, well, then I might have a problem. But an outlaw can be defined as somebody who lives outside the law, beyond the

law, not necessarily against it. And it's pretty ancient. It goes back to Scandinavian history. People were declared outlaws and they were cast out of the community and sent to foreign lands—exiled. They operated outside the law and were in communities all over Greenland and Iceland, wherever they drifted. Outside the law in the countries they came from—I don't think they were *trying* to be outlaws . . . I was never trying, necessarily, to be an outlaw. It was just the place in which I found myself. By the time I started *Hell's Angels* I was riding with them and it was clear that it was no longer possible for me to go back and live within the law. Between Vietnam and weed—a whole generation was criminalized in that time. You realize that you are subject to being busted. A lot of people grew up with that attitude. There were a lot more outlaws than me. I was just a writer. I wasn't trying to be an outlaw writer. I never heard of that term; somebody else made it up. But we were all outside the law: Kerouac, Miller, Burroughs, Ginsberg, Kesey; I didn't have a gauge as to who was the worst outlaw. I just recognized allies: my people.

Interviewer: The drug culture. How do you write when you're under the influence?
Thompson: My theory for years has been to write fast and get through it. I usually write five pages a night and leave them out for my assistant to type in the morning.

Interviewer: This, after a night of drinking and so forth?
Thompson: Oh yes, always, yes. I've found that there's only one thing that I can't work on and that's marijuana. Even acid I could work with. The only difference between the sane and the insane is that the sane have the power to lock up the insane. Either you function or you don't. Functionally insane? If you get paid for being crazy, if you can get paid for running amok and writing about it . . . I call that sane.

Interviewer: Almost without exception writers we've interviewed over the years admit they cannot write under the influence of booze or drugs—or at the least what they've done has to be rewritten in the cool of the day. What's your comment about this?
Thompson: They lie. Or maybe you've been interviewing a very narrow spectrum of writers. It's like saying, "Almost without exception women we've

interviewed over the years swear that they never indulge in sodomy"—
without saying that you did all your interviews in a nunnery. Did you
interview Coleridge? Did you interview Poe? Or Scott Fitzgerald? Or Mark
Twain? Or Fred Exley? Did Faulkner tell you that what he was drinking all the
time was really iced tea, not whiskey? Please. Who the fuck do you think
wrote the Book of Revelation? A bunch of stone-sober clerics?

Interviewer: In 1974 you went to Saigon to cover the war. . .
Thompson: The war had been part of my life for so long. For more than ten
years I'd been beaten and gassed. I wanted to see the end of it. In a way I felt
I was paying off a debt.

Interviewer: To whom?
Thompson: I'm not sure. But to be so influenced by the war for so long, to
have it so much a part of my life, so many decisions because of it, and then
not to be in it, well, that seemed unthinkable.

Interviewer: How long were you there?
Thompson: I was there about a month. I wasn't really a war. It was over. Nothing
like the war David Halberstam and Jonathan Schell and Philip Knightley had
been covering. Oh, you could still get killed. A combat photographer, a friend
of mine, was killed on the last day of the war. Crazy boys. That's where I got
most of my help. They were the opium smokers.

Interviewer: You hoped to enter Saigon with the Vietcong?
Thompson: I wrote a letter to the Vietcong people, Colonel Giang, hoping
they'd let me ride into Saigon on the top of a tank. The VC had their camp by
the airport, two hundred people set up for the advancing troops. There was
nothing wrong with it. It was good journalism.

Interviewer: Did you ever think of staying in Saigon rather than riding in on
a Vietcong tank?
Thompson: Yes, but I had to meet my wife in Bali.

Interviewer: A very good reason. You're famous for traveling on assignment
with an excess of baggage. Did you have books with you?

Thompson: I had some books with me. Graham Greene's *The Quiet American* for sure. Phil Knightley's *The First Casualty.* Hemingway's *In Our Time.* I carried all these seminal documents. Reading *The Quiet American* gave the Vietnam experience a whole new meaning. I had all sorts of electronic equipment—much too much. Walkie-talkies. I carried a tape recorder. And notebooks. Because of the sweat I couldn't write with the felt-tip pens I usually use because they would bleed all over the paper. I carried a big notebook—sketchbook size. I'd carry all this stuff in a photographer's pack over my shoulders. I also carried a .45 automatic. That was for weird drunk soldiers who would wander into our hotel. They were shooting in the streets . . . someone would fire off a clip right under your window. I think Knightley had one, too. I got mine from someone who was trying to smuggle orphans out of the country. I couldn't tell if he was on the white slave or the mercy market.

Interviewer: Why only a month in Saigon?
Thompson: The war was over. I'd wanted to go to Saigon in 1971. I'd just started working for *Rolling Stone.* At a strategy summit meeting that year of all the editors at Big Sur, I was making the argument that *Rolling Stone* should cover national politics. Cover the campaign. If we were going to cover the culture, to not include politics was stupid. Jann Wenner was the only person who half-agreed with me. The other editors there thought I was insane. I was sort of the wild creature. I would always appear in my robe. For three days I made these passionate pitches to the group. At the end of it I finally had to say, "Fuck you, *I'll* cover it. I'll do it." Dramatic moment, looking back on it.

Well, you can't cover national politics from Saigon. So I moved lock, stock and barrel from here to Washington. Took the dogs. Sandy, my wife, was pregnant. The only guy willing to help me was Timothy Crouse, who at the time was the lowest on the totem pole at *Rolling Stone.* He had a serious stutter, almost a debilitating stutter, which Jann mocked him for all the time, really cruel to him, which made me stand up for him more and more. He never had written more than a three-hundred-word piece on some rock'n'roll concert. He was the only one who volunteered to go to Washington. "Okay, Timbo. It's you and me. We'll kick ass." Life does turn on so many queer things . . . ball bearings and banana skins . . . a political reporter instead of a war correspondent.

Interviewer: Crouse eventually wrote a bestseller about the press and the campaign—*The Boys on the Bus.*

Thompson: He was the Boston stringer for *Rolling Stone.* He had graduated from Harvard and had an apartment in the middle of Cambridge. Strictly into music at the time. He was the only person who raised his hand in Big Sur. We covered the 1972 campaign. I wrote the main stories and Tim did the sidebars. Then there was that night in Milwaukee when I told him I was sick, too sick to write the main story. I said, "Well, Timbo, I hate to tell you this but you're gonna have to write the main story this week and I'm gonna write the sidebar." He panicked. Very bad stuttering. I felt I had to deal with that. I told him he had to stop stuttering. I told him that it's not constructive. "Goddamn it, spit it out!"

Interviewer: "Not constructive?" Easy for you to say.

Thompson: Well, I saw that he lacked confidence. So I made him write the Wisconsin story, and it was beautiful—suddenly he had confidence.

Interviewer: In your introduction to *A Generation of Swine,* you state that you spent half your life trying to escape journalism.

Thompson: I always felt that journalism was just a ticket to ride out, that I was basically meant for higher things. Novels. More status in being a novelist. When I went to Puerto Rico in the sixties William Kennedy and I would argue about it. He was the managing editor of the local paper; he was the journalist. I was the writer, the higher calling. I felt so strongly about it that I almost wouldn't do journalism. I figured in order to be a real writer, I'd have to write novels. That's why I wrote *Rum Diary* first. *Hell's Angels* started off as just another down-and-out assignment. Then I got over the idea that journalism was a lower calling. Journalism is fun because it offers immediate work. You get hired and at least you can cover the fucking City Hall. It's exciting. It's a guaranteed chance to write. It's a natural place to take refuge in if you're not selling novels. Writing novels is a lot lonelier work.

My epiphany came in the weeks after the Kentucky Derby fiasco. I'd gone down to Louisville on assignment for Warren Hinckle's *Scanlan's.* A freak from England named Ralph Steadman was there—first time I met him—doing drawings for my story. The lead story. Most depressing days of my life. I'd lie in my tub at the Royalton. I thought I had failed completely as a journalist. I thought it was probably the end of my career. Steadman's drawings were in place. All I could think of was the white space where my text was supposed to be. Finally, in desperation and embarrassment, I began to rip the pages out of my notebook and give them to a copyboy to take to a fax machine down the street. When I left I was a broken man, failed totally, and convinced I'd be exposed when the stuff came out. It was just a question of when the hammer would fall. I'd had my big chance and I had blown it.

Interviewer: How did *Scanlan's* utilize the notebook pages?
Thompson: Well, the article starts out with an organized lead about the arrival at the airport and meeting a guy I told about the Black Panthers coming in; and then it runs amok, disintegrates into flash cuts, a lot of dots.

Interviewer: And the reaction?
Thompson: This wave of praise. This wonderful . . . pure gonzo. I heard from friends—Tom Wolfe, Bill Kennedy.

Interviewer: So what, in fact, was learned from that experience?
Thompson: I realized I was on to something: maybe we can have some fun with this journalism . . . maybe it isn't this low thing. Of course, I recognized the difference between sending in copy and tearing out the pages of a notebook.

Interviewer: An interesting editorial choice—for *Scanlan's* to go ahead with what you sent.
Thompson: They had no choice. There was all that white space.

Interviewer: What is your opinion of editors?
Thompson: There are fewer good editors than good writers. Some of my harshest lessons about writers and editors came from carrying those edited stories around the corridors of Time-Life. I would read the copy on the way up and then I would read it again after the editing. I was curious. I saw some of the most brutal jobs done on the writers. There was a guy there, Roy Alexander, a managing editor . . . oh God, Alexander would x-out whole leads. And this was after other editors had gone to work on it.

Interviewer: Did anybody do that to your copy?
Thompson: Not for long. Well, I can easily be persuaded that I'm wrong on some point. You don't sit in the hotel room in Milwaukee and look out the

window and see Lake Superior, which I've written by mistake. Also, an editor is a person who helps me get what I've written to the press. They are necessary evils. If I ever got something in on time, which would mean I'd let it go from this house and *liked* it . . . well, that's never happened in my life . . . I've never sent a piece of anything that's finished . . . there's not even a proper ending to *Fear and Loathing in Las Vegas.* I had several different endings in mind, another chapter or two, one of which involved going to buy a Doberman. But then it went to press—a two-part magazine piece for *Rolling Stone.*

Interviewer: Could you have added a proper ending when it was published as a book?
Thompson: I could have done that but it would have been wrong. Like rewriting the letters in *The Proud Highway.*

Interviewer: Would it help if you wrote the ending first?
Thompson: I used to believe that. Most of my stuff is just a series of false leads. I'll approach a story as a subject and then make a whole bunch of different runs at the lead. They're all good writing but they don't connect. So I end up having to string leads together.

Interviewer: By leads, you mean paragraphs.
Thompson: The first paragraph. The last paragraph. That's where the story is going and how it's going to end. Or else you'll go off in a hundred different directions.

Interviewer: And that's not what happened with *Fear and Loathing?*
Thompson: No. That was very good journalism.

Interviewer: Your book editor at the time of the earliest stages of what was to become *Fear and Loathing in Las Vegas* was Jim Silberman at Random House—a lot of correspondence between the two of you.
Thompson: The assignment he gave me to do was nearly impossible: to write a book about the Death of the American Dream, which was the working title. I looked first for the answer at the Democratic National Convention in Chicago in 1968, but I didn't find it until 1971 at the Circus-Circus Casino in Las Vegas. Silberman was a good, smart sounding board for me. He believed in me and that meant a lot.

Interviewer: *Fear and Loathing in Las Vegas* is one of the great titles. Did that come to you suddenly or did someone suggest it?

Thompson: It's a good phrase. I noticed it last night in one of my letters from 1969. I'd never seen it before or heard it. People accuse me of stealing it from Kierkegaard or Stendhal. It just seemed like the right phrase. Once you get that kind of title down, once you see it on paper, there's no way you're going to change it.

Interviewer: What about Raoul Duke? How did the alter ego come about, and why and when?

Thompson: I started using him originally in what I wrote for *Scanlan's*. Raoul comes from Castro's brother, and Duke, God knows. I probably started using it for some false registration at a hotel. I learned at the Kentucky Derby that it was extremely useful to have a straight man with me, someone to bounce reactions off of. I was fascinated by Ralph Steadman because he was so horrified by most of what he saw in this country. Ugly cops and cowboys and things he'd never seen in England. I used that in the Derby piece and then I began to see it was an extremely valuable device. Sometimes I'd bring Duke in because I wanted to use myself for the other character. I think that started in *Hell's Angels* when I knew that I had to have something said exactly right and I couldn't get any of the fucking Angels to *say* it right. So I would attribute it to Raoul Duke.

Interviewer: Are the best things written under deadlines?

Thompson: I'm afraid that's true. I couldn't imagine, and I don't say this with any pride, but I really couldn't imagine writing without a desperate deadline.

Interviewer: Can you give an example?

Thompson: I'd agreed for a long time to write an epitaph for Allen Ginsberg. I was going to go to the memorial in Los Angeles. Then I thought it would be a good idea to have Johnny Depp go and deliver it. And he agreed. A bad deadline situation. What I wrote arrived just before Depp went on stage. He was calling me desperately from a payphone in the halls of the Wadsworth Theater in L.A. So Depp goes out and reads the thing which he just got a half hour before . . .

[Thompson asks us if we would like to see the result. He switches on the large screen TV set. Johnny Depp is introduced and speaks from behind a podium.]

This is . . . from the Good Doctor . . . it's hot off the presses: "Dr. Thompson sends his regrets. He is suffering from a painful back injury, the result of a fateful meeting with Allen Ginsberg three years ago at a sleazy motel in Boulder, Colorado, when the deceased allegedly flipped Thompson over his back and into an empty swimming pool after a public dispute about drugs. Ginsberg, sixty-nine at the time, accused Thompson, in court papers now permanently sealed because of the poet's recent death, of 'destroying my health and killing my faith in drugs.' Ginsberg was hysterically angry, sources said, because Thompson had deliberately and deceitfully lured him into an orgy of substance abuse and random sex that ended after three days and nights when the poet was crushed against the wall by a large woman on roller skates in an all-night Boulder tavern. Then admitted to a local hospital, treated for acute psychosis and massive smoke inhalation, Ginsberg also claimed that Thompson had 'maliciously destroyed my last chance for induction to the poetry hall of fame' by humiliating him in public, secretly injecting him with drugs and eventually causing him to be jailed for resisting arrest and gross sexual imposition. Dr. Thompson denied the charges, as always, and used the occasion of Ginsberg's death to denounce him as a dangerous bull-fruit with the brain of an open sore and the conscience of a virus. The famed author said that Ginsberg had come on to him one too many times, and was a hopeless addict. 'He got too strong with all that crank,' Thompson said. 'When he got that way, being in front of him was like being in front of the Johnstown Flood . . . Allen had magic,' he said. 'He could talk with the voice of an angel and dance in your eyes like a fawn. I knew him for thirty years and every time I saw him it was like hearing the music again.' Thompson added that he was shocked by Ginsberg's crude charges and violent behavior and would have the alleged court papers buried deeper than Ginsberg's spleen. 'He was a monster,' Thompson said. 'He was crazy and queer and small. He was born wrong and he knew it. He was smart but utterly unemployable. The first time I met him in New York he told me that even people who loved him believed he should commit suicide because things would never get better for him. And his poetry professor at Columbia was advising him to get a pro-frontal lobotomy because his brain was getting in his way. "Don't worry," I said "so is mine. I'm getting the same advice. Maybe we should join forces. Hell, if we're this crazy and dangerous, I think we might have some fun . . ." I spoke to Allen two days before he . . . died. He was gracious as ever. He said he'd welcome the Grim Reaper . . . because he knew he could get into his pants.' "

[After applause and questions as to how the audience in the theater reacted to the somewhat odd eulogy ("They liked it"), the interview was continued.]

Interviewer: The lead to *Fear and Loathing in Las Vegas,* "We were somewhere near Barstow on the edge of the desert when the drugs began to take hold . . . " When did you write that? Did you write that first?

Thompson: No, I have a draft . . . something else was written first, chronologically, but when I wrote that . . . well, there are *moments* . . . a lot of them happen when nothing else is going right . . . when you're being evicted from the hotel a day early in New York or you've just lost your girlfriend in Scottsdale. I know when I'm hitting it. I know when I'm on. I can usually tell because the copy's clean.

Interviewer: Most people . . . losing a girl in Scottsdale or wherever, would have a drink somewhere and go crazy. It must have something to do with discipline.

Thompson: I never sit down and put on my white shirt and bow-tie and black business coat and think, Well, now's the time to write. I will simply get into it.

Interviewer: Can you describe a typical writing day?

Thompson: I'd say on a normal day I get up at noon or one. You have to feel sort of overwhelmed, I think, to start. That's what journalism did teach me . . . that there is no story unless you've written it.

Interviewer: Are there any mnemonic devices that get you going once a deadline is upon you—sharpening pencils, music that you put on, a special place to sit?

Thompson: Bestiality films.

Interviewer: What is your instrument in composing? You are one of the few writers I know who still uses an electric typewriter. What's wrong with a personal computer?

Thompson: I've tried. There is too much temptation to go over the copy and rewrite. I guess I've never grown accustomed to the silent, non-clacking of the keys and the temporary words put up on the screen. I like to think that when I type something on the *[pointing to the typewriter],* when I'm finished with it, it's good. I haven't gotten past the second paragraph on a word processor. Never go back and rewrite while you're working. Keep on it as if it were final.

Interviewer: Do you write for a specific person when you sit down at that machine?

Thompson: No, but I've found that the letter form is a good way to get me going. I write letters just to warm up. Some of them are just, "Fuck you, I wouldn't sell that for a thousand dollars," or something, "Eat shit and die," and then send it off on the fax. I find the mood or the rhythm through letters, or sometimes either reading something or having something read— it's just a matter of getting the music.

Interviewer: How long do you continue writing?

Thompson: I've been known to go on for five days and five nights.

Interviewer: That's because of deadlines, or because you're inspired?

Thompson: Deadlines, usually.

Interviewer: Do you have music on when you write?

Thompson: Through all the Las Vegas stuff I played only one album. I wore out four tapes. The Rolling Stones' live album, called *Get Yer Ya-Ya's Out* with the in-concert version of "Sympathy for the Devil."

Interviewer: At one point, Sally Quinn of the *Washington Post* got after you for writing about specific events, but only 45 percent is actually the truth . . . how do you reconcile journalism with that?

Thompson: That's tough one. I have a hard time with that. I have from the start. I remember an emergency meeting one afternoon at Random House with my editor about *Fear and Loathing in Las Vegas*. "What should we tell the *New York Times*? Should it go on the fiction list or nonfiction?" In a lot of cases, and this may be technical exoneration, but I think in almost every case there's a tip-off that this is a fantasy. I never have quite figured out how the reader is supposed to know the difference. It's like if you have a sense of humor or not. Now keep in mind I wasn't trying to write objective journalism, at least not objective according to me. I'd never seen anybody, may-be David Halberstam comes closest, who wrote objective journalism.

Interviewer: You can write anywhere, can't you? Is there a place you prefer?

Thompson: Well, this is where I prefer now. I've created this electronic control center here.

Interviewer: If you could construct a writer, what attributes would you give him?

Thompson: I would say it hurts when you're right and it hurts when you're wrong, but it hurts a lot less when you're right. You have to be right in your judgments. That's probably the equivalent of what Hemingway said about having a shock-proof shit detector.

Interviewer: In a less abstract sense, would self-discipline be something you would suggest?

Thompson: You've got to be able to have pages in the morning. I measure my life in pages. If I have pages at dawn, it's been a good night. There is no art until it's on paper, there is no art until it's sold. If I were a trust-fund baby, if I had any income from anything else . . . even fucking disability from a war or a pension . . . I have nothing like that, never did. So, of course, you have to get paid for your work. I envy people who don't have to . . .

Interviewer: If you had that fortune sitting in the bank would you still write?

Thompson: Probably not, probably not.

Interviewer: What would you do?

Thompson: Oh . . . I'd wander around like King Farouk or something. I'd *tell* editors I was going to write something for them, and probably not do it.

Still Gonzo after All These Years

Jeff Kass / 2000

From *Rocky Mountain News,* December 31, 2000, pp. 7A, 11A, 13A.
Reprinted with the permission of the *Rocky Mountain News.*

Hunter S. Thompson is hot. Again.

The gonzo journalist, who has called Aspen home for some thirty years, is presiding over the publication of two books—*Fear and Loathing in America: The Brutal Odyssey of an Outlaw Journalist,* the second volume in a planned trilogy of his letters; and *Screwjack,* a rerelease of three short stories. He is on the cover of the latest *Paris Review,* the first living author to earn that honor.

The December 10 *New York Times Book Review* made him a cover boy as well, commissioning a drawing by Thompson's one-time book cohort, Ralph Steadman. And *Vanity Fair* excerpted several of his letters, along with the observation from Pulitzer Prize-winning journalist David Halberstam that the world needs Thompson's kind of instinct-based journalism.

All of this means a new round of attention is being heaped on Thompson, whose literary legend started in 1966 with *Hell's Angels* and continued to build with *Fear and Loathing in Las Vegas* and *Fear and Loathing: On the Campaign Trail '72.* Along the way, he has written for *Rolling Stone,* run for sheriff of Pitkin County, faced charges ranging from assault do driving while impaired, and survived decades of drug-and-alcohol-soaked escapades.

"I think that sometimes, when you're an American original, which Hunter is, it takes a while to notice you," said presidential scholar Douglas Brinkley, who has edited both of Thompson's letters compilations.

Thompson is sixty-three now and a grandfather, heading into his fourth decade of twisted celebrity. Age, however, hasn't softened him. His answer to published reports that he's given up drugs is off the record. Draw your own conclusions. He canceled a round of high-profile New York interviews and parties, including a dinner in his honor at the home of *Paris Review* editor

161

George Plimpton, because of a cold. And when the Denver *Rocky Mountain News* arranged to interview him at his Woody Creek home, about ten miles outside Aspen, the process turned into a thirty-six-hour endurance test.

While an appointment with Thompson may be helpful, it is not destiny. This is two stories-one about the peculiar ritual required to meet with Thompson, the other about the state of Hunter S. Thompson at the dawning of 2001, after all these years.

Monday, December 18, 11:30 A.M., Denver:
I buy Thompson a bottle of Chivas Regal. In a commemorative tin.

Hunter S. Thompson fires a shotgun at a propane canister, sending a huge fireball arcing toward a poster of Ronald Reagan dressed as a cowboy. A large photo of this scene hangs on a far wall of Thompson's kitchen. It is called "The Death Bomb," and it captures the concoction of violence, humor and politics that is pure Thompson.

"That is a risky mix that will sooner or later lead you to cross the wrong wires and get shocked, or even burned to a cinder," he writes in *Fear and Loathing in America.*

Thompson has captured world events, from presidential elections to Super Bowls, with a human flashbulb. But instead of relying on the photo to write his story, he has used the negative. The resulting image is always filled with silvery darkness and gross exaggeration. "That's the genius of Hunter," says Brinkley. "A gift of making his exaggeration seem more realistic than cold truth."

Thompson now has a two-and-a-half-year-old grandson, Will, born to Thompson's son, Juan, and his wife, Jennifer, who live in Denver. Will calls Thompson "Ace," at Thompson' suggestion. What does he like to do with his grandson?

"Drive heavy machinery," Thompson deadpans. He is proud of Will, touting his smarts. But he insists being a grandfather has not changed him. Thompson surely is heavier and slower-moving than the younger man portrayed on the cover of the letters book, but make no mistake. He remains a serial whiskey-sipper able to jerk reporters around like marionettes, and enthrall readers.

Noon Monday, somewhere in Golden, westbound on Interstate 70:
I reach Thompson by cellphone. He invites me to watch Monday Night Football *with him at his Woody Creek home. But no photographs, he warns. This is a problem. Photographer Steven R. Nickerson is en route, carrying three grapefruits from his eighty-five-year-old aunt as a present to Thompson.*

Thompson is holding court in his kitchen. He sits at the counter with a typewriter, a plate of oysters, and a large glass of Chivas on ice. Anita Bejmuk, his twenty-eight-year-old girlfriend, flits in and out, alternately putting out a bowl of grapes and kissing Thompson on the top of his head. He wears black and white batik-print cotton pants, after-ski boots and a pink button-down. He will later don a black leather Indianapolis Colts jacket (team owner Jim Irsay is a fan) to round out the ensemble before heading out. The television is tuned to ESPN sports highlights, and when Thompson means to turn up the volume and cannot instantly find the remote control, he lets out a series of desperate squawks that sounds like a pack of hysterical monkeys.

The kitchen is part office, part shrine to Thompson's career. It is a salon, as *The Paris Review* notes, "where people from all walks of life congregate in the wee hours for free exchanges about everything from theoretical physics to local water rights." The ranch house and rustic property Thompson calls a "fortified compound" is also worth $1.34 million, according to records. Copies of the drawing on the cover of the *New York Times Book Review* by Steadman, who has collaborated with Thompson for years, hang throughout the kitchen. Three whisks, a ceremonial gold key from his hometown of Louisville, Kentucky, a pair of handcuffs, a stethoscope, a thick chain and a dagger hang above the counter. Spectacles, a presidential tie clip, a photo of two lithe young women and a "Made in India" tag are all somehow attached to a large white lampshade. The top of the refrigerator is a sea of booze bottles. And in case anyone has mistaken the court of gonzo for an artsy LoDo coffeehouse, a homemade sign above one doorway reads, "Polo is my life."

6:30 P.M. Monday, down the road from Thompson's house at the Woody Creek Tavern:

We had expected to meet Thompson at the Woody Creek Tavern before heading to his house for the game. He is not here. So we decide to call and coyly say—surprise—that we just happen to be at the Tavern. How about we come up to the house for a chat? But a flurry of calls to his personal assistant reveals that Hunter is "down," i.e., asleep. He keeps the hours of a vampire.

Thompson describes his book of letters, which run from 1968 to 1976, as historical documents that reflect on a whacky period in history. "The '70s, it was unbelievable and wild. That was rock 'n' roll," Thompson says. "It would be hard to explain or even imagine now, because it was a different time." That history provides a lesson for readers, he says. "I'd like them to be afraid to know that their world can become like this; a jungle of savagery and violence and drugs," he says. "It was the '70s; this can happen to you."

Thompson doesn't expect a repeat of the '70s under President-elect Bush. But that doesn't mean he thinks matters will be fine. "Bush will bring in a plague of political maggots," he says. "He'll try to settle in in the next two years, but midterm elections will be so brutal; we're just taking a pause in the political brawl."

Thompson hasn't stopped his commentary, or his letter-writing. "I sent a letter to my agent the other day accusing him of negligence, fraud, malfeasance," he says. "Well, let's see, two and a half weeks later, he came up with $88,000." Agent Andrew Wylie said he did not have time to comment.

While the letters may be a historical window into the '60s and '70s, they also document Thompson's wit. Here, in a 1971 letter to his editor at Random House, Thompson explains his expenses for *Fear and Loathing in Las Vegas:* "No doubt some of these expenses are 'unreasonable.' Like renting a white Cadillac convertible and then soaking the (expletive) with the hard-crusted, sun-baked scum of 100 grapefruits and 2 dozen coconuts and 26 pounds of catsup and french fry residue—along with a layer or so of vomit and a goodly number of bad dings, dents and scrapes that were covered, thank Christ, by an extra $2 a day for total insurance. . . . Anyway, the point is that you can't send a man out in a (expletive) Pinto or a VW to seek out the American Dream in Las Vegas."

There is debate over how much fiction Thompson inserts in his writing. But he depends on real backdrops-the Vietnam War, the 1972 presidential campaign. "Muhammad Ali, one of my very few heroes, once took the time to explain to me that 'there are no jokes,' " Thompson writes in *Fear and Loathing in America.* " 'The truth is the funniest joke of all.' " Thompson knows he looks at life differently. "I see a sheen of darkness on things," he says, "which I think is kind of funny. But basically, I'm just a hired gun; a writer. The weird stuff goes with the territory. I just learned to think that way."

Thompson says his mad-cap career wouldn't have been for everyone. "I don't know if I would recommend it as a way of life," he says. "Don't try this at home. I've never advocated what I do, necessarily." If he hadn't found journalism, what would Thompson have become? "A tight end," he says, "a wide receiver for the 49ers. I had speed in those days."

9:30 P.M. Monday, at the Kenichi sushi restaurant, Aspen:
With chopsticks in hand amid crab rolls and tuna, we have taken to calling Thompson "our prey." We try some gonzo math: If he went to bed at 4 P.M. and

got ten hours of sleep, he should be up by 2 A.M. So we can go to bed at 10:30 P.M.,
wake up at 2 A.M., and call him. But Thompson won't want to see us the first
hour or so after waking up, so we could set our alarms for 4 A.M. Or we could
just wake up at 6 A.M., call him and say, "Hey, wanna grab breakfast?"
Meantime, we fear the grapefruits may freeze.

Thompson may seem annoyed by the latest round of publicity, which
sometimes means a half-dozen interviews a day. "It's supposed to sell books,
I guess," he says. He says he feels at home in New York City, but prefers to live
in Woody Creek for the wide-open space. "I get away from the mobs and
crowds," he says. Then, sarcastically, "This is a good place to hide."

Brinkley thinks Thompson's home in the Colorado mountains cements
his appeal. "In a sanitized age, there's something about a lone voice typing
away in the Rockies," he says. "There's a frontier, individualistic, maverick
streak, and a trickster in Hunter. Too often those mavericks are co-opted.
Hunter has stayed true to the beat of his own drum."

Tuesday, December 19, 6:07 A.M., Aspen:
Thompson's answering machine picks up. We leave a message. We know he
will not automatically answer the phone, even if he is awake. We call again at
7:30 A.M. Nothing. Finally, we connect with Thompson's longtime assistant, Debra
Fuller, at 9:15 A.M. She is confident the interview will happen.

Curtis Robinson, the Aspen-based publisher of the Mountain Gazette and
a self-described "Hunter crony," is credited in the letters book for
"brainstorming with Dr. Thompson and creating subheads." He is also our
guide through Thompson's world. Standing in the kitchen, Robinson is
partaking of a classic Woody Creek pastime: reading aloud one of Thompson's
works, this one a column from ESPN.com, one of Thompson's current gigs.

"George W. Bush is our President now, and you better start getting used
to it," Robinson reads in his southern drawl. "He didn't actually steal the
White House from Al Gore, he just brutally wrestled it away from him in the
darkness of one swampy Florida night. He got mugged, and the local cops
don't give a damn. Where did Al Gore think he was-in some friendly civics
class?"

There is talk of heading down to the Tavern, which caters to Thompson's
whims. Thompson calls ahead to get the lay of the land. "You see any pretty
little girls?" he asks with a fiendish laugh.

"There's three ugly guys at the end of the bar," the bartender replies over
the speakerphone.

2:45 P.M. Tuesday:
Fuller calls. She says Thompson is waking up. He will call us around 6 P.M. "Maybe Hunter will have masterminded a plan," Fuller says. Thompson finally calls at 6:25 P.M. He is ready, but not for the photographer. Nickerson must circle in a holding pattern at the Tavern.

Local newspaper clippings on Thompson read more like a petty rap sheet. "Writer Thompson Wounds Aide." "Writer Cleared in Shooting." "Thompson Fined for Stunt with Fire Extinguisher." "Hunter Thompson's DWI Settled; He says Agreement Serves as Restraint to 'Crooked Cops as Well as Dangerous Drunkards.' " Thompson says he was targeted in some of the cases. But the misadventures often find their way into his work. "That's not so bad, when you can get paid for that instead of getting put in prison," he says.

9:30 P.M. at Thompson's house in Woody Creek:
We finally interview Thompson, without the photographer. Afterward, he agrees to head down to the Tavern. He wears a safari hat with a badge on the front. The Tavern is empty and the chairs are stacked. The bartender is the only employee there. We find Nickerson, who has been waiting four and a half hours, in the back. Thompson arrives at 11:30 P.M. He lets Nickerson take pictures, but makes him ask permission before each frame.

Some critics point out that Thompson's "new works" are actually letters written years ago and the rerelease of earlier work. It doesn't bother Thompson. He says the critics aren't paying attention to his continuing work, which includes two books, *Generation of Swine: Tales of Shame and Degradation in the '80s* and *Better Than Sex: Confessions of a Political Junkie.* For his next trick, Thompson says he wants to work on the movie version of his 1998 book *The Rum Diary.*

But now it is near midnight, the deadline for our interview to end. We ask Thompson whether he is more proud of *Screwjack* or the letters. He bristles. "That's a question like a raccoon would ask," he says.

He is recovering from a cold, and a droplet of clear mucous hangs under his nostril. He wipes it away and goes through a coughing jag that he quiets with quick sips of different drinks, each a different color.

With that, the clock strikes 12. Thompson walks out of the Tavern, and into the night.

But his day is not over.

Fear and Writing

Seth Mnookin / 2000

From *Brill's Content,* December 2000/January 2001, pp. 116–19, 169–70.
Reprinted with the permission of Seth Mnookin.

Thirty years ago, Hunter S. Thompson, like H. L. Mencken before him, forced America to look at journalism as an organic literature. He wrote as if he had to bare his soul: The inherent chaos of his style (run-on sentences, bizarre addenda, personal digressions) and the breadth of his subject matter (the Kentucky Derby, presidential politics, orgiastic binges) made Thompson's writing as intimate as it was revelatory.

This month brings the publication of *Fear and Loathing in America,* the second volume in a planned trilogy of Thompson's letters. The seven hundred-plus-page book spans from 1968, one year after the release of *Hell's Angels,* a savage account of life with the legendary outlaw biker club, made Thompson an instant icon of America's edgy, subjective New Journalism, to 1976, by which time Thompson had literally become a cartoon character, the inspiration for Doonesbury's "Uncle Duke." In between, the 1971 publication of *Fear and Loathing in Las Vegas,* Thompson's quasi-fictional account of a drug-soaked adventure covering a motorcycle race and district attorneys' conference, confirmed Thompson as an American genius, a satirist and cultural critic to be compared with Mark Twain and Norman Mailer; and *Fear and Loathing: On the Campaign Trail '72,* Thompson's coverage of the 1972 presidential election, became a brilliant, if not baroque, display of political reportage. Reviewing *Las Vegas* in the *New York Times,* Crawford Woods wrote that Thompson had "written himself into the history of American literature in what I suspect will be a permanent way. . . . [H]e moves with the cool integrity of an artist indifferent to his reception." The cool artist, the fiery populist, the inimitable agitator and the drugged-out freak all live on in this new volume of letters, with writing as vivid as anything Thompson has ever produced.

It was Thompson—not Woodward and Bernstein, not Ben Bradlee, not James "Scotty" Reston nor Jimmy Breslin nor Mike Royko—who fueled my dreams of becoming a journalist. One story in particular sealed the deal: "The Great Shark Hunt," which appeared in *Playboy* in December 1974. I was sixteen when I first read it and have returned to it—as a way of recharging my professional batteries—at least two dozen times since then. It's a long, twisted tale that starts in the hours before dawn, when many of his stories begin, with Thompson staring at the ocean from a hotel room. Within a couple of pages, Thompson describes the adventure that will consume the rest of the narrative: He and his "technical advisor," Yail Bloor, need to escape from Cozumel, Mexico, without ponying up for any of their numerous hotel, rental car, or other sundry bills, all of which are left unpaid when the PR team for a local fishing tournament decides Thompson is "too weird" to be what he claims—a writer on assignment for America's premier men's magazine. In his relentless, jackhammer prose, Thompson uses himself as the fulcrum for a portrait of "white trash run amok on foreign shores; an appalling kind of story, but not without a certain human-interest quotient." Of course, Thompson did not journey to Mexico only to cover a sport-fishing event: A month earlier he had left fifty units of pure MDA, a hallucinatory tranquilizer, stashed in the shark pool of a Cozumel aquarium.

As journalism, "The Great Shark Hunt" falls far short of the sublime level Thompson achieves elsewhere; uncovering the depravity of rich, tasteless gringos isn't exactly a scoop. And the writing, although invigorating and often hysterically funny, isn't up there with Thompson's best. But the exuberance is infectious—the love of adventure palpable—and the realization that you could make a career seeking this kind of adventure sold me more than clandestine encounters with Deep Throat ever could.

And then there were the drugs. Thompson's clear-eyed debauchery, and the immediacy with which he described it, thrilled me, as it has many acolytes over the past three decades. As the writer Timothy Ferris, Thompson's former *Rolling Stone* colleague, says, "Hunter has remained out on the frontiers of extreme and indulgent behavior when most people either rode back or perished. In terms of drugs, and high-speed driving, and alcohol, and explosives, and firearms, in terms of that constellation of risk, very few people ever get into all of that in the first place. A vanishing few stay there and survive for decades. . . . Hunter's living for a lot of people now.

I think there's a certain vicarious identification, particularly [among] males, who think they would like to do what he does but can't."

Indeed, Thompson has long served as a kind of inspirational anti-hero, an embodiment of youthful disdain for the establishment. That Thompson's conclusions often feel so much fresher, so much more prescient and insightful than those of quotidian journalists, gives him a gravitas missing from the countless writers who seem to write about drugs for drugs' sake. Thompson's writing has a wild-edged brilliance and comes with the apposite implication that his reckless indulgence fueled, if not fermented, his best work. Take the ending of "The Great Shark Hunt," in which Thompson, ripped on a ferocious combination of acid, speed, cocaine, and booze, staggers through customs in San Antonio, Texas, leaving a trail of bright-orange amphetamine pills in his wake: "Well a lot of madness has flowed under our various bridges since then, and we have all presumably learned a lot of things. John Dean is in prison, Richard Nixon has quit and been pardoned by his hand-picked successor, and my feeling for national politics is about the same as my feeling for deep-sea fishing, buying land in Cozumel or anything else where the losers end up thrashing around in the water on a barbed hook."

As a teenage journalist-to-be, I wanted to write like Thompson: ellipses signifying the ever-charging quality of my thinking, capitalized words broadcasting Greater Truths. I wanted to live like Thompson: too many drugs, too much whiskey, too loud rock 'n' roll. I emulated his affectations, smoking Dunhill cigarettes—the brand Thompson still chain-smokes—with a small cigarette holder, which he has made his trademark. And for a long while I thought that drugs would help make me a great writer, would help me bypass the necessary years of labor and tortured revisions. It took years, and many painful lessons, to rid myself of this notion. But that's another story.

I was thinking about "The Great Shark Hunt"—about drugs and adventure and losers thrashing around on a hook—as I drove down Snowmass Mountain one moonless night this August on my way to Owl Farm, Thompson's myth-besotted compound outside Aspen. The trip had the feeling of a pilgrimage, but one that was coming a decade too late. I was going to Owl Farm to talk to Thompson about *Fear and Loathing in America,* and about his legacy, and about journalism, and I didn't know what to expect or even what I wanted to find. It's been years—decades, really—since Thompson has written anything that truly inspired me. Most contemporary

profiles of Thompson are made up of either rank lionization or
condescending mockery; for a generation of journalists raised on the
mythologies of Hunter S. Thompson, he is either a god or a hack, an idol or a
childish fancy. I wasn't sure which caricature I was hoping for: Would I prefer
to find Thompson a half-mad, incoherent buffoon? Or would I rather that
Thompson continue to confound expectations, a sixty-three-year-old
committed degenerate who's still the smartest guy in town?

Fear and Loathing in America provides as vital a snapshot of American
journalism in the '60s and '70s as any book ever will. As a historical
document, it offers copious raw material. Magazines were born—*Rolling
Stone, Scanlan's Monthly, Aspen Wallposter, True*—and many of those
magazines died. Journalism reached the peak of its power with the
resignation of Richard M. Nixon. Political movements, such as the hippie-,
biker-, and youth-fueled "Freak Power," erupted and then just as suddenly
flamed out. And Thompson was in the midst of it all, squabbling with Jann
Wenner, *Rolling Stone's* publisher and one of Thompson's earliest and most
ardent boosters, over money and insurance; running for sheriff of Colorado's
Pitkin County on a Freak Power ticket; threatening to sue the *Washington
Post's* Sally Quinn for having flippantly misquoted him in *Esquire* to the
effect that "at least 45%" of what he writes is true.

But *Fear and Loathing in America* is more than a document of the times.
Thompson put as much energy and care into his epistolary efforts as he did
into his journalism (and, with an eye toward the future, saved carbon copies
of his correspondence). And although Thompson's prose often seems to be
spun from whole cloth, a kind of primal outpouring of twisted genius, the
letters show just how much the originator of Gonzo journalism—who once
professed that his aim was "to buy a thick notebook and write everything
down as it happened, and then send it in, unedited"—struggled with his
craft. In a long 1970 missive to Jim Silberman, his editor at Random House,
Thompson wrestles with a follow-up assignment to *Hell's Angels.* In the letter,
Thompson tries to work through some of his ideas about journalism and his
own craft. "I've had a lot of trouble with the notion of mixing up a fictional
narrative with a series of straight journalistic scenes," he writes. "I'm
convinced it can work, and I've done it before, but the problem now is that
I'm so self-conscious about the mixture that I can't let it work. The fiction
part strikes me as bulls–t and the journalism seems dated and useless [. . .]

It's embarrassing to think that I can't compete, in book form, with cop-outs like [the films] *Medium Cool* and *Easy Rider* . . . but the compulsion to write something better and more real than those things has left me with what amounts to nothing at all—except a bundle of weird article carbons."

Another letter to Silberman, written a year later, contains what seems to be *Fear and Loathing in America*'s biggest revelation: that Thompson was not on drugs during either the "reporting" or writing of *Las Vegas,* a book with this legendary opening line: "We were somewhere around Barstow on the edge of the desert when the drugs began to take hold." The book goes on to describe the contents of a car trunk filled with "two bags of grass, seventy-five pellets of mescaline, five sheets of high-powered blotter acid, a salt shaker half full of cocaine, and a whole galaxy of multi-colored uppers, downers, screamers, laughers . . . and also a quart of tequila, a quart of rum, a case of Budweiser, a pint of raw ether, and two dozen amyls." In the June 1971 letter, Thompson writes that he is depressed that Silberman says he can tell the book's drug use is a contrived pose: "All I ask is that you keep your opinions on my drug-diet for that weekend to yourself. As I noted, the nature (& specifics) of the piece has already fooled the editors of *Rolling Stone* [where the piece originally ran as a two-part series]. They're absolutely convinced, on the basis of what they've read, that I spent my expense money on drugs and went out to Las Vegas for a ranking freakout. Probably we should leave it this way; it makes it all the more astounding, that I could emerge from that heinous experience with a story."

It's unlikely that these letters are the ones that will receive the most attention. The ferocious back-and-forths with Wenner will interest gossip columnists more, and the correspondences with Jimmy Carter and Pat Buchanan will interest the history buffs. But it's Thompson's letters about the writing life that the myth of Hunter S. Thompson as a drugged wild child, vomiting out perfect prose. In fact, he has always been more of a workman—and stylist—than he is given credit for. While still in his twenties he would sit at his typewriter and copy pages from Hemingway and Faulkner and Fitzgerald word for word, just to get the feel for the rhythms of the language. He still refuses to write on a word processor, because he believes that computers divorce writers from their labor.

It was that last letter to Silberman that Thompson was reading when I first walked into his kitchen that moonless night in August. *Fear and Loathing in*

America was scheduled to be released in less than four months, and
Thompson was still culling the volume's final selections. Marysue Rucci,
Thompson's editor at Simon & Schuster (and a friend of mine—she was my
entrée into Owl Farm), was there, as was Douglas Brinkley, the University of
New Orleans historian who was overseeing the project. Anita Bejmuk, one of
Thompson's two full-time assistants, was serving oysters and booze, and a
couple of local Thompson aficionados were making suggestions and filming
the proceedings. The television was turned to ESPN, and taped to each side
of the set was a hand-lettered sign that read "No Music + Bad TV = Bad
Mood + No Pages." Thompson's house is a kind of living museum, with
faxes and postcards and photographs and scribblings attached to every
available surface. As I walked in Thompson was saying, about that day's
squabble with Jann Wenner, "I'm clearly the most reasonable person, maybe
in the nation, to deal with." (Thompson and Wenner communicate like an
old married couple, bickering with a fond familiarity. The next night,
Thompson cracked that Wenner's autobiography could be titled *I Screwed
Them All.*)

Thompson was wearing an Indianapolis Colts jersey with his name on the
back, a gift from owner Jim Irsay, who is one of the writer's ardent fans.
There's something almost gentle about the six-foot-three Thompson in his
home, framed by a lampshade strung with reading glasses and a wall adorned
with pincers he used to grab objects following a hip replacement a couple of
years ago. Thompson stays for the most part perched in one chair facing the
television and is always swaying and bobbing, his arms constantly swimming
through the air. He's usually surrounded by an array of remote controls:
for the TV, the air conditioner, the stereo. As I quickly learned, being around
Thompson can be infantilizing to both parties. He has come to expect that
his needs are attended to, and most people—myself included—seem inclined
to go along with his demands rather than risk an outburst.

That first night, everyone took turns reading Thompson's letters out loud.
I didn't say much, and I couldn't stop thinking I'd come late to the party. I quit
drinking and drugging years ago and knew that Thompson would spend the
weekend smoking hash, snorting coke, and drinking Chivas Regal. Instead of
boozing with my onetime idol, I'd be sipping seltzer water and soft drinks. The
night ended at about 4 A.M. Thompson wanted to go up the road for a swim.

The next night everyone was a little more at ease. We started earlier—at
about 7—and at 10, Brinkley, Rucci, Thompson, and I went for burgers at the

Woody Creek Tavern. By now Thompson seemed to have decided that I was acceptable company, and at one point he asked me when I was going to interview him, adding, "Let's get this thing over with." I began by asking Thompson about his legacy, which is not a subject he likes to talk about, and when I pressed throughout the night, he would either ignore me, stop talking, or whack his fist against the table. "I knew this question was going to come right up," he said the first time I asked him about his influence on journalism. "I don't think I'm the one who should be assessing my influence. More-qualified people have." Later he turns the question back on me: "It's assumed that I have had a large impact or influence, is it not?"

Of course, Thompson is not unaware of his impact or his image. When I ask him about publishing his letters, he says he knows that writers don't usually get epistolary retrospectives until they're dead. (Implicit, at least to me, is the corollary: and not writing anymore.) It reminded me what my friends asked when they heard I was going to visit Thompson: Is he a brain-dead acid casualty? But Thompson is not a sorry product of the drug era. He seems as smart—and as twisted—as ever, and, although he's not pounding the pavement or on the campaign trail, he still writes a lot, churning out letters and occasional pieces for national magazines. "A lot of outlaws have been killed," he says." I probably should have been killed a while ago. I would have been a lot more popular. . . . I kind of feel a little bit like the Rolling Stones. I don't think they thought they'd be on the road in 2000."

Still, Thompson's best Gonzo journalism seems to be in his past. Part of that has to do with the circus that results when Thompson makes one of his rare appearances outside Colorado. "I've never quite figured out a way to capitalize on or enjoy fame," he says. "I can't resent and curse it. I'm not sure what to do about it." It's a hackneyed line, but there's truth in it. Thompson never got rich off his work and for the most part stays secluded in Woody Creek, shunning the groupies and rubberneckers who flock to his occasional readings. When I asked him whether he considered going out and covering this year's presidential race, he said, "When I went out it was a job, and this time it would have been sort of an appearance . . . Once I signed more autographs in a room than the candidate, then I got a little edgy about it."

A couple of weeks later, I called Thompson and asked him about the letter to Silberman in which he says he wasn't on drugs during the conception of *Las Vegas*. "People make too much of it," he said. "At that time, it wasn't outlandish to sample even the drugs that I mention. It actually seemed quite logical: We lived in a drug culture, so if you go to Las Vegas, let's have some drugs. Now it would be like you had rabies."

Indeed, the drug use in *Las Vegas*—and in all of Thompson's work—does seem almost preordained. It's part of what makes *Las Vegas* a vital historical document as well as one of the best pieces of writing in the past thirty years. The world Thompson was writing about was confused and often illogical. "Drug use, in a way, was about controlling your environment. That's always been important to me."

"I think he's a very dangerous man. We're all afraid of him. He's irresponsible and reckless as a human being, and so we all live in fear," says Walter Isaacson, the managing editor of *Time* magazine, about the man he refers to as Doctor Thompson. Isaacson met Thompson a couple of years ago and sometimes tries to persuade him to write for his magazine. Isaacson has succeeded only once, in 1997, when Thompson wrote "Doomed Love at the Taco Stand: Fear and Loathing in Hollywood" for *Time.* Isaacson's delight at Thompson's antics is as pure as any fan's. Talking of "Fear and Loathing in Hollywood," Isaacson describes the scene that unfolded at deadline: "He showed up with the piece and with Johnny Depp and with a bottle of whiskey, and perhaps some other substances that I made clear weren't appropriate for my office. Soon there was a crowd, and Johnny Depp was reading the piece out loud while a dozen staffers crowded around and the good Doctor was playing air drums to accent the rhythm of his writing as Depp was reading it. And then Lyle Lovett somehow showed up because he was part of the good Doctor's entourage, and it was a totally surreal closing night."

And like any fan, Isaacson wishes there were more new material coming out of Owl Farm. "I'd love to see what happened if he dove into the Net," Isaacson says. "He writes off the top of his head in a sort of electric way, and the best dose of Doctor Thompson is unfiltered, which is what the Web is all about." I had asked Thompson about the Web when I was at Woody Creek, and he blanched. "It seems to me like more of a—and this is simplistic—but more of a 'me, me, me, me' thing," he says. "Like a teenager, you know, self-centered. And you don't really learn much about the subject . . . . I'm sure people got tired of some of the 'me, me' in my campaign coverage, but it was important. It was a building block of the story." So Isaacson makes do with the missives that sputter out from his fax machine. "The joy of trying to get him to do a story is mainly the faxes back and forth, or mainly forth. It's just this full-throttle thinking," Isaacson says. "If he could just put into print what he's able to put into his faxes, he'd be more productive."

In a way, that's what Thompson is doing with these volumes of letters. Since he was a teenager, Thompson has treated writing as his life's work, and he says there's a certain "poetic justice coming home to roost" that he's getting paid for writing he did thirty years ago. "Writing letters was not going to pay the rent back then. And little did I know that it would be paying the rent now . . . . I think [it's] a wonderful thing . . . . I'm a workman. I've always been a workman. I think God is a workman."

Thompson and Rucci and Brinkley finished editing down the final selection of letters just before 2:30 in the morning on my second night in Woody Creek. There was some champagne, some absinthe (sent from Europe by Johnny Depp), and I raised a glass of water and then drove off. Hunter S. Thompson is a sybarite, and a drug fiend, but above all he's a workman. It's what I didn't understand when I was growing up; somehow I thought Thompson's genius was connected to drugs. I was confused when dropping acid (or shooting dope, for that matter) didn't have the same effect on me. "Drugs snatch us out of everyday reality," Octavio Paz wrote in *Alternating Current,* "blur our perception, alter our sensations, and, in a word, put the entire universe in a state of suspension." Very few people can translate this new reality into literature. Thompson is one of a handful of American writers over the past century who have pulled off the feat.

Bedtime for Gonzo

J. Rentilly / 2003

From *Razor Magazine,* January 2003, pp. 76–80. Reprinted with the permission of J. Rentilly.

The first time you speak with Hunter S. Thompson, he's got a bad case of gas and he's not shy about letting you know it. Non-verbally. It's 4:30 in the afternoon and he's waiting for his breakfast, trying to wake up. He's already got hashish on his mind, and blow-up dolls, too. He wants to know your preference: old-fashioned inflatable—the $19.95 cheapie with the triad of donut-shaped pleasure ports, or the $5000 customized latex Real Doll with Barbie-hair pubes, heat-able pink parts, and Sandy Duncan eyes that throw back in the sockets when you fuck it hard. On the phone from Owl Farm, his acres-large ranch in Woody Creek, Colorado, just south of Aspen, the sixty-three-year-old Thompson comes exactly as advertised: a grouchy, mumbling, flatulent, Dunhill-smoking, Patron-gulping chemical laboratory who plays disoriented when it suits him, maintains a nocturnal lifestyle, and gets by despite—or because of—the "foul and odd temperament" to which he confesses this afternoon. This is the writer, after all, who once suggested that the only way to kill the pain of being a man is to become a beast.

Then there's the second phone call, the one that comes pre-dawn from Thompson's live-in companion, Anita Bejmuk, who tends to the writer's personal, professional, and pharmaceutical affairs. "Taking care of me is a job that requires a helluva lot sometimes," says Thompson. "And I try to take care of her, too." Early this morning, Bejmuk announces that Thompson will be ready to talk later in the day. The day passes without a word from Thompson. So does the next. Thompson is promised, then fails to appear. Icons, apparently, are frequently indisposed. And then you finally get him on the line.

JR: Hello, Mr. Thompson. How are you?
HST: I'm not done waking up and I'm not very, uh, awake and I'm watching this World Series game.

JR: Is this a bad time for you?

HST: Uh, it's not a good time. I don't really feel very smart. But what do you want to talk about?

JR: I want to talk about the new book, *Kingdom of Fear,* and . . .

HST: I tell you, I could do this a lot better if, uh . . . (belch) . . . excuse me . . . goddammit . . . if I could wake up and feel a little better. I'm not feeling very well.

JR: You want to pick another time?

HST: Let's say something like . . . Oh, I don't know . . .

And suddenly you feel it all going south again, and fast. Thompson wants to finish the ball-game, and you figure after that it'll be something else and then some other thing again. With deadline approaching, you're left to ponder the possibilities of writing a story about Hunter S. Thompson, father of Gonzo journalism, the legendary counterculture, anti-authoritarian figure, who has forged a career and a reputation guzzling drugs, juggling broads, rattling cages, naming names, shucking convention and etiquette, digging up bodies, and shitting on all things sanctimonious and false in seminal works of non-fiction like *Fear and Loathing in Las Vegas, Fear and Loathing: On the Campaign Trail '72,* and *Hell's Angels,* and in unrefined, hard-boiled fiction tomes like *The Rum Diary* and *The Curse of Lono.*

If deadline comes to shove, you can always make easy jokes about how Woody Creek, Colorado, is eight thousand feet above sea level and so Thompson, the notorious, self-professed dope fiend, is always quite literally "high." You can paint a picture of Thompson's famous peacocks roaming freely around Owl Farm amid the buckshot. Thompson, an avid gun collector, occasionally unloads into the nighttime, an existential acting-out abetted by artillery. You can report on the giant American flag Thompson says hangs from his front porch to keep away the Nazis and—simultaneously, perhaps ironically—the Wagner music he claims to blare into the wilderness through a sound system that boasts more than eighty speakers. You can pontificate on the pages Thompson has recently written, wherein he refers to the current Presidential administration as The Fourth Reich run by "a goofy child-President," and wherein he laments that we "are about to start paying for the sins of (our) fathers and forefathers, even if they were innocent . . ." and that "we are down to our last cannonball."

But none of it's right. None of it could be right. At least not entirely right. Trying to imagine the "real" Hunter S. Thompson is like trying to imagine the American Dream itself, which Thompson in his writing has alternately embraced, defined, redefined, and utterly annihilated. In Thompson's new book, *Kingdom of Fear: Loathsome Secrets of a Star-Crossed Child in the Final Days of the American Century,* a collection of some of his most recent and perhaps greatest writing, Thompson describes himself as "a professional journalist and a writer of books about life in the weird lane."

Maybe. But beneath the gruff, inaccessible exterior—the beast that conceals the pain of being the man—Thompson hides a sincere and noble heart, even if it is dosed with a bit of Percocet. The truth about Thompson: he is a Romantic in the grand, old-school tradition of the word. A man who in his writing and his lifestyle has perpetuated a larger than life persona, a loud and sometimes fearsome, apocalyptic but ultimately truthful voice and attitude and philosophy. Like Lord Byron or William Blake before him— political activists, incorrigible in their passions, who pushed life to the outer limits where most people become terribly uncomfortable or at least very, very afraid.

As Thompson writes in *Kingdom of Fear.* "It may be that every culture needs an Outlaw God of some kind, and maybe this time around I'm it. Who knows?" *Razor* found out when Thompson finally opened up during a savage journey to the heart of the American Dream.

JR: You're a tough man to track down. I was beginning to think you just don't like doing interviews. That couldn't be the case, could it?
HST: Oh, no, no. I'd just rather not do some sort of negative junk, but uh . . . I don't know. I'm just not in a very . . . I'm not in an articulate mood. My tongue hurts and it's hard to talk.

JR: When we first spoke a couple weeks ago, you were fairly preoccupied with blow-up dolls and hashish. Are these truly at the forefront of your thinking these days, or is that just a way to tell a journalist to get fucked?
HST: Oh, I'm always preoccupied with hashish. And what else?

JR: Blow-up dolls.
HST: At any given moment, blow-up dolls can come up on my mind. I think I might've been writing about blow-up dolls when we were talking.

JR: In your new book, *Kingdom of Fear,* you write bout "adding up the score" on your life. I thought that kind of self-inventory and soul-searching was best left for old guys and dying men.

HST: I don't know. I've been adding up the score all along. I've been keeping score.

JR: What is the score for Mr. Thompson?

HST: Well, I'm comfortable. Yeah. See, I noticed something being forced to put something on paper for this book for what's been almost two straight years now. Try being my age and being forced, more or less, to take your life for—not for granted, but—the confrontation that it's been. Anyone in their sixties or seventies—hell, anyone in their forties—has to confront themselves I suppose. But this writing—this book—is doing it intentionally. This is a forced march through everything in my life. I have storyboards all over my house with big pictures of me in different times of my life. I'm so tired of myself. I'm having to explain all these pictures, all these episodes in my life. I have to explain me somehow.

JR: Does mortality have much to do with what you're up to in a day? *Kingdom of Fear* is taking account of where you've been and what you've done.

HST: That's not my inclination. But it was the publisher's. Things like memoirs always seem easy. Everybody's got a couple good stories about themselves, don't they? But the unsettling part of this is the examination of your life, the real voluntary articulation of it, talking about people, talking about things you've done and maybe the wrong way. It's always been my cover, keeping it all under tight wraps and only explaining myself when I really had to.

JR: In your writing you've always seemed like a man who has moved straight ahead. It must be strange looking back as much as you do in the new book.

HST: Well, what I've noticed is that, uh, I'm either the most steadfast, reliable man, with a natural level of integrity and loyalty or . . . I guess that sounds like gibberish, but you know what I'm saying: I'm either good, wise, brave, strong, all that. Or I'm just the stupidest man who's ever lived. I haven't learned anything since I was fifteen years old. My positions and my basic stances, my, my . . . Fuck, I need help . . .

JR: Your values, principals.

HST: Yeah, I can't see that I've really changed anything. I guess a man likes to think he's changed, but I just don't see it. I don't change much.

JR: You write a lot about your juvenile delinquent childhood, about pushing a Federal mailbox into the path of an oncoming school bus and other sundry peccadilloes from your youth. In the new book, you write: "I was cursed with a dark sense of humor that made many adults afraid of me, for reasons they couldn't quite put their fingers on."

HST: Yep.

JR: How do you think that's informed your writing, being a rotten kid?

HST: Oh, I think it's a pretty strong factor. Gave me a kind of, I don't know, an anti-authoritarian kind of a position. Which I think has worked out pretty well for me.

JR: Anti-authority? Yeah, that seems to have panned out for you.

HST: Yeah. I've done all right, considering you can get put up against the wall and executed at any minute in this country for so much less than I've done in my lifetime.

JR: Hunter Thompson might get away with it, but most of us don't dare question authority too much these days.

HST: Yeah. This is turning into one of the most dangerous regime governments in the world—anywhere in the world—since Adolf Hitler.

JR: It is a frightening time. I'm thirty-one. I've got two little boys. Just getting through a day is scary sometimes.

HST: Well, that is . . . That would be, uh . . . Man, I don't envy you where you're at. See, you're part of the first generation that's going to do worse than your parents did. And your kids, probably worse than you. I would be feeling very unhappy if I were thirty-one and had two kids.

JR: You say we're having kind of a "national nervous breakdown." You've referred to yourself as Dr. Thompson. Is there a prescription for this?

HST: Well, I usually have one. I don't have one right now. We're obviously going in the wrong direction right now. And, uh, I go back and forth between wondering if there really are more Nazi bastards out there now on any city block in America than there used to be. And I wonder: if everybody in America voted would we have the same government we have now? I have a feeling that barely a 50 percent turnout at the polls is a large factor in who ends up controlling the government.

JR: Not being able to count those ballots doesn't help, either, does it?
HST: These Nazis have created this system. They've very slowly built a very, uh, relentless, merciless system.

JR: By "Nazis," are we talking about the current administration only, or the Republican Party in general? That may be an important distinction.
HST: Nah, we're talking about . . . Well, Yeah, it's been a Republican fact of life since, uh, Nixon I guess. Reagan is really where it started. Those same people were in there with Nixon and Reagan, some of them. And they brought Reagan in; he didn't bring them in. That's where it's all began.

JR: Reagan actually said in 1985 that "this may be the generation that will have to face the end of the world."
HST: Yep.

JR: I know you're no fan of Baby Bush, but I have to ask: Do you think the enemy is any more clearly defined or identifiable today than it was in the 1970s?
HST: Are we talking about the sand niggers over there or the Nazis at home? Look out for all of them.

JR: We used to be told that there was nothing to fear but fear itself. Now I wonder, what isn't there to be afraid of?
HST: What isn't there? Well, let's see . . . Well, you can watch the World Series without fear of who's going to win or lose the games. Uh . . . No, every development internationally, in politics or in this continuing war, is nothing to be optimistic about. I don't see anything to be optimistic about. I'm not sure what all these politicians are afraid of. I know what you're afraid of, what I'm afraid of. But what could they possibly be afraid of when they spend all their time talking about having total war everywhere?

JR: What do you think about war in Iraq? Is sending off 200,000 boys with rifles really the answer to our international problems and the victory to this so-called War on Terror?

HST: It'll help us out, sure. There's real strategy there, probably. I've been giving this some thought. The basic reasoning for this foreign war fetish is, basically, it's better to fight a war on the other side of the world.

JR: Don't shit where you eat, in other words.

HST: Yeah. That's kind of a cynical way to explain it. It doesn't really cheer the people whose sons and daughters and parents and all that are routinely butchered over there, but it is over there.

JR: At least it's not our skyscrapers coming down.

HST: (laughs) Yeah. Right.

JR: According to some of the books you wrote in the '70s, we're on borrowed time anyway. In *Fear and Loathing in Las Vegas,* you suggested we wouldn't even be around in 2000.

HST: Well, boy, what I did say is "there will be no year 2000 . . ."

JR: ". . . Not as we know it."

HST: Well, that's almost right on, right there.

JR: Did you really see any of this coming—the Elections, 9/11, this utter madness?

HST: Well, yeah. I mean I'm not some kind of a warlock. I don't get my wisdom from piles of dead animals that I put up in the kitchen area. There's just a terrible logic to it all.

JR: The subtitle of *Kingdom of Fear* references the end of the American Century. The century closed . . .

HST: The century's done. It ended with the election (in 2000). The numbers are right in front of our face. So the century's over. All done. But boy, I didn't expect the door to slam shut like a bank vault, like some mechanical door. Just a giant clang gone slamming shut on us. That's what the book's about. It's been kind of necessary to define wherever the American Dream was at the end of the last century. Because it's certainly not going to be like it was not ever again.

JR: I can't even imagine how to describe the American Dream right now. Can you?

HST: Uh . . . I don't know. It's hard to . . . It's kind of a naïve faith that talent . . . God, this is a horrible conversation for me to be dealing with right now . . . You must have a naïve faith that right will prevail, that it could succeed.

JR: It's faith, ultimately.

HST: Naïve faith.

JR: Relationships sometimes take that kind of faith, too. You've had some amazing friendships in your life. You've said that your "most amazing talent is your ability to choose good friends."

HST: I don't know if I'm deserving of it, but I do have some good friends. That's one of the most valuable things in life. Unimaginable pleasure I get from the friends I have.

JR: I bring up your friendships because, very prematurely and unexpectedly, many of them are slipping away. Ginsberg left us a few years ago. Warren Zevon is one of the great, underrated musical artists ever, and a good friend of yours, and he could very well be dead by the time this interview is published.

HST: Warren is what being a good friend is all about. Oh, yeah. Warren has flown across the country at his own expense to back me on political rallies and all that. He makes public stands on issues that I've chosen to be involved in myself. He's high risk. You can count on Warren. I already miss him. He is hanging on, I guess, I just treat it like a bad phase, you know. He may go tomorrow, I don't know. It's a day-to-day basis for all of us. I'm very amazed that I'm still bumming around and having a good time.

JR: I think you sell yourself short when you refer to yourself as "an elderly dope fiend off in the wilderness by himself." You've put out this image that betrays the heart you truly hold.

HST: Well, I always try to understand how somebody's parents would look at me. For example, Anita's mother when she heard that her daughter went off with a truly dangerous brute. It would not be my first desire or choice to have my daughter run off into the mountains with a . . . I don't know, what would you call me, Anita?

Anita: *A teenage girl trapped in the body of an elderly dope fiend.*

JR: At sixty-three, do you still get as loaded as you used to? You've been rattling around with a bottle of Percocet as long as we've been on the phone. But have you slowed it down a little?
Anita: *(laughs hysterically)*

JR: What's in the pillbox for today's consumption?
HST: Oh, I'm not called a doctor for nothing.
Anita: *Fresh-squeezed orange or grapefruit juice every morning. And his cholesterol is better than his doctor's.*

JR: Excellent. Is there anything to which we should "just say no"?
Anita: *Warm beer.*
HST: Cheap whiskey. Uh, let's see, I still enjoy a visit with just about anything.

JR: I'd like to close by talking about something from the new book that's really stuck with me the last couple days: "Morality is temporary. Wisdom is permanent."
HST: What the hell is that?

JR: You wrote it.
Anita: *Yeah, you did.*
HST: Yeah. I don't really know how to respond to that.

JR: Can you give me an example of what you mean by that?
HST: Did I really say that?
Anita: *Yeah.*

JR: You wrote it. It's in the book.
HST: Fuck, man.

JR: I know. Sometimes . . .
HST: Let's see, I guess morality is present-tense thinking. It's current. Wisdom is the luxury, perhaps, of hindsight.

JR: It's that, "if only I'd done it another way." Is that wisdom?
HST: A lot of it is exactly that. Wisdom is more like, "Jesus Christ, that was dumb." You do something and you know you shouldn't have. You should've

stuck with your instinct. Basically, that's one of my most important things, going on instinct.

JR: Is there anything you'd take back?
HST: Take back?

JR: Anything you'd do differently? Regrets, I mean.
HST: Oh. The question is: would you do it again? That's the reality. You can underline that one. Would you do it again? That's the test, maybe the final test, looking back on anything. I've been saying that for many years. That's the aging fruit of the aging person. That's about the only rule I've found that I can put on things is that question: would you do it again? Let's try one right now. Let's see, uh . . . I don't know you that well, your station in life . . .

JR: Something from my life?
HST: An example for you. See, I know nothing about you or what your proclivities are.

JR: See, we could go very basic and ask "would I get married again?"
HST: That's a good one. Would you?

JR: Yes.
HST: Okay. Okay, that's a good one. But when I ask, "would you do it again?" it comes with a rule. The rule is "would you do it again, not knowing what you know now, not knowing what the outcome will be." There's none of that. You know what you know now and life's a safer bet all the way around. So you've got to ask the question like this, "would you get married again even if it meant getting beat bloody three times on various occasions by the police?" or something like that.

JR: I'll just go on the record and say that I'd get married again no matter what it took. I've got a good woman and I'm a very, very lucky man.
HST: Oh, well you are blessed. Love. That's a very valuable thing.

JR: Yeah.
HST: But who knows what might happen, you know some kind of a nightmare might come along . . .
Anita: *Hunter!*

HST: Oh, never mind. (laughs) I tell you, my lifestyle, I tend to make strange, whiskey decisions and I would hate to lose my faith that I can keep doing what I've been doing all my life. But not everything pays off immediately. I'm often flogged. Risk is not just a four-letter word. It's something where bad things can happen. Love is like that. You get behind the wheel at 150 miles per hour in the night. Things might happen there that wouldn't happen, maybe, if you were at 75 miles per hour.

JR: Sometimes it's just waking up in the morning.
HST: Yeah. You can't expect everything to go all right, but it all does balance. I just look at it like this: if I wouldn't do it again, it means that I wasted that time.

JR: Doesn't seem like you've wasted a lot of time in your life.
HST: Oh, I feel like I've wasted a lot of moments. Yeah. I'm a pretty horrid taskmaster. I've been to jail a few times. I'd do that again. There are probably a few things I would rather not do again, but overall if I've got the feeling that I'd take something back or that I'm full of regret over something, it means that I was wrong. It's like with Alcoholics Anonymous and you have to confess you're a hopeless alcoholic for the rest of your life and that your life was wrong for as long as you remember and that it always will be. You have to say you're wrong, that your life was fucked up all the way along.

JR: You've never been through AA.
HST: No. But I get asked all the time to help people through. I've been personally involved here and there, counseling people who are prone to turning their backs on whole periods of their lives. You can't throw yourself on the mercy of other cripples who are also living wrong. You just can't do that. I've had a couple moments where I've wished I never started drinking gin or that it was a terrible mistake to get into drugs, but I don't regret it. I've occasionally had some difficult times with them, but that just goes with the territory. Yeah, this is how I look at it: if it produces pages, it has to be right.

JR: That sounds like a final word.
HST: I see it like this: whatever you're doing, even if it's crazy, if you get paid for it, well that can't be insane. There's insane that's functional, and there's insane that's dysfunctional.

Hunter S. Thompson

John Glassie / 2003

From *Salon.com*, February 3, 2003. Reprinted with permission of John Glassie.

He calls himself "an elderly dope fiend living out in the wilderness," but Hunter S. Thompson will also be found this week on the *New York Times* bestseller list with a new memoir, *Kingdom of Fear: Loathsome Secrets of a Star-Crossed Child in the Final Days of the American Century.*

Listening to his ragged voice, there is some sense that Thompson, now sixty-five, has reined in his outlaw ways, gotten a little softer, perhaps a little more gracious now that he's reached retirement age. "I've found you can deal with the system a lot easier if you use their rules," he says. "I talk to a lot of lawyers."

But do not be deceived. In *Kingdom of Fear* and in a telephone interview with *Salon* from his compound in Aspen, Colorado, Thompson did what he's always done: speak the truth about American society as he sees it, without worrying much about decorum. "Who *does* vote for these dishonest shitheads?" he writes, referring to the people currently occupying the white House. "They are the racists and hate mongers among us—they are the Ku Klux Klan. I piss down the throats of these Nazis."

That's his enduring attitude in this new age of darkness: a lot more loathing than fear.

The godfather of gonzo believes America has suffered a "nationwide nervous breakdown" since 9/11, and as a result is compromising civil liberties for what he calls "the illusion of security." The compromise, he says, is "a disaster of unthinkable proportions" and "part of the downward spiral of dumbness" he believes is plaguing the country.

While the country's spinning out of control, Thompson says his own lifestyle has been a model of consistency. He still does whatever the hell he wants. In fact, his new book was *supposed* to be a "definitive memoir of his

187

life," a long look back by the man who rode with the Hell's Angels, who experienced the riots at the 1968 Democratic Convention, and who has smoked more cigarettes, driven more fast cars, fired more weapons, and done more drugs than most living people, let alone most living authors. But the book is much more than memoir.

Thompson has long been an outspoken and vigorous champion of civil liberties, at least since a well-publicized 1990 case in which he was charged with sexual and physical assault and possession of illegal drugs—charges that were ultimately dropped due to an illegal search and seizure.

Of course, the writer has distrusted power all his life, and it may come as no surprise that he now believes the administration is "manufacturing" the Iraqi threat for its own political gain and the economic gain of the "oligarchy" (read: the military-industrial complex).

Perhaps Thompson's most disturbing charge is aimed at the American people—only half of whom exercise their right to vote. "The oligarchy doesn't need an educated public. And maybe the nation does prefer tyranny," he says. "I think that's what worries me."

In the end, however, Thompson is not and has never been that easy to pigeonhole. He's friends with Pat Buchanan and has a lifetime membership in the National Rifle Association. In his own mind, if not in others', he is "one of the most patriotic people I've ever encountered in America."

JG: Your new book, *Kingdom of Fear,* is being called a definitive memoir—although almost all of your books seem to be autobiographical in one way or another. What's the difference between the written accounts—of drug use, run-ins with the law, sex, fast cars, guns, and explosives—and real-life events?
HST: I don't really see any difference. Telling the truth is the easiest way; it saves a lot of time. I've found that the truth is weirder than any fiction I've seen. There was a girl that worked for me a long time ago, who graduated third in her class from Georgetown Law School, and was from some kind of uptown family in Chicago, and instead of going to work for some big-time firm, she came to Aspen and ends up working for me out here in the wilderness. A year or so later her mother or father were coming out to visit. I've had some understandable issues with parents—really all my life. And I'd be worried about my daughter, too, if she'd run off with some widely known infamous monster. And so I asked her—just so I could get braced for this situation, meeting the parents and having them come to the house: "Given

what you know about me and what you hear about me, which is worse?" She finally came out and said there was no question in her mind that the reality was heavier and crazier and more dangerous. Having to deal with the reality is no doubt a little more traumatic.

JS: Indeed, your author blurb says you live in "a fortified compound near Aspen, Colorado." In what sense is it fortified and why does it need to be?
HST: Actually, I live in an extremely pastoral setting in an old log house. It's a farm really. I moved here thirty years ago. I think the only fortification might be my reputation. If people believe they're going to be shot, they might stay away.

JG: Yes, I understand you're a gun enthusiast, to put it euphemistically. But do you support more restrictive gun laws? Do you support a ban on assault weapons?
HST: I have one or two of those, but I got them before they were illegal. In that case, if I were sure that any tragedies and mass murders would be prevented, I'd give up my assault rifle. But I don't really believe that. Do I have any illegal weapons? No. I have a 454 magnum revolver, which is huge, and it's absolutely legal. One day I was wild-eyed out here with Johnny Depp, and we both ordered these guns from Freedom, Wyoming, and got them the next day through FedEx. Mainly, I have rifles, pistols, shotguns; I have a lot of those. But everything I have is top quality; I don't have any junk weapons. I wouldn't have any military weapon around here, except as an artifact of some kind. Given Ashcroft and the clear blueprint of this administration to make everything illegal and everything suspicious—how about suspicion of being a terrorist sympathizer? Goddamn, talk about filling up your concentration camps. But, yeah, my police record is clean. This is not a fortified compound.

JG: So, just to clarify, how do your views stack up with the NRA's?
HST: I think I'm still a life member of the NRA. I formed a gun club out here, an official sporting club, and I got charter from the NRA. That made it legal to have guns here, to bring guns here, to have ammunition sent here, that sort of thing. I've found you can deal with the system a lot easier if you use their rules—by understanding their rules, by using their rules against them. I talk to a lot of lawyers. You know, I consider Pat Buchanan a friend. I don't agree with him on many things. Personally, I enjoy him. I just like him.

And I learn from Pat. One of the things I'm most proud of is that I never had anybody busted, arrested, jailed for my writing about them. I never had any—what's that?—collateral damage.

JG: But speaking of rules, you've been arrested dozens of times in your life. Specific incidents aside, what's common to these run-ins? Where do you stand vis-à-vis the law?

HST: Goddammit. Yeah, I have. First, there's a huge difference between being arrested and being guilty. Second, see, the law changes and I don't. How I stand vis-à-vis the law at any given moment depends on the law. The law can change from state to state, from nation to nation, from city to city. I guess I have to go by a higher law. How's that? Yeah, I consider myself a road man for the lords of karma.

JG: In 1990, you were put on trial for what you call "sex, drugs, dynamite, and violence." Charges were eventually dropped. Since then, you've been outspoken on Fourth Amendment issues: search and seizure, the right to privacy. I assume you've taken a side in the civil liberties debate that's come up in the aftermath of 9/11?

HST: It's a disaster of unthinkable proportions—part of the downward spiral of dumbness. Civil liberties are black and white issues. I don't think people think far enough to see the ramifications. The Patriot Act was a dagger in the heart, really, of even the concept of a democratic government that is free, equal, and just. There are a lot more concentration camps right now than Guantanamo Bay. But they're not marked. Now, every jail, every bush-league cop can run a concentration camp. It amounts to a military and police takeover, I think.

JG: Well, as some have pointed out, Lincoln suspended habeas corpus during the Civil War. Is some suspension of civil liberties ever appropriate or justified in a time of war?

HST: If there's a visible, obvious threat like Hitler, but in my mind the administration is using these bogeymen for their own purposes. This military law is nothing like the Constitution. They're exploiting the formula here: The people are afraid of something and you offer a solution, however drastic, and they go along with it. For a while, yeah. My suspicions are more justified every day with this manufacturing of dangerous killer villains.

The rest of the world does not perceive, I don't think, that some tin-horn dictator in the Middle East is more of a danger to the world than the U.S. is. This country depends on war as a primary industry. The White House has pumped up the danger factor because it's to their advantage. It's to John Ashcroft's advantage. There have always been pros and cons about the righteousness of life in America but this just seems planned, it seems consistent, and it seems traditional.

JG: What do they get out of it?
HST: They get control of the U.S. economy, their friends get rich. These are not philosopher-kings we're talking about. These are politicians. It's a very sleazy way of using the system. One of the problems today is that what's going on today is not as complex as it seems. The Pentagon just asked for another $14 billion more in the budget, and it's already $28 billion. [Defense spending in the 2003 budget rose $19.4 billion, to $364.6 billion]. That's one sector of the economy that's not down the tubes. So, some people are getting rich off of this. It's the oligarchy. I believe the Republicans have never thought that democracy was anything but a tribal myth. The GOP is the party of capital. It's pretty basic. And it may have something to do with the deterioration of educational system in this country. I don't think Bush has the slightest intention or concern about educating the public.

JG: Many people would say you're un-American and unpatriotic.
HST: I think I'm one of the most patriotic people that I've ever encountered in America. I consider myself a bedrock patriot. I participate very actively in local politics, because my voice might be worthwhile. I participate in a meaningful way—not by donations, I work at it.

JG: Well, what do you prescribe? What do you advocate?
HST: All the blood is drained out of democracy—it dies—when only half the population votes. I would use the vote. It would seem to me that people who have been made afraid, if you don't like what's happening, if you don't want to go to war, if you don't want to be broke, well for God's sake don't go out and vote for the very bastards who are putting you there. That's a pillar of any democratic future in this country. The party of capital is not interested in having every black person in Louisiana having access to the Ivy League. They don't need an educated public.

JG: So what took place during this past election?

HST: I believe the Republicans have seen what they've believed all along, which is that this democracy stuff is bull, and that people don't want to be burdened by political affairs. That people would rather just be taken care of. The oligarchy doesn't need an educated public. And maybe the nation does prefer tyranny. I think that's what worries me. It goes back to Fourth Amendment issues. How much do you value your freedom? Would you trade your freedom for some illusion of security? Freedom is something that dies unless it's used.

JG: This is coming from someone who's described himself as "an elderly dope fiend who lives out in the wilderness" and also as a "drunken screwball."

HST: A *dangerous* drunken screwball.

JG: Right. Sorry. So why would anybody listen to you?

HST: I don't have to apologize for any political judgments I've made. The stuff I wrote in the '60s and '70s was astonishingly accurate. I may have been a little rough on Nixon, but he was rough. You had to do it with him. What you believe has to be worth something. I've never given it a lot of thought: I've never hired people to figure out what I should do about my image. I always work the same way, and talk the same way, and I've been right enough that I stand by my record.

JG: But is there a sense in which your views are, by definition, going to be seen as fringe views—views that can just be discarded?

HST: That is a problem and I guess *Fear and Loathing in Las Vegas* might have colored the way people perceive me. But I haven't worried that people see me as "dope fiend," I'd rather get rid of the "elderly" rather than the "dope fiend."

JG: What's the best example of something you were right about?

HST: Christ, the Hell's Angels certainly. Police agencies regarded that book as a major primary resource on motorcycle gangs. I started covering presidential politics after I realized how easy it was to manipulate the political machinery in this county—or almost officially doing it—by running for sheriff. I saw that there might be some serious fun in politics. I covered Goldwater's convention in 1964. And I went from Nixon to Kennedy to Nixon. I wanted to have some say in events, just for my own safety.

JG: You have famously attached yourself to the word "fear" since you wrote *Fear and Loathing in Las Vegas*. Now you've written *Kingdom of Fear*. Will you explain?

HST: This country has been having a nationwide nervous breakdown since 9/11. A nation of people suddenly broke, the market economy goes to shit, and they're threatened on every side by an unknown, sinister enemy. But I don't think fear is a very effective way of dealing with things—of responding to reality. Fear is just another work for ignorance.

JG: You write in *Kingdom of Fear* about the passing of the American century—

HST: That's official, by the way. The American century was the twentieth, so sayeth Henry Luce. And when it ends, Christ, you can't avoid thinking: "Ye Gods!"

JG: To whom or what is the twenty-first century going to belong?

HST: That's something I have not divined yet. Goddammit, I couldn't have told you in 1960 what 1980 was going to be like.

JG: You've also referred to your beat as the "Death of the American Dream." That was the ostensible "subject" of *Fear and Loathing in Las Vegas*. Has it just sort of been on its deathbed since 1968?

HST: I think that's right.

JG: A lot of people would argue with you about that anyway, and believe that the American Dream is alive and well.

HST: They need to take a better look around.

JG: But in a way, haven't you lived the American Dream?

HST: Goddammit! [pause] I haven't thought about it that way. I suppose you could say that in a certain way I have.

JG: You said back in 1991 that you were "as astounded as anybody" that you were still alive. Still drinking, smoking, and doing drugs?

HST: I guess I'd have to say I haven't changed. Why should I, really? I'm the most stable neighbor on the road here. I'm an honest person. I don't regret being honest. I did give up petty crime when I turned eighteen, after I got a look at jail—I went in there for shoplifting—because I just saw that this stuff doesn't work. There's a line: "I do not advocate the use of dangerous drugs, wild amounts of alcohol and violence and weirdness—but they've always worked for me." I think I said that at a speech at Stanford. I've always been a little worried about advocating my way of life, or gauging my success by having other people take up my way of life, like Tim Leary did. I always quarreled with Leary about that. I could have started a religion a long time ago. It would not have a majority of people in it, but there would be a lot of them. But I don't know how wise I am. I don't know what kind of a role model I am. And not everyday is made for this life.

JG: In fact, you've experienced more than your share of dangerous situations. You've been beaten by the Hell's Angels. You were in the middle of the 1968 Democratic Convention riots. You've been shot at. What's going on with that?
HST: By any widely accepted standard, I have had more than nine lives. I counted them up once and there were thirteen times that I almost and maybe should have died—from emergencies with fires to violence, drowning, bombs. I guess I am an action junkie, yeah. There may be some genetic imperative that caused me to get into certain situations. It's curiosity, I guess. As long as I'm learning something I figure I'm OK—it's a decent day.

JG: Is there anything you regret?
HST: That goes to the question of would you do it again. If you can't say you'd do it again, it means that time was wasted—useless. The regrets I have are so minor. You know, would I leave my Keith Richards hat, with the silver skull on it, on the stool at the coffee shop at LaGuardia? I wouldn't do that again. But overall, no, I don't have any regrets.

Man of Action: Hunter S. Thompson Keeps Moving

Jesse Jarnow / 2003

From *Relix*, April–May 2003, pp. 59–65. Reprinted with the permission of Zenbu Media LLC.

Hunter S. Thompson's eyes lit up when he saw the fireworks. "Hot damn, you've got *Action!*" he said, fondling the tightly packed bomb, running his fingers down its elegant spine-fuse and around its bulbous body. "This is real good shit. Real good." Owing to the agreeable weather and it being the Chinese New Year and all, I'd suggested that we hop a cab over to Central Park and set off some fireworks.

Thompson pondered this and placed the firework on the bar, amidst the slowly accumulating clutter between drink tumblers: two pairs of eyeglasses (one reading, one tinted), cigarettes (one half-smoked and burning, one mostly full pack of Dunhill's), an ugly brown cigarette holder (retrieved for him by his assistant, Anita, after he let forth a high-pitched squeal), a round plastic receptacle containing a white powder (ingested orally through a short sipping straw), several lighters (though he later pilfered my associate's), and a copy of his new book, a memoir titled *Kingdom of Fear* (presented to Kevin, the bartender at Elaine's, a New York City hangout for cops, writers and unrepentant smokers).

"You guys are gonna set that off outside, right?" Kevin asked nervously, remembering the time Thompson gargled Bacardi fire-balls at the bar, nearly setting the place ablaze. He amiably refilled our glasses anyway, apparently without our noticing. Likewise, Thompson laid out his goods with a sleight of hand. One moment, we were sitting at the bar with just our drinks, the next moment, Thompson had a small arsenal of employable props. Each could be dissected as some key fragment of Thompson's public persona, the character he carved for himself in half-mad, cocksure journalistic novels and autobiographical dispatches from his self-assigned beat, "the Death of the American Dream."

In *Hell's Angels* (1967), *Fear and Loathing in Las Vegas* (1971), *Fear and Loathing on the Campaign Trail '72* (1973), *The Great Shark Hunt* (1979), and countless articles and straight acidic screeds, Thompson laid into American culture with broad fangs and endless bravado. It was this combination that turned him into a legendary figure forever associated with the fringe—drugs, guns, and nearly vengeful hippiedom—and caricatured, to Thompson's eternal displeasure, as Uncle Duke in Garry Trudeau's *Doonesbury.*

At sixty-five, Thompson is still raffish. His cartoony bow-legged walk is tempered slightly by the use of a hard wooden cane—though, lest anyone read it as a sign of deterioration, Thompson also used the cane to measure the fear instincts of nearby civilians by *thwacking* it soundly against the side of the bar.

Just over the frontal lobe of his brain, at the center of his white buttoned brim fishing cap, was a small cream-colored pin with the closest thing Thompson has to a logo: a sharp image of a cross formed by the intersection of a work in black text and a six-fingered fist stemming down to a dagger-like point and clenching an asterisk-shaped peyote button. The word, which crosses just below the palm, is "Gonzo."

It is rare for a writer and a single word to be so conjoined. Attributed to him in the Oxford English Dictionary, it describes both an attitude and a form of reportage he championed. Based on William Faulkner's notion that the best fiction is more accurate than any fact, Gonzo provided the theoretical gas to spark Thompson's blowtorch prose. As a literary style, it had two main tenets: total subjectivity and a first draft/best draft approach that jibed perfectly with the post-Beatnik literary world of the late 1960s.

Thompson threw himself into his stories recklessly, riding with Hell's Angels, getting drunk with Kentucky Colonels at the Derby in his native Louisville, and talking football with Satan himself, Richard Milhous Nixon. Most famously, he (with friend and Chicano activist Oscar Acosta) set out on a multi-day drug rampage in Las Vegas. It was a chaotic fear experiment, as he explained to his editor at the time, where he and Acosta gave "dollar bills to 'boys' for quick unctuous service" and went "roaring into the Circus-Circus in a huge Coupe de Ville [in order to] know the insanity of watching people jump and run and salute and all that crap."

Thompson describes himself as a hillbilly. And, like a lot of things, he means this far more literally than one might first suspect. He rarely leaves the

Colorado highlands. When he does—such as for the whirlwind promotional tour of book signings, television appearances and interviews that landed him in New York following the publication of *Kingdom of Fear*—he seems incredibly ill at ease. When his attention drifted, it wasn't hard to imagine his mind wandering back to the quiet dark of the hills.

Reductively, Thompson has always been the old man from the mountains who stumbles out of the underbrush every few years to wreak havoc and pass judgment, before growing exasperated and cantankerously trundling back to the hills to be with his guns and books and peacocks. The birds stalk the night at Owl Farm, Thompson's home of forty years, squawking creepily as they navigate between twisted pieces of metallic sculpture and the wreckage of whatever Thompson's been using for targets lately.

Owl Farm is often referred to as a "fortified compound", and there seems some kernel of truth to that. Memorabilia of all kinds line the walls, remnants of Thompson's long career. There are weapons and drugs, but most of them are books. Thompson is a man of letters, and dishes out references with aplomb: H. L. Mencken and Mark Twain, Bob Dylan and the Book of Revelations, enlightened men and porn moguls, learned philosophers and speed freaks—a vast panoply of the wizened and weird.

Amidst the clutter are also Thompson's extensive archives—carbon copies of everything he has written, including several thousand letters— haphazardly organized by dozens of assistants over the years, which only necessitates new assistants to untangle the filing systems of previous ones. A third volume of his collected letters is currently being prepared, and he is playing an active role in a film adaptation of *The Rum Diary,* a novel he wrote in the late 1950s. Set to again star Johnny Depp and Benicio Del Toro, along with Val Kilmer and others, the movie will go into production sometime next year.

Inside, Thompson works on his beloved typewriters, never upgrading to a computer, despite a weekly column on ESPN's website. His brain works only as fast as he can type on a vintage Selectric. In conversation, he speaks in tight bursts, quickly stopping and starting, as if allowing his hands time to type. "I'veneverunderstood. Whatamemoir. Reallyis." When he stumbles, which is frequent, the impression is that he's stuck on a word. The constant derailments can be explained, perhaps, as lingual crossroads: how to write the story. When presented with an object of desire or potential Action he barrels ahead, his body language changing and thoughts focusing.

"I leave [Colorado] once every two months," Thompson said. "In the past six months, I've been to Hawaii and LA. It's getting harder and harder because of the planes. I fly first class, with all the advantages I can get, but—goddamn—it's just getting more and more horrible. That's intentional, I believe. That's part of the overall plan to dumb the population down. A frightened population is obedient. They're confused. They're afraid. A fearful population is going to be easier, more malleable, more compliant. I wasn't personally hassled [on the way to New York], but the breakdown of the system hassles everybody."

"Politics is the art of controlling your environment," Thompson is fond of saying. For Thompson, politics is the base level at which humans communicate and it deeply bothers him when people make no attempt to engage.

"If you don't do it—if you don't participate in your life—someone else will. You're either going to be aware of what's happening around you, or you're going to be a slave to it." For his part, Thompson ran for sheriff of Aspen in 1970, waging a ridiculous (and widely documented) campaign on the Freak Power ticket, whose promises included renaming Aspen "Fat City" (to discourage tourism) and very nearly won. More recently, he has played an active role in the Fourth Amendment Foundation, founded in 1990 after he was acquitted in a privacy issues case to protect citizens from unlawful searches of their homes.

Thompson is an avowed enemy of Timothy Leary's "turn on, tune in, drop out" mantra. "I believed that the thing to do with acid was to eat it and go out and get involved in the public life." He built steam. "Leary, that son-of-a-bitch, that fraud . . . I think he was the most horrible person to come out of all of the '60s. He advocated his way, which was the Guru way. You had to have a guide, and had to do things in a certain way, be in a room with certain lights, and have a certain high priest leading you. And that would be him, of course. I denounced Leary right from the beginning, even when I didn't know that he was a working, hired informant for the FBI."

When Thompson offers an unsympathetic account of the '60s, he's not being a revisionist. He said the same thing at the time, as he fermented in the same San Franciscan ooze as the Grateful Dead and Jefferson Airplane. He bemoans the lack of a contemporary counterculture. "Jerry Garcia was a friend," he said. "He and I used to argue. He was totally against politics. He had nothing but contempt for my involvement, my running for Sheriff. But I believe that until you personalize politics, you're not gonna get anywhere. This war is not some distant thing. If every Deadhead voted, the country would be a different place."

Thompson speaks of politics like an old General ready to fetch his tank in an age of personal rocketships. He calls music his "fuel": Favorite albums like Bob Dylan's *Bringing It All Back Home* and Los Lobos' *Kiko* are valuable not because they are pleasurable escapes, but because they push him on.

Several times throughout *Kingdom of Fear* there appears a quote, attributed alternately to Robert Kennedy, an eighteenth-century British political theorist named Edmund Burke, and Thompson himself: "The only thing necessary for the triumph of evil is for good men to do nothing." When Thompson recited the dictum in the bar, his voice rose, as if looking for other patrons to join him in a moment of old-time solidarity.

Men of Action are needed. Taken as such, Gonzo is not too far removed from the bliss of the Beats, the Grateful Dead, or even Walt Whitman: being able to fully appreciate the capital-M Moment. Where Thompson splits with them, though, is his willingness to hone in on both ugliness and its consequences.

"My idea [for *Vegas*] was to buy a fat notebook and record the whole thing, *as it happened,* then send in the notebook for publication—without editing," he proclaimed, describing undiluted Gonzo. Thompson has inspired more bad journalism than perhaps any other American writer. " 'All you have to do is drink a little whiskey, smoke a joint, eat some acid, and *you too can write like this!* ' " Thompson groused. "That's as stupid as it sounds."

At his best, a Gonzo journalist works not unlike an improvising musician. Just as a soloist must be able to spontaneously formulate coherent music from a knowledge of theory, form and historical vocabulary, a Gonzo journalist should be able to parse a story in real-time. It is a way of experiencing things with open antennae, fully aware of the mechanisms grinding under a scene's surface, both subjectively and objectively.

And, sure, the drugs help, too. Gonzo is a primal manifestation of what might be deemed "the authentic American Dream." In recent years, the phrase "the pursuit of happiness" has come to mean, basically, the right to be left the fuck alone. Rather, as historian Gary Wills has posited, Thomas Jefferson meant something more classical. Being a good American didn't mean engaging in self-absorbed quests for money. It meant being an active citizen, which would inevitably lead to a rich happiness. The simplest step one can take is to become aware of what's going on around him.

In other words: Shit, if you're gonna light off fireworks in the middle of a major metropolitan area, you should be damn sure of what the law is, the history of the flying dirt you turn up, and who you might piss off. "What kind of ordinances do you have around here?" Thompson asked, nearly as soon as he saw the fireworks. "What kind of permits do you have?"

"Do We have a sunroof?" Thompson barked at the limo driver, who had parked in front of the bar. "I have some rockets that you can shoot out of cars," he explained. He turned a cardboard mortar over and paused. "This is not one of them. The ones I've got are Marine rockets. They really light things up—forty miles for forty seconds with forty thousand candlepower. They really hang up there."

The sunroof whirred open quietly, air pouring in. Thompson looked up, then out the windows at the passing Upper East Side traffic. "I'd just as soon do it right here," he announced, and took another hit off the bowl. "I'm a law abiding citizen." A loose theme of *Kingdom of Fear* is Thompson's life-long relationship with the Law, beginning with a childhood incident. "To live outside the law, you must be honest," he writes, quoting Dylan.

"I don't think it's the *right* and *duty* of Americans to carry a gun," he said. "We know that the more guns that are left around, the more trouble you're gonna have. I live out in the wilderness, far out in the wilderness. They're tools. I'm not a murderer. I don't go around and shoot people. It's stupid to shoot people. It's not beneficial. Or necessary.

"Where I stand leads to an elitist point of view, and not entirely democratic. My gut feeling is that I should have firearms, and not everybody else should. You can see the elitism in that. But it's true. I have a proven record of forty years."

Since his pivotal political coverage in the '70s, Thompson's output has been notoriously erratic, publishing sporadically in *Rolling Stone*, *Playboy*, and numerous sports magazines. For a time in the 1980s, he penned a media criticism column for the *San Francisco Examiner*. During this time, Thompson mutated into an icon, more often invoked as a character reference than an actual writer.

Thompson's writing has suffered in recent years, often coming off as unfocused and paranoid; or, more often, as simply a mix-n-match of stock invective—swine, twisted, fear, bastards, atavistic, Nazi—interspersed with great Ideas and proclamations that employ Capital Letters and imply some insane Mix of drug Frenzy and early Protestant political writings.

When applied well, Thompson's use of capital letters plugs his writing into much older stories. When he writes of firemen fighting Fire, they aren't simply extinguishing a blaze, they are engaging in battle with a Biblical plague. Thompson frames the Bush regime similarly. "It's a simple Plot," he says, capital letters evident by the tone of his voice. "These are old-time Procedures: take over the government and loot the Treasury."

To Thompson, the Bush regime is pure Fire, one that he'll Fight from his new platform at *Vanity Fair,* where he says he'll soon begin publishing (while according to Thompson, he continues his effort to get his name removed from the *Rolling Stone* masthead). Despite a generally chilly reception (the *New York Times* called it a "haphazard journalistic yard-sale"), *Kingdom of Fear* was an instant hit, selling out its first printing and quickly rising onto the *Times'* own best-seller list. Simply, Thompson is still an agitator with a clarion message, which is why he remains relevant, as a character, a public figure and a writer.

And he's managed to do it without tempering his message. "I piss down the throat of those Nazis," he writes of the Bush administration, and means it. Lately, he's been rereading William Shirer's classic study, *The Rise and Fall of the Third Reich.* "I would think it would be pretty difficult to understand what's going on now in terms of history without reading this. You'll see the parallels between Nazi Germany and this country. It's scary."

While *Kingdom of Fear* isn't exactly a return to form, Thompson is still capable of a fantastic dissent. "It was the death of fun, unreeling right in front of us," he writes of September 11th's aftermath "unraveling, withering, collapsing, draining away in the darkness like a handful of stolen mercury. Yep, the silver stuff goes suddenly, leaving only a glaze of poison on the skin."

Andre Breton called surrealism a "new vice." "There is every reason to believe that it acts on the mind very much as drugs do," he wrote, and the same might be said of Gonzo. It is said that after Bill Murray portrayed Thompson in 1980's *Where the Buffalo Roam* (an amusing, though deeply flawed, biopic), he began to take on Thompson's personal characteristics, donning dark glasses, smoking cigarettes through a filter, and becoming increasingly volatile. Similar rumors circulated about Johnny Depp after his appearance in Terry Gilliam's 1998 adaptation of *Vegas.*

Rallying the troops in bars, Thompson knows full well that his actions will be duly reported in the gossip pages. "Those fuckers didn't even mention I had a new book!" he kvetched about coverage of his colorful appearance at an Aspen peace rally. Out and about, Thompson is a self-conscious public figure and, thus, a performer.

One of the tasks of Thompson's assistants is to transcribe tapes. Like his old friend Nixon, he records a lot—phone calls, conversations, and the like. He is no doubt conscious of the permanent record. There were two tape machines running at the bar. One was strapped to Thompson, the other to me. Mysteriously, Thompson's cut off as soon we stepped outside, and returned exactly when we reentered the bar. "I wanna eat some of that salad before we light this off," Thompson can be heard saying. "Let's go back inside, we can do it between the salad and the main entree."

As Thompson's tape cuts back in, he is telling his Handlers that he's extremely stoned. At other points, Thompson wanders off to consult with members of his entourage about whether or not to contact bookies, or ask where his hash is. Exactly spliced, the recording seems an invitation to eavesdrop on Thompson's other conversations. Indeed, the Handlers play an important role in Thompson's current mythology. He uses them as a public prop just as well as any cane, cigarette holder, or tin that may be filled with common sugar.

Following his introduction on *Late Night with Conan O'Brien* several days later, Thompson appeared from behind the curtain, beverage in hand, and began to walk in the wrong direction. Several men appeared, nudge towards O'Brien, only to have him walk behind the set's furniture, causing further chaos. It is a common ploy for Thompson as tapes of appearances with David Letterman often feature him entering the stage several seconds after his cue. On one hand, it might be simple intoxication.

On the other hand, it might be read as a conscious attempt to throw things off—which, in a way, seems to be exactly the goal of Thompson's professional drug use: to produce Action. "I'm not a drug *abuser*," he insisted. "I'm a drug *user*. I've always said that drugs are no excuse. Being drunk is no excuse. If that's how you're gonna operate in the world, don't try to blame it on some weird shit."

And why not? Drugs are fun. Fireworks are fun. They can be beautiful, especially in such an ugly, paranoid climate. What else besides strange wonder could one feel if he saw, for no instantly discernible reason, a crystally spark shower with no other witnesses to verify it?

After the explosion, there will be *silence,* and in that silence there exists the possibility for a better world where anything can happen, because something just *did* happen.

Action points towards Rest. There are fast cars in Thompson's stories, very fast, but they almost always take Thompson to a deserted beach for a moonlit swim or someplace else where he can enjoy the afterglow of Speed and Chaos. The most common setting for Thompson's work is late at night, usually in a hotel room, the rest of the world at slumber, where he can reflect thoughtfully. Writing itself becomes a sublime act.

Though he'd deny it to the end ("We won't get anywhere if we talk about Utopia!" he snapped, as if someone might overhear), Thompson reveals the heart of a dreamer. Moments are made transcendental not because he has a sense of what is wrong and can articulate it (though he does), but because he has a sense of what is undoubtedly perfect and magical. "There was a fantastic universal sense that whatever we were doing was *right,* that we were winning," he writes in *Vegas.*

Thompson reflected on the reputation that has acted as an open invitation for people to continuously show up in his life with weed and explosives and sounded more than a little bit weary, though he glared longingly at the sunroof as he said it.

"It gets boring, every time that cartoon runs, that *Doonesbury* thing. It's a little bit of fun, maybe, to be taken as a lunatic. It colors people's perceptions. If you call the President a 'shit-eating dog' and then you say he should 'get the fuck out of Iraq', it may give the 'get the fuck out of Iraq' a crazy tinge. 'Oh, the messenger is a little stoned, so whatever it is, it can't be true!'" Thompson looked at the sunroof once more and heaved himself out of the limo.

If action points to Rest, then Rest—such as, say, sitting in a bar, walking outside to a limousine, then walking back inside the bar—surely points right back at Action, a great circle. Each needs the other, and Thompson needs Rest, because he needs to write. So he creates Action. It's passive-aggressive, really.

Inside, Thompson reconvened with the Handlers. "Anita AnitaAnitaAnitaAnita!" he called, voice rising in pitch. "Where's my hammer?" Anita retrieved an exaggerated plastic hammer that, when force was applied, reproduced a crash of shattering glass via a cheap, distorting sound chip. Thompson hit me over the head.

After the salad, before the main entree could even be discussed, Thompson was swept off by the Handlers to deal with a phone call. I was left with a bag of fireworks and a head full of ways to use them.

Index

205